JESUS
Among the Theologians

JESUS
Among the Theologians
Contemporary Interpretations of Christ

✳ ✳ ✳

WILLIAM J. LA DUE

TRINITY PRESS INTERNATIONAL

Trinity Press International, P.O. Box 1321, Harrisburg, PA 17105
Trinity Press International is a division of the Morehouse Group.

Cover photo of Leonardo Boff by Mev Puleo. Photo of Karl Barth courtesy of Neukirchener Verlag. Photo of Jürgen Moltmann courtesy of SCM Press. Photo of Elisabeth Schüssler Fiorenza courtesy of Fortress Press.

Cover design: Corey Kent

Library of Congress Cataloging-in-Publication Data

La Due, William J.
    Jesus among the theologians : contemporary interpretations of Christ./ William J. La Due.
        p. cm.
    Includes bibliographical references and index.
    ISBN 1-56338-351-9 (alk. paper)
    1. Jesus Christ – Person and offices. I. Title.
BT203 .L3 2001
232'.09'04 – dc21

                                                    2001027247

Printed in the United States of America

01   02   03   04   05   06   10   9   8   7   6   5   4   3   2   1

Contents

Introductory Note

No study comes closer to the core of Christian life than the study of Jesus. His days on earth, although reasonably brief, represent for his followers the richest, fullest expression of humanity and the clearest window into God. Over the years Christology has been a perennial object of fascination, for it is the keystone of theology for serious Christians. In the last five decades or so there has been a flowering of research prompting the publication of countless works on the life and mission of Christ. The descriptions of Jesus and the explanations of his identity have traveled in many, sometimes conflicting directions, leaving even educated, inquiring minds rather perplexed at times.

During my active priestly ministry and also in my seventeen years of working in the secular world, I have encountered many such Christians, eager to learn more about recent approaches to Jesus, but having neither the time nor the occasion to access the wide spectrum of studies. The purpose of this work is to summarize the efforts of twenty-three Catholic and Protestant theologians. It is not intended as a survey of the entire field of contemporary Christology. However, the choice of theologians does reflect a representative range of current thought. Serious readers and students will thus be introduced to the works of these scholars in an abbreviated and readable format. My hope is that these observations might assist other believers to sort out their own thoughts and to pursue those thinkers who especially attract them. Most important, it is my desire to provide them with the opportunity to reflect once more upon the person who stands at the center of our Christian universe and offers the key to our future.

You will note that a number of prominent scholars have not been included here. The omission of Paul Tillich, Yves Congar, Hans Urs von Balthasar, Schubert Ogden, and others will seem unforgivable to some. Nonetheless, I have chosen these particular theologians because they have crossed my path at certain strategic moments and have left a special imprint upon my consciousness and my faith. Permit me to share them with you.

✳ *Chapter 1* ✳

Surveying the Christological Scene

Notable Catholic Contributors

The Christology of the past two generations can be roughly described as falling into two general categories. The traditional approach, "from above," begins with the descent of the Son of God from the heavens and then takes up the human life and activity of the Word made flesh, Jesus of Nazareth, culminating in his death, resurrection, and his return to the Father. This is the pattern clearly revealed in the Gospel of John and, according to a good number of scholars, in the hymns of Philippians 2:6–11, Colossians 1:15–20, and in several other New Testament passages.[1] The challenge for this descending Christology is to preserve and defend the genuine character of the humanity of Jesus in every significant respect, for unless he is truly human, his role as mediator for humankind is seriously compromised. The other approach, Christology "from below," establishes first the full humanity of Jesus, and then proceeds to describe the divinity of the Son in various ways that need not directly call for his actual preexistence from eternity. This Christology from below is observed in the speeches of Peter in the early chapters of the Acts of the Apostles and is crystallized in Acts 2:36, "this Jesus whom you crucified, God has constituted as both Lord and Christ." This ascending Christology was popularized by the liberal theologians of the nineteenth century and has found new proponents in the twentieth. Though it is easier for Christology from below to defend the full and genuine humanity of Christ as being like us "in all things but sin," its explanations of the divine in Jesus are not as adequate or satisfactory. This study attempts to outline some of the efforts of various Catholic and Protestant theologians in the past fifty or sixty years to address a number of these christological dilemmas. Although many other scholars' works have been well received and even critically acclaimed, the authors selected for this work have

1

particularly challenged and fascinated me during this period as a lifelong student in the pursuit of the true meaning of Jesus.

My narrative begins in the autumn of 1951 on taking up formal theological studies at the Gregorian University in Rome. Almost contemporaneous with my arrival in the Holy City came the publication of Pope Pius XII's encyclical, *Christ, the Eternal King,* on September 8 to commemorate the fifteenth centenary of the Council of Chalcedon, which took place in the fall of 451. More than any other event in the early church, Chalcedon formulated in rather lapidary phrases the ecclesiastical doctrine regarding the identity of Jesus Christ. Those formulations have remained the standard and the litmus test of belief for Catholics, Orthodox, and Protestants for fifteen centuries. The encyclical proclaimed itself as a celebration of the anniversary of Chalcedon, stressing its importance in the development of our faith understanding of Christ.

According to Pius XII, then in the thirteenth year of his long pontificate (1939–58), the encyclical was to stress two points: the Roman primacy that had been given noble expression at Chalcedon, and the importance of the dogmatic definition concerning the nature and person of Christ.[2] Pius proceeded to describe in some detail the circumstances leading up to the gathering at Chalcedon. It was the priest Eutyches (ca. 378–454), the head of a monastery of monks and a popular preacher in Constantinople, who precipitated the whole dispute by proclaiming that Christ did not possess a true human nature, since the Word had absorbed the humanity in such a way that there was only one nature in Jesus, the divine nature of the Son. Several attempts were made in the East to address the errors of Eutyches, but he had powerful friends who shared his view that there was but one nature and one person in Christ. Finally at the instigation of a new eastern emperor, Marcian (451–57), a council was called to settle the controversy, which had been raging for a number of years. Approximately six hundred bishops gathered at Chalcedon, situated across the Bosporus Strait within sight of Constantinople. All the bishops were from the East with the exception of two from Africa, while Pope Leo I (440–61) was represented by five delegates, three of whom presided over the proceedings.

Pius XII then identified the condemnation of the errors of the monk, Eutyches, as the central project of the conciliar delibera-

tions.³ A letter written on the subject by Pope Leo some years
before 451 to Patriarch Flavian of Constantinople was read aloud
in the third session and approved enthusiastically by all present.
At the fifth session a new definition of faith was presented to the
Fathers and approved by unanimous consent. The 1951 encyclical
then repeated the heart of the christological definition:

> [F]ollowing the traditions of the holy Fathers we teach that
> all with one voice confess that the Son ... and our Lord Jesus
> Christ are one and the same, and that he is perfect in his di-
> vinity, perfect in his humanity, true God and true man, made
> of a rational soul and a body, consubstantial with the Father
> in his divinity, and the same [i.e., consubstantial with us] as
> regards his humanity ... having two natures without confu-
> sion, change, division or separation; the distinction between
> the natures was not removed by the union, but the proper-
> ties of each remain inviolate and are joined together in one
> person.⁴

Pius XII noted with regret the rise of the monophysite confession after Chalcedon. It is they who maintain that there is but one
nature in Christ. Even today, he added, there are separated monophysite bodies in Egypt, Ethiopia, Syria, Armenia, and elsewhere,
who refuse to accept the definition of Chalcedon.⁵ According to
the pontiff, the differences separating mainstream Christians from
the Monophysites are principally the result of misunderstandings
in the use of words such as *nature* and *essence, person* and *hypostasis,* and he expressed the hope that these differences can and
should eventually be settled. In the encyclical, Pope Pius also lifted
up "another enemy of the faith of Chalcedon" which he referred
to as the "kenotic doctrine."⁶ He did not explain this fully, but
one gathers that he was opposing the various tendencies in play
since the 1800s to reduce Christ to the state of a mere man, thus
eliminating his divinity. Although the pope encouraged continued
research on the humanity of Jesus, even those studies that attempt
to clarify Christ's psychological profile, he warned scholars not to
desert the ancient teachings.

Pius then proceeded to lay out several New Testament quotations that point to the divine nature of Christ, along with a number
of statements from the writings of Pope Leo I that corroborate the
Chalcedonian definition. He again urged the eastern Christians to

return to communion with Rome, reminding them that he and his predecessors had protected their liturgical rites, promoted the study of their history, enacted laws for them, and even bestowed the cardinal's hat on their brother, the (Uniate) patriarch of the Armenians.[7] It was the pope's feeling that at this point all parties could revisit and review the events of the past more calmly, and he hoped that this would bring all back together again under the banner of Chalcedon.

This was roughly the state of christological thought among the majority of Catholics and Protestants alike in 1951. Most Catholic theologians in their manuals followed the formulas of Chalcedon very closely and structured their presentations accordingly. There was some discussion, however, between such scholars as Paul Galtier and Pietro Parente, as to whether or not there is a human consciousness in Christ that is distinct from the divine consciousness of the Word. As a matter of fact, a last-minute change was made in paragraph 31 of the 1951 encyclical to leave open the question of the possibility of a separate human consciousness in Jesus. Apart from issues such as this, the tract *On the Word Incarnate* had experienced few major changes for perhaps several hundred years. The warning by Pius XII regarding "kenotic doctrines" in Christology was in all likelihood addressed to scholars, inspired in one way or another by the liberal theologies of the nineteenth century who portrayed Jesus as a man sent by God, and very close to God, but not God.

Bernard Lonergan

In the fall of 1953 my classmates and I were introduced to the treatise on Christology under the tutelage of a new Gregorian University professor, Bernard Lonergan (1904–84), who came from Regis College in Toronto. Lonergan at that time was completing his masterpiece, *Insight*, a monumental study of the processes of human understanding. His 1953–54 lectures in Christology, apart from several of his unique touches, for example, on the desirability of the Incarnation, were largely patterned after Charles Boyer's *De Verbo Incarnato*, which came out in a second edition in 1952.[8] It was not long, however, before Bernard Lonergan prepared his own text for his Gregorian University lectures on the subject of Christology.[9] His second edition "for the use of students" was published in 1961. Lonergan divided the material as follows:

Part 1: Christ, True God and True Man, from the New Testament

Part 2: The Doctrine of the Councils, from Nicaea through the Seventh Century

Part 3: The Hypostatic Union, Theological Conclusions

Part 4: The Grace and the Knowledge of Christ

Part 5: The Redemption

In his demonstration of the divinity of Christ (thesis 1), Lonergan pays considerable attention to the more recent adversaries such as Immanuel Kant (1724–1804), George W. F. Hegel (1770–1831), and Rudolf Bultmann (1884–1976), all of whom were unable to accept the Chalcedonian understanding of Jesus' divinity. The authority that Christ asserted over the Mosaic law, his power over sin, his miracles, the resurrection, and finally the assertions in John and Paul regarding his preexistence are set forth as proofs for the divinity of Jesus. The author then makes much of the frequent use of the designation "Son of man" in the gospels to demonstrate the true humanity of Christ (thesis 2).

In the presentation of the conciliar developments, Lonergan's text goes into considerable detail outlining the positions of the principal early contributors to the debate, such as Athanasius (ca. 298–373), Theodore of Mopsuestia (350–427), and Cyril of Alexandria (ca. 375–444), who prepared the way for the definitions of Ephesus and Chalcedon: that there is but one person in Christ, who is both truly God and truly man (thesis 3). Moreover, after the Incarnation these two natures, the divine and the human, remained unconfused and unchanged, as was stated clearly at Chalcedon (thesis 4). As a consequence of the two distinct natures, there are two wills and two natural principles of operation in Christ according to the declarations of the Council of Constantinople III (680–81). Lonergan adds a note on Honorius I (625–38), defending the pope's position regarding Monotheletism, but the weight of history seems inclined to view Honorius's statements as favoring one will in Christ (thesis 5).

Part 3, on the hypostatic union, is developed by Lonergan in several closely reasoned theses. The first (thesis 6) argues that the human nature assumed by the Word is not a person, but only an individual human essence that lacks its own proper act of existence, for otherwise Christ would have been a human person as well. Although there are two natures, two natural sets of properties, two natural wills, there is a single act of existence, and that is the divine existence (thesis 7). The person of the Word is the subject of the actions of the assumed human nature (thesis 9). The author then declares his position regarding two consciousnesses in Jesus, whereby the same person is present to himself as both divine and human. Lonergan thus parts company with some of his scholastic colleagues in asserting that although there is but one person in Christ, there is also a distinct human subjectivity that results from the fact that Jesus has two intellectual natures. Without that distinct human subjectivity, something would be lacking in Christ's humanity that, according to Chalcedon, is indeed a perfect humanity (thesis 10). In Christ the two consciousnesses are united in the one psychological subject, that is, the person of the Word. The author proceeds to pose the question as to whether or not the Son of God was, through his human consciousness, aware of himself as divine. Lonergan's response is rather complicated. Although Jesus through his human consciousness was aware of his personhood (which is divine), he was not explicitly aware of his divinity. Potentially, however, his human consciousness could indeed have known that he was God, in that Christ's human intellect always enjoyed the beatific vision.

Part 4 of Lonergan's study treats the grace and the knowledge of Jesus. His possession of sanctifying grace was uniquely full and superabundant. It is from him that all grace proceeds. All saving grace has its source in the grace of Christ, which in him was perfect from the first moment of his human existence (thesis 11). Concerning Christ's human knowledge, Lonergan holds as theologically certain that Jesus enjoyed the beatific vision, that is, the immediate vision of God, from the moment of his conception, since this was commonly held by all theologians (thesis 12). Of course, Christ in his human intellect does not possess a comprehensive knowledge of God because his human nature is finite. There were some things he did not claim to know, such as the day and the hour of the final judgment (Mark 13:32). However, the author concedes that to maintain the position that Christ's human knowledge was limited is still somewhat problematic, since he did possess, in addition to the beatific vision, infused and acquired knowledge. Nevertheless, Lonergan does affirm that, regarding the human psychology of Jesus, we are not yet in a position to explain some of these concepts very clearly.

The question of Christ's sinlessness is treated in the conventional scholastic fashion. Jesus was not only free from all sin, but was unable to sin due to his divine personhood. Nor was there any inclination to sin in Jesus (thesis 13). The question of his freedom in spite of his lifelong possession of the beatific vision is analyzed by Lonergan at some length, but his presentation of the issue is not especially satisfying. As a matter of fact it seems to be a rather torturous exercise in logic.

The fifth and final section of the author's tract *De Verbo* deals with the redemption, which is portrayed as a ransom of sorts to God, so that humankind might again experience the opportunity to be restored to grace. Christ's mediation consists principally in his passion, death, and resurrection (Rom. 4:23–25). If he had not risen we would still be under the judgment of sin (1 Cor. 15:17). After departing, Jesus promised that he would send the Holy Spirit (John 16:7–13), the Advocate, the Spirit of truth, who would lead believers into the full range of truth (thesis 15). The satisfaction of Christ, which was full and pleasing to the Father in every way, was touched upon by the Council of Trent but, according to Lonergan, was never adequately defined.[10] Anselm's theory, which focused for the most part on the compensation due to the offended God, was based on the assumption that either there would be full satisfaction, or humankind would be forever penalized. According to the author, however, these were not the only options. God conceivably could have freely forgiven humankind's sin or exacted a minimal satisfaction from Christ short of his passion and death (thesis 16).

The final thesis of the work affirms that Christ died and rose again according to the divine plan, not just to lift humankind out of the evils that are the wages of sin, but to convert and transform this evil into good (thesis 17). The self-emptying of Jesus resulted in his exaltation—which is the theme of Philippians 2:7–11—and becomes the pattern and the example for all believers. The author concludes with a corollary on the goal of the Incarnation, which is identified as the restoration of the good order of the universe as intended by God.

In 1956 Bernard Lonergan had published a little volume on the subject of the ontological and psychological composition of Christ that paved the way for the treatment in part 3 of his *De*

Verbo.[11] His conclusions were fairly similar but the exposition of the subject was somewhat more detailed. For example, in the 1956 work he held that Christ as man is conscious of himself as man, and as a divine person he is conscious of himself as divine. Further, in his human consciousness he is aware of himself as a divine person. There can be only one psychological subject in Jesus because there is only one ego, the divine ego. And yet, in a certain sense one is inclined to affirm that he has a human ego, inasmuch as he has two natures and two consciousnesses. Lonergan, however, does not hold that there is a distinct human ego in Christ because there is only one psychological subject. The two consciousnesses communicate with one another so that Christ as God knows that he is this man, and Christ as man knows that he is the natural Son of God. The one person is the same psychological subject of both consciousnesses. The author distinguishes himself from the position of his colleague, Paul Galtier, who seemed to say that the immediate subject of the human operations in Christ is the human nature rather than the psychological subject, who is the Word. This allowed Galtier to affirm that Christ did have something like a distinct human ego, separate from the divine ego of the Word. As a consequence, according to Galtier, it is not necessary to affirm that the personal subject (i.e., the Word) is perceived by Christ's human consciousness. Lonergan, on the other hand, holds that the psychological subject of the human operations of Jesus is the Word, rather than the human nature of Christ. These kinds of complicated intellectual exercises are necessary in order that the proponents of a Christology from above can attempt to present Jesus the man in a reasonably credible and convincing manner for believers.

In a later study, published in 1967, Lonergan reaffirms that Christ is a single subject of both a divine and a human consciousness, while in the Godhead there are three subjects of a single, dynamic, existential consciousness.[12] In a lecture delivered at Laval University in 1975, Lonergan revisits the issue of the meaning of "person" at Chalcedon (451) and declares that in Christ there is only one identity, the identity of the Word. The man, Jesus, has an identity, not in himself but in the Word. Moreover, he reminds us that we must find a way to assert that a divine person can have a fully human life. Though his identity was divine, Jesus possessed a truly human subjectivity that grew in wisdom, age, and grace (Luke 2:52) and was similar to us in all except sin.[13]

Karl Rahner

The name of Karl Rahner (1904–84) was not especially honored in Rome during the 1950s. Although the ordinary professor of dogmatics at the University of Innsbruck had given a number of visiting lectures in the Holy City over the years, he had difficulties with the Roman authorities which began in 1949 when he wrote a lengthy article on the subject of concelebration. Rahner argued for concelebration rather than the endless multiplication of private masses that seemed to him to be counterproductive and, perhaps, fostered as much for the multiplication of stipends as for any other reason. As a result of this study, Rahner was forbidden by the Holy Office to speak further on the subject of concelebration. In 1951 he wrote a monograph, which was never fully published, on the subject of Mariology, as a response to the November 1, 1950, dogmatic definition of the Assumption of Mary by Pope Pius XII. Rahner sought to soften some of the elements of the definition, in view of the rather thin historical evidence available, and to address the numerous European objections to the new dogma by putting the affirmations concerning Mary within the wider context of the final consummation of all the faithful, which he believed involved a corporeal dimension of some sort. Threats to place all of his future writings under censorship were made by his Jesuit superiors after he wrote a study on the virgin birth in 1960 in which he set forth a moral rather than a biological definition of virginity. However, through the intervention of Cardinal Döpfner, this never came to pass. As a matter of fact, in March of 1961 Pope John XXIII appointed Rahner as a consultor to one of the conciliar preparatory commissions, and in October of 1962 he was appointed by the pope as an expert, or *peritus*, to the Second Vatican Council.[14]

In the early 1960s Karl Rahner's work attracted attention in the United States. Several of his shorter studies in the Disputed Questions series, such as his *Inspiration in the Bible*, *On the Theology of Death*, and *The Episcopate and the Primacy* (which was coauthored with Joseph Ratzinger), introduced him to a larger audience that accepted his fresh approaches with considerable enthusiasm. Rahner became one of the four or five most influential theologians in the course of the deliberations of Vatican II. In 1961 the first volume of his *Theological Investigations* series appeared in English; the English edition eventually came to twenty-three volumes. One of the more important studies in the first volume was entitled "Current Problems in Christology," which he wrote on the occasion of the fifteenth centenary of the Council of Chalcedon in 1951.[15] This study, which has been so frequently cited by others, begins with the observation that although the Chalcedonian doctrine has lasting value for us due to its clarity, every formula is limited and can never be considered as an adequate articulation of the reality behind it. Rahner asks whether the Christology of the Acts of the Apostles, which begins with the human experience of Jesus (a Christology from below), should be considered as a merely primitive formulation, or whether it has something valuable to add to classical Christology, which begins from above. Is there an element that the classical Christology lacks or does not communicate with the same freshness and vigor that we find in the Christology of the early chapters of Acts? In this connection, the Christ portrayed in the classical Christology is one often misunderstood by believers. For many he has become a kind of mythological figure—a divine being walking about in human attire, but not really a full-fledged human like us at all.

Rahner insists on affirming the existence in Jesus of a genuine human self-consciousness that is only aware of its hypostatic union with the Word or Logos by virtue of an objective communication that is presented to his consciousness by the beatific vision. He criticizes those theologians (e.g., Boyer) who fail to understand that the two distinct and unconfused natures in Christ imply a certain duality of a psychological sort, between what he calls the I-center in the man Jesus and the consciousness of the Word. Without a distinct personal center, Jesus could not be truly man, and hence his ability to mediate for us in freedom before God would be illusory. His humanity cannot simply be envisioned as a pure instrument of the Word, for this would clearly vitiate the quality of his mediation. In the light of the hypostatic union, how do we assert and preserve the free, human character of Christ's mediational activity on our behalf? Without this do we not find ourselves in the realm of myth?

Rahner underlines the importance of moving beyond the one person/two natures formula to a new statement that can communicate the truth of Christ's reality in a more meaningful way for us, yet with equal clarity. His choice is what he terms *transcendental Christology*. For him the Incarnation of the Word is identified as the one ultimate goal of the movement of creation itself. God is gradually taking hold of the world and bringing it to himself. Jesus Christ is the high moment of this convergence—creature and Creator coming together. Rahner expanded this christological approach in his later writings. Another approach to a new Christology could be the revitalization of biblical theology which, in his judgment, has greatly overused a few biblical texts to do nothing more than substantiate the conclusions of Ephesus and Chalcedon, leaving much of the richness and variety of the New Testament evidence relatively untouched. He returns again to the issues of Christ's human consciousness, which had to experience the immediate vision of God as a consequence of his hypostatic union with the Word, but he noted that this vision need not always be "beatifying." The union of the two natures in the person of the Word has traditionally assumed that the change is completely on the side of the human nature. But how can the Incarnation, the convergence point of all creation, not affect God in some way? Are we caught up here in a sort of desperate dilemma? What kind of real convergence can there be if the one side is utterly unaffected by it? Rahner insists that the Word, although remaining unchanged in itself, truly comes to be in the human nature that he takes to himself, and which remains united and yet distinct from him.

The issue of a transcendental anthropology surfaces again and again in Rahner's work. Humankind is a reality that is absolutely open upward. It attains its highest perfection when the Word becomes flesh in the world. There is in human nature an "obediential potency" to communion with the divine, which has been revealed to us in Jesus, and it is he who provides the starting point for a new approach to Christian anthropology. Humankind is so open-ended that it was possible for a human being (i.e., Jesus Christ), by being human in the fullest conceivable sense, to be God's essence in the world.

Rahner concludes his 1951 essay by lifting up some of the key challenges for contemporary Christology:

> Although there is in mankind an openness to the transcendent, the Incarnation cannot be considered an event which is in any way owed to humanity.
>
> There is an abiding monophysitic undercurrent in classical Christology that tends to swallow up the human in Christ

in the face of the divine. Further, there is no well-formulated theological position regarding Christ's abiding role as man.

It must be said that there is not a great deal of attention paid to the mysteries of Jesus' human life. What really occurred at the transfiguration or the ascension? Also, the daily life of Jesus involved an ongoing revelation of God in one way or another. We have yet to probe that matter adequately.

We must reexamine in greater detail the inner structure of the redemption itself. Jesus' death put him into a totally new relationship with the world. He was no longer limited to a single place or a single point in time.

It is essential to reaffirm that there is only one Christ in our world history. This unique convergence of the human and the divine is a once-and-for-all event. The Incarnation was the decisive act of history, the watershed that gives ultimate meaning to all that went before and all that comes after. Our challenge is to grow toward an ever-expanding realization and actualization of that occurrence in our history and in the history of mankind.

About twenty-five years later Karl Rahner produced a summary of his theological endeavors, which he entitled *Foundations of Christian Faith*.[16] American theologian David Tracy considers this volume to be "the clearest and most systematic presentation by Rahner of his own position."[17] Rahner's treatment of Christology in chapter 6 constitutes about one-third of the book and is invaluable for our understanding of his developed theology of the Incarnation. He identifies his position as an ascending Christology, beginning with the historical Jesus, but there is also a great deal of descending Christology in his approach, inasmuch as the idea of a God-man coming into our history is a very prominent feature of his presentation. At the outset, Rahner stresses the need to articulate our faith in such a way that it is reasonably reconcilable with the horizons of understanding of our age (1 Peter 3:15). We must take seriously the affirmation that the Word was made flesh, and not resort to what he terms a *mythological understanding*, that is, the humanity of Jesus being viewed as a mere instrument of the Word. At the same time, Rahner considers the hypostatic union as the beginning of humankind's self-transcendence into God through God's self-communication to humankind. The Incarnation, then, is viewed as the beginning of the divinization of the entire universe.

Karl Rahner was of the mind that matter has an intrinsic pull to develop into spirit. There is an "energy" in matter to surpass itself, to surge into something essentially higher. On the basis of his evolutionary view of the world, he projects what he refers to as an *a priori* approach to Christology. Presupposing that the goal of the universe is God's self-communication to it—which occurs at certain junctures along the time/space continuum—the author posits the appearance of one whom he calls the "absolute savior," whose role is to initiate the irreversible salvation in history. He would be the absolute promise of salvation and, at the same time, the complete and total acceptance of that salvation. The subject of the hypostatic union is identified as the absolute savior, and this is Jesus Christ. God has truly become flesh (John 1:14). Of course the Incarnation was not a necessary part of God's plan for the world, but if it had not occurred, the self-transcendence of matter would have been deprived of that final completion that was achieved in the Incarnation, and can be shared by humankind in and through the possibility of this self-transcendence offered to all in Christ. The immediate vision of God that the human soul of Christ always enjoyed is really the goal and the objective of all men and women who approach him as savior. According to Rahner, sanctifying grace in us, and the hypostatic union in Jesus, can only be understood in relation to one another.

Although the idea of the absolute savior is only one christological approach among many that have their ground in the New Testament, it deserves to be given fuller attention in that it seems to accord well with Rahner's transcendental anthropology. However, there are some problems. For example, what is our justification for identifying the concept of absolute savior with Jesus alone? What of the possibility of another individual—past, present, or future—being considered as one who is a bearer of humankind's final salvation? This transcendental Christology is rooted in four basic assertions:

> Humankind is essentially directed toward the mystery we call God.
>
> Men and women must be hopeful and even confident that their being is open to the self-communication of God.

> This self-communication of God must come to us in the context of human history.

> With sincere hope then, we search throughout history for that promise of divine self-communication as actualized in a member of the human race.

Humankind is defined by this limitless orientation toward the infinite. Rahner affirms that there is an obediential potency for the hypostatic union in the fabric of human nature. If we accept these premises, we are in a position to construct a transcendental Christology that can stand as a counterpart and a complement to the classical Christology of the schools. But in our description of the absolute savior, the God-man, we must avoid any explanation of the Incarnation in which the humanity of Jesus would be merely the instrument of God. This would simply take us back to the heresies of the early centuries such as Docetism, Apollinarianism, Monophysitism, and Monotheletism.

Rahner then addresses the question of the historical ground of our faith in Jesus. Against the view of the Enlightenment—that our salvation cannot be dependent on a contingent set of historical facts—he replies that although historical facts call forth a lesser degree of certitude, the claim to an absolute commitment of one's life, based on a certain construct of historical facts, is clearly justifiable. What, then, for this theologian are the minimal historical presuppositions regarding the life and activity of Jesus Christ?

> Jesus was identified with the religious life and culture of his people. He participated in that life and set himself up as a religious reformer.

> He was a radical reformer who criticized the domination of the law that had been elevated in importance above God.

> He sensed that he was very close to God whom he called Father, and he identified himself with the outcasts of Jewish society.

> He understood himself as the last of the line of prophets—as the one who was bringing definitive salvation.

> He became aware that his mission was creating opposition among the religious and political authorities of his day.

In spite of this, he pursued his objective and faced the prospect of his death, realizing that somehow it would be the result of his mission.

His preaching and healing were a call to conversion. The kingdom of God was drawing near and he intended to gather together a group of disciples.

In his human self-consciousness, Jesus had to learn that his message was to be rejected by many. The singular character of his relationship with the Father must have been the result of an "abiding unreflexive consciousness" of a radical closeness to God. He sensed that there was only a brief period before the in-break of God's rule on earth. And perhaps in this regard, Rahner feels that we might speak of an error in judgment concerning Christ's anticipation of the imminent coming of the kingdom. In light of the proximity of the advent of the kingdom, Jesus encouraged his hearers to a radical change of heart, a *metanoia* (Matthew 5–7). Not only did he experience this intimate relationship with the one whom he called Father, but he wanted to share this relationship with others. It is in this sense that Jesus could have experienced himself before his death and resurrection as the absolute savior. There is no question that he went to his death freely, and that he saw his death as the ultimate destiny of his life as a prophet among his people. Whether Jesus saw in his death a deeper meaning, some kind of expiatory significance, is not clear from the New Testament evidence.

With respect to the miracles of Christ, Rahner affirms that the Lord was indeed a miracle-worker of some sort. Although historical criticism has notably changed our view of his miraculous activity, what can be said concerning such phenomena as his sudden cures? Today we clearly do not understand what a miracle is. However, we can say that it is a sign of God's saving action, frequently addressed to a definite person at a given point in time. In the miraculous event, the subject experienced in a dramatic way the self-communication of God that was not necessarily evident to anyone who might have been a witness to the event. There is no doubt that miracles are clearly presumed to have occurred, according to those sayings of Jesus which have been shown by scholars to have been certainly his.

In addressing the subject of the resurrection, Rahner describes it as the definitive and complete salvation and validation of the humanity of Jesus—the final demonstration of his identity as the absolute savior. This is what we mean when we say that Jesus is risen into the faith of his disciples. Christ's victory is in a true sense the anticipation of our victory over death. All of us are continually confronted with the prospect of our own mortality. We have to concede that life as we know it is not such that we would want it to go on forever. Yet we yearn for something more, a new existence that arises out of death, not simply a continuation of what we experience now. What we know of the resurrection of Jesus can serve as a prototype of the kind of victory we might hopefully achieve after death. Reviewing the resurrection experiences shared by the early disciples, we encounter a good many reports of the appearances of Jesus that are very difficult to harmonize into a continuous narrative. One issue is certainly clear. These men and women were very aware of the fact that what Rahner refers to as "Easter experiences" were events that they encountered in the world outside of them. They were not purely internal experiences.

The religious Jews of Jesus' day—except perhaps for the Sadducees—had a general belief in the resurrection, and they held out the hope that it would be the ultimate destiny of everyone. The original theology of the resurrection of Christ among his followers was that his victorious return constituted the complete vindication of his claim to be the final prophet and the absolute savior. They believed that the risen Christ is no less than the definitive self-disclosure of God in the world, and that his resurrection, of which they were witnesses, was in some fashion a pledge of their own total victory if they persevered in faith and charity. In the later writings of the New Testament, a redemptive dimension was ascribed to the death of Jesus, and the notion of placating the offended God by means of an expiatory sacrifice was developed (e.g., Hebrews 5–10). Such an approach, according to Rahner, offers little help for us today.

Without attempting to set forth the official classical Christology as articulated in the Councils of Nicaea, Ephesus, and Chalcedon, Rahner diagnoses this approach as a descending Christology, a Christology from above, which develops out of the idea that the Word, the eternal Son of God, became man. This rationale presupposes the classical trinitarian theology wherein Father, Son, and Holy Spirit are three persons in one God, and are distinct from one another relationally. The Word, at the appointed time, assumed a complete human nature in a union that has been termed *hypostatic*, with no intermingling of natures, but both existing unseparated from the Word. The official teaching of the church has not attempted to expand on the character of this hypostatic union in its dogmatic pronouncements. Rahner notes that none of the efforts to explain this union more fully in the Middle Ages has found very wide acceptance in the church. In the clarification of the union of the human and divine in Jesus, there is always the Nestorian danger of predicating two subjects in Christ, and the monophysitic danger of making the humanity of Jesus a mere instrument of the Word. This latter danger is the much more common aberration of believers today. The human nature of Jesus must always be affirmed as a created, conscious, and free humanity, with a created subjectivity distinct from the subjectivity of the Word. This created subjectivity faces God at "a created distance" in freedom and obedience.

The classical soteriology has really not developed much beyond the New Testament presentation of the subject. In the West the expiatory sacrifice thesis of St. Anselm of Canterbury (1033–1109) has been widely espoused and, according to Rahner, has even found its way into some of the official church pronouncements dealing with the redemption. Further, there can be no doubt that there are limitations to the classical presentation of Christology. There is the abiding danger of mythologizing Christ so that his humanity is not fully accounted for, and this attenuates his role and function as mediator between God and humankind. Further, we must respect the classical definitions as we seek out new formulations that will be more sensitive to the contemporary intellectual and cultural horizons. The traditional Christology from above, which was no doubt adequate for earlier ages, may not be sufficient for believers today who want to see the fullness of Christ's humanity given greater attention and prominence. Rahner urges us to expand our vistas and our thought patterns so that we can express the truth of the ancient formulas in a more credible fashion for our age.

Perhaps the overtures in the area of transcendental Christology can be developed, as well as the possibilities of a new approach to a Christology from below that begins with humankind's boundless openness upward, and humanity's obediential potency for the be-

atific vision. Such an offer of the immediate vision of God would
have to be made in history—discovered, identified, and responded
to in history. Rahner's final thoughts are directed to the challenges
raised recently by the preexistence of the Son. His response is that
if Jesus Christ is the absolute event of salvation, embodying the
definitive offer of God's own self and (at the same time) the free,
created acceptance of that offer, then, he reasons, the one who
offers himself—that is, God—must be preexistent.

In a study written in the fall of 1961, Rahner probes somewhat
more deeply into the questions of the human knowledge and the
self-consciousness of Christ.[18] He asserts that the 1943 encyclical,
Mystici Corporis, attributed to Jesus an explicit knowledge concerning all the members of the Mystical Body of all ages from the
first moment of his Incarnation.

> For hardly was He conceived in the womb of the Mother
> of God, when He began to enjoy the beatific vision, and in
> that vision all the members of his Mystical Body were con-
> tinually and unceasingly present to Him.... In the crib, on
> the Cross, in the unending glory of the Father, Christ has all
> the members of the Church present before Him and united
> to Him.[19]

Rahner comments that these declarations seem contrary to the real
humanity of Jesus, since in the gospels he is described as growing
in wisdom and knowledge (Luke 2:52), and as confessing ignorance regarding certain decisive saving events of the future (Matt.
24:36). The theologian then attempts to present a scenario that
is in accord with the statements of the magisterium on the matter of Christ's human knowledge. He asks why it is that we feel
compelled to ascribe to the earthly Jesus the beatific vision, since
a direct presence to God would not always necessarily have to
be "beatific." Can one seriously maintain that in his death agony
on the cross, when he felt forsaken by God, Jesus enjoyed the
beatitude of the blessed?

Although the immediate vision of God is unquestionably an essential element of the hypostatic union, this vision does not of
necessity have to be beatific. The earthly Jesus possessed what Rahner terms an unobjectified consciousness of his divine sonship and
a consciousness of a direct presence to God. But this awareness was
situated at the subjective pole of our Lord's consciousness and was

not the vision of an object. This consciousness evolved only gradually during his earthly life. The self-understanding of his situation and his identity occurred day by day, in and through the unfolding events of his human history. Thus he grasped more and more what he truly was and what he in some fashion already knew. In light of this immediate vision of God at the subjective pole of his human consciousness, Rahner did not believe it critical to posit infused knowledge in Christ. Also, he concludes that a lack of knowledge on various occasions on the part of Jesus regarding certain events and happenings would have been consistent with this immediate vision of God, which only gradually deepened and expanded during his time on earth. The genuine humanity of Christ requires that growth in knowledge be a part of his human experience. At the same time, the doctrinal statements of the church demand that we affirm that the human soul of Jesus shared in the direct vision of God during his earthly life, although the precise nature of this vision remains unclear. Karl Rahner's efforts to reconcile the data of the church's doctrine with our contemporary understanding of human consciousness, and what that understanding demands of us today when we say that Christ is indeed truly man, represent, within the context of the classical Christology from above, a very distinctive and precious contribution.

Gerald O'Collins

One of the more representative contemporary contributions of the Christology from above school is the 1995 study published by Gerald O'Collins, currently a professor at the Gregorian University.[20] The author begins with a review of the pertinent biblical data, that is, the Old Testament roots, the human history of Jesus as reflected in the New Testament, and an extended treatment of the resurrection. He then delves into the principal titles referring to Christ, such as Son of God, Lord, Savior, God, and Spirit, and proceeds to outline the history of the theological development from the Fathers of the church, the councils, especially Ephesus and Chalcedon, and the progress of christological thought from the medieval to the modern period. For O'Collins, the Council of Chalcedon constituted the defining moment for the discipline by setting forth the formulas and the language (e.g., person, nature, hypostasis) that would remain normative from the fifth century to the present, although it failed to define the terms it employed. That was not unusual since councils often do not attempt to define the philosophical terms that they use in their declarations. However, in this instance, the fifth-century uses of the words *person, nature,* and *hypostasis* were so varied, especially between East and West, that it is now quite challenging to determine what such theologians as Theodore of Mopsuestia, Cyril of Alexandria, and even Pope Leo I meant when they employed such language.

In the section on the medieval period, O'Collins deals extensively with the Christology of Thomas Aquinas (ca. 1224–74), concluding that Thomas's greatest achievements were his emphasis on Christ's free and loving consent to undergo death, his application to Jesus of the titles "priest, prophet and king," his emphasis on the human story of Christ (largely ignored after Trent), and his consistent emphasis on a Christology from above. For Thomas, the humanity of Jesus simply had to have the best of everything, for example, every conceivable resource in the area of knowledge— the beatific vision and infused knowledge as well as acquired knowledge. And Christ's beatific vision involved for Aquinas a comprehensive grasp of all creatures, present, past, and future, and all their possible actions. Apparently Thomas had no trouble reconciling this awesome knowledge with the fact that Jesus bore the limitations of humankind.

During the Reformation both Catholic and Protestant scholars were more concerned about the issue of the justification of sinners than about the doctrine of the Incarnation. Both Martin Luther (1483–1546) and John Calvin (1509–64) held fast to the positions of Chalcedon and were not especially interested in metaphysical Christology. Nor was there a great deal of christological development in Catholic circles during the sixteenth and seventeenth centuries. The quest for scientific objectivity and the turn toward the conscious subject initiated by René Descartes (1596–1650) changed the direction of the academic world and opened the way for the Enlightenment that, from a theological point of view, was predominantly deistic in tone. These eighteenth-century thinkers repudiated such phenomena as the miracles and the resurrection of Christ. After Immanuel Kant (1724–1804) had insisted that we are not able to know such things as the existence of God and the immortality of the soul through the light of natural reason, Friedrich Schleiermacher (1768–1834) preached a Christianity based upon feelings and an approach to faith as a feeling of absolute dependence upon God. His Christology revolved around his conviction that the uniqueness of Jesus consisted of his singular "God consciousness," which animated his entire earthly existence. Following the Enlightenment, the nineteenth century was punctuated by a flurry of "lives of Jesus" especially out of Germany, which in the estimate of Albert Schweitzer (1875–1965) portrayed Jesus according to the various authors' own likes and values. O'Collins complains that this very same kind of reductionism and subjectivism is happening again in our day.

After this extensive background, O'Collins directs himself to the more central christological issues such as the divinity and the humanity of Christ. He states that we recognize in Jesus certain divine characteristics, and we can respond to these in one of two ways. There are soft accounts of the Incarnation in which God is said to be definitively disclosed and revealed in Jesus. But O'Collins asks, is Christ nothing more than a window, or is he truly God? It is his conviction that a full doctrine of the Incarnation requires that Jesus be identified not just as God's final and complete revelation, but as one who is actually, substantially divine. We cannot, he says, accept a Christ who merely represents God for us, while not truly being divine himself. In dealing with the humanity of Jesus O'Collins sets forth certain properties which, in his judgment, essentially constitute what it is to be human: a bodily existence, rationality, free will, affectivity, and memory. If all of these properties can be predicated of Christ as man, then he must be recognized as sharing our condition. This sidesteps the question of the integrity and wholeness of Christ's created subjectivity and his distinctive reality as a limited, created member of the human race who is identified with us.

O'Collins addresses the problem of the one single subject being both divine and human. He does not agree with Schleiermacher, who held that one individual cannot possibly share two very different natures. The two essences, according to O'Collins, are not mutually exclusive, and consequently the Incarnation does not present itself to human reason as obviously "incoherent." The relationship between the divine consciousness of the Word and the separate human consciousness of Jesus is not treated by the author in detail, as Karl Rahner did. O'Collins does affirm that Christ was aware of his distinct human identity and his unique relationship with the Father. He disagrees, however, with James D. G. Dunn, who said that only in the Gospel of John is there an unambiguous claim of Christ's preexistence.[21] According to O'Collins, 2 Corinthians 8:9, Philippians 2:6–8, Colossians 1:15–17, and Hebrews 1:1–3, 9:26, 10:5–10 also assert the preexistence of the Word who became flesh in Jesus. In contrast to such theologians as Walter Kasper, Hans Küng, Wolfhart Pannenberg, and Edward Schillebeeckx whom he considers as proponents of a Christology from below, O'Collins proudly places his work in the Christology from above category, due to his emphatic affirmation of the preexistence of the Word who became man.

Although the English theologian John Macquarrie has recently taught that preexistence would threaten the genuineness of Christ's humanity, he does allow that in a certain fashion Jesus did preexist in the plan and foreknowledge of God from the beginning.[22] O'Collins counters this position categorically, asserting that the preexistent Christ in John's Prologue, Philippians 2:6–8, and Colossians 1:15–20 cannot be reduced to a mere intention in the mind of God, since preexistence in the divine intention could well be true of all of us. O'Collins also roundly criticizes American scholar Roger Haight for his claim that preexistence is incompatible with Chalcedon's teaching that Jesus is consubstantial with us. According to Haight, what is preexistent to Jesus is God, who became man in Christ.[23] O'Collins retorts that the God who became incarnate in Jesus is not God as such, but the second person of the Trinity.

Regarding the question of a distinct human consciousness in Jesus, O'Collins teaches that the fact that there is but one person in Christ does not rule out the existence of "a distinctive assemblage of traits" that together constitute the human personality of Christ. It is in this sense that Jesus possessed, and possesses, a human personality. He enjoys a divine consciousness as well as a human consciousness, but the ontological unity of his person calls for a single self-aware center of reference for his actions and experiences. This can only be the ego of the Word operating through the divine and the human consciousnesses. Rahner's description of the divine and the human subjectivities seems more convincing and more credible than O'Collins's analysis of the ego of the Word on the one hand, and that "distinct assemblage of traits" constituting the human personality of Jesus on the other.

Does the human ego of Christ know that he is a divine subject? O'Collins responds that during his earthly life, Jesus had a limited human understanding of his divine identity but no awareness of his eternal preexistence. Although his human knowledge was finite and temporal, he coexperienced the Infinite and Eternal as the One to whom he was related as Son to Father. The author deals at some length with the faith of Jesus, that is, Jesus as a believer. He reminds us that Aquinas had taught that Christ was not a believer, since he possessed the beatific vision from the first moment of his human existence.[24] O'Collins is unable to accept Thomas's view that the human Jesus enjoyed the beatific vision. Otherwise, how could he have suffered? How was his human will free? How were the temptations he experienced anything more than a facade? This would call into question the true character of Christ's human knowledge that, according to Chalcedon, was genuinely human. The New Testament evidence, he says, leads us to the same conclusion (Mark 5:30–32, 13:32). In the Synoptics, Jesus' unique relationship with the Father (Abba) was the ground for his human awareness of his divine sonship and his saving mission. Further, this awareness expanded as he proceeded through life. O'Collins probes more deeply into the faith of Christ, which he says is alluded to in Hebrews 12:2. Although Jesus did not have to believe in his divine sonship or in his redemptive mission of which he had direct knowledge, he did have faith in the saving history of his own people. He also believed in his own future and had confidence in the positive outcome of his own mission, wherever that would lead him. In O'Collins's Christology from above, he not only asserts that Jesus' sinlessness is revealed in the New Testament, but also his incapacity to sin since he was a divine person. His temptations were real inasmuch as Christ probably was not aware that he was incapable of sinning. The author's treatment of the grace of Christ follows the classical Christology fairly closely, attributing to him the grace of the hypostatic union, habitual grace, and the grace of headship whereby all grace flows to humanity through him.

O'Collins vigorously and explicitly defends the virginal conception of Jesus against such theologians as Edward Schillebeeckx and Hans Küng who opt for more symbolic interpretations.[25] He maintains that both Luke and Matthew regarded the virgin birth as historical, although he admits that their views of what is historical were quite different from ours. The point of the infancy narratives was to give a trinitarian face to the story of Jesus from the outset.

Gerald O'Collins notes that over the years there has been little doctrinal clarification regarding the redemptive function of Christ. The effects of sin in the world are many, that is, alienation from God and from one another, illness and death, ignorance, error. According to Paul and John the key to the redemptive effort is divine love (Rom. 5:10–11; John 3:16–17) that has been poured out on us in Christ through the Spirit. The Letter to the Hebrews develops the image of Christ as priest and victim after the pattern of Isaiah 53. But it is the theme of love, according to O'Collins, which prevails in the New Testament as the primal force of the redemption. The story of the prodigal son (Luke 15:11–32) provides an exquisite paradigm of salvation, with love as the central theme. Out of love come reconciliation, reunion, and restoration. That this redemption effected by Christ is available to all humankind is a recurring theme in the New Testament (e.g., 2 Cor. 5:14–15; Col. 1:15–20; Acts 17:22–31; Matt. 28:18–19), and has been proclaimed by a number of the Fathers of the church such as Justin, Irenaeus, Athanasius, and Gregory of Nyssa. O'Collins makes much of the last judgment scene in Matthew's gospel (25:31–46) in that it lifts up the authentic and active love of neighbor as the ultimate criterion of salvation, which carries a strong inference of the universalism of the redemption in Christ. O'Collins ends his treatment of Christology by attempting to outline a theology of presence, Christ-presence, built on the theme suggested in Matthew 28:20, "behold I shall be with you always," but the presentation is neither especially forceful nor does it seem to contribute very much to his overall approach. This 1995 study by O'Collins, however, does fairly represent the state of thought from the point of view of those theologians who propose a Christology from above.

Influential Protestant Theologians

Karl Barth

The Swiss scholar Karl Barth (1886–1968) has been called by many the most important Protestant theologian in the first half of the twentieth century. He came out of the liberal Protestant school of the nineteenth century but experienced a radical change of heart in August of 1914 when he learned that two of his teachers, Adolf Harnack and J. W. Herrmann, had formally endorsed the aggressive militarist policies of Wilhelm II, emperor of Germany from 1888 to 1918. In a lecture delivered at a meeting of Swiss Reformed ministers in September 1956, Barth analyzed what had occurred in 1914.[26] Evangelical theology had become anthropocentric and humanistic, having little to say about God. This situation had to be turned around and God had to become once again the center of theological interest. It was the "holy Other" breaking in from above that alone mattered. Schleiermacher had to be "stood on his head!" Other factors were involved, of course, in the rejection of liberal theology by Barth and others—the pessimism in Europe just prior to the outbreak of World War I, and the growing feeling that the pervasive nineteenth-century belief in progress had stalled.

According to Barth, the nineteenth century had accomplished little in terms of a fresh understanding of Christian revelation and was too much inclined to canonize the secular ideas of the age. Faith gave way to philosophy since liberal theology's more notable spokespersons saw themselves as philosophers first and theologians second. The liberal approach to theology, although beneficial in some respects, resulted in leaving God almost out of the equation. Although the emphasis upon the historical character of Christianity was important and constituted an achievement, most of the Protestant biblical and historical scholars of the last century worked more as scientists than as men of faith. For the most part, they did not see themselves as operating within the community of believers, but were criticizing the Christian phenomenon from the outside. Their work was seen by the world as scholarship in the history of religions, rather than as the efforts of Christian biblicists, theologians, and historians.

Barth sensed that it was time to change direction. His clarion call was his commentary on the Epistle to the Romans which appeared in 1918 and was thoroughly revised in 1922.[27] It was in effect the magna charta of a new theology, affirming the word of God over human efforts at constructing religious meaning. In his analysis of Romans 9:1–5 Barth says:

> God the pure and absolute boundary and beginning of all that we are and have and do; God, who is distinguished qualitatively from men and from everything human . . . who is never

a known thing in the midst of other known things; God, the
Lord, the Creator, the Redeemer,—this is the living God. In
the Gospel, in the message of Salvation of Jesus Christ, this
hidden, living, God has revealed Himself as He is.[28]

Barth is not particularly concerned with textual criticism. His
concentration is on the word of God as revealed in scripture.

For Barth theology begins and ends with Jesus.[29] As a matter of
fact, for this author there are no Christian truths independent of
Christology, which is the center of everything. The New Testament
always assumes the genuine humanity of Jesus who is qualitatively
different from all other humans. Before he became flesh, he was
the Son of God the Father and, by nature, God. The earthly Jesus
did not ally himself with any of the religious or political factions
of his day, but he did feel free to criticize them when they had
strayed from the truth. He regarded the Jerusalem temple as his
Father's house (Luke 2:49), although its significance was not permanent (John 4:21), and he participated in the religious rituals
of the Galilean synagogues (Luke 4:16–17). According to Barth
Jesus came to fulfill the law (Matt. 5:17), and he acknowledged
the authority of the scribes and Pharisees (Matt. 23:1–2) in spite of
the fact that he frequently disagreed with them. Christ did not see
himself as a political or economic reformer (Mark 12:17; Matt.
20:1–16). He recognized the jurisdiction of Rome and that of the
Jewish rulers, though he did call Herod a fox (Luke 13:32). The
Lord did not consider the Sabbath regulations as absolutes since
the Sabbath was made for humans (Mark 2:27).

Barth teaches that Jesus stands between God and humankind
as the mediator who brings redemption and salvation. He became
man to plead our case. Because he is God, however, he is human
in a different way from all other men. He suffered for us and bore
the penalty of sin that was to fall upon each of us. Christ as God
can act in an absolute way and also in a finite way. He assumed
a worldly form without giving up his own divine form. In no way
did he dishonor himself when he went "into the far country" in
the form of a servant. The most important thing we can say about
Jesus, according to Barth, is that he is the Son of God, since this
title reveals to us most completely who he truly is. Barth assures
us that God does not cease to be God in the Incarnation. That is,
Jesus is authentically human only as the Son of God, and there is

no question of any human personhood in Christ. Moreover, this lack of human personhood does not in any way destroy the true humanity of Jesus.[30]

According to Barth, Jesus took the place of sinful humankind. Through his passion and death, he reestablished the covenant between God and humanity that had been broken, not just by Adam and Eve but by all of us. Christ made himself the target of the divine judgment that humankind deserved because of unfaithfulness. He actually took our place. As the Son of God he had the authority to make this substitution and to permit this to happen to him. Humankind was pronounced righteous because of what he suffered, freeing us from inevitable doom and destruction. Barth teaches that redemption for us consists in acknowledging that our sinfulness is really dead, though we are powerless to cleanse ourselves. There has been realized in Christ a new beginning for all humankind which is quite beyond our powers. God has let himself be known to us in and through the humanity that Jesus assumed. God speaks to us when this man speaks, and acts when this man acts, since God himself came among us in his Son. It is the Holy Spirit who discloses to men and women that because they are in Christ and with Christ, they can themselves be called children of God.

In his *Church Dogmatics*, volume 1, part 1, Barth clearly establishes that the divinity of Christ is to be understood in the sense that he reveals the Father. To reveal the Father is to reveal God, and who can reveal God but God himself?[31] To confess Jesus as the privileged revelation of the Father is to affirm him as essentially equal in divinity to the Father. According to the revelation set out in the scriptures, humankind has wantonly abandoned communion with God and has found itself in a situation in which God has turned away from us. The work of the Son, however, constitutes a new revelation. Jesus the reconciler consummates a second divine act, that is, the act of reconciliation, which follows upon the act of creation. Although the Son follows upon the Father, this act of reconciliation is no less divine than the act of creation.

The affirmation of the eternal divinity of the Son is a fundamental statement that the Reformers never thought of compromising in any way whatsoever. The creed of Nicaea-Constantinople stands as an indispensable norm for Christian faith. The Father and the Son are not two independent essences. Rather, they exist in two different ways in the same independent essence.[32] For Barth, the Son's consubstantiality with the Father is the most critical dimension of the dogma. He sees Father and Son as two distinct and equal modes of the one essence. Barth is not comfortable with the use of the word *person* as applied to the Father, the Son, and the Holy Spirit. He is convinced that this designation was accepted in the early centuries on the basis of certain linguistic presuppositions that are no longer valid today. There was no intention to imply that in God are three different personalities, with their own special self-consciousness, cognition, volition, and activity. The one personality of God is Father, Son, and Holy Spirit. There are three different modes of being to which the term *person* was applied. In three different modes God exists as the one personal God.

In *Church Dogmatics*, volume 4, part 1, Barth deals in detail with the journey of the Son "into the far country." Christ willed to be obedient to the Father and to become the servant of all. There can be no doubt about the full and authentic humanity of the man Jesus. However, every pericope of the New Testament portrays this genuinely human being as the one who is qualitatively different from all other humans. His disciples saw him as absolutely unique. Jesus did not simply become "any flesh," he became Jewish flesh, and the high moment in the history of God with the people of Israel. This identification of Jesus as a Jew of this time and place closes the door on every species of Docetism. In addition to being the electing Creator, God has now become the elect creature. He is not only the giver but also the recipient of grace who accepts personal responsibility for all the rebellion and unfaithfulness of his people. Taking on the mantle of a sinner, he is not accepted by the Father. In Christ it is God himself who takes the place of sinners and allows the bitterness of their guilt and suffering to fall upon himself.

This man, Jesus, who was born like all of us in time, who was in fact tempted and suffered and died, did not cease to be God, and experienced no diminution of his divine nature. The Son did not give up being God by becoming man, but at the same time, as man he was not omnipotent and eternal but limited in time and space, not glorious but lowly.[33] Yet, on the other hand, of what value would his deity be to us if he had left that deity behind in coming to us? If God has revealed himself in Christ as the one who enters into our condition, we must correct our notions concerning the being of God, in light of the fact that he has accomplished this. Indeed, he thus shows himself to be greater and more sovereign than anyone could imagine. The Incarnation reveals that for God it is just as natural to be lowly as to be exalted. The world cannot achieve its own act of atonement, standing as it does in need of radical reconciliation. Anyone less than the true God could not atone for the alienation separating the human race from the Deity. In the Godhead there is One who obeys and the Other who is obeyed. This "subordination" belongs to the inner life of God. It is a differentiation within the Godhead of the modes of divine being.[34]

Barth asks how an event that occurred a very long time ago can be judged as important for us now. His answer is that we must accept the significance of Christ's death and resurrection from the testimony of the church, and ultimately from the biblical witness.[35] Thus, he does not consider the problem of the German philosopher Gotthold Lessing (1729–81)—that is, the issue of historical distance—to be a genuine obstacle, because these critical happenings in the life of Jesus have an abiding, once-and-for-all impact on humankind. Barth distinguishes the event of the cross, which has a component of human willing and acting, from the resurrection that was purely an act of God. Nonetheless, the raising of Christ from the dead was a happening in time. Although there is no historical ground for proving the resurrection to the "historicists," it did take place in time just as surely as the crucifixion.

The forty days between the resurrection and the ascension gave to the disciples a sure and higher place from which they could look back on the life and death of Christ with an enlightened awareness of the act of God that took place here. They were also given a grace-filled opportunity to look forward in order that they might determine how the rest of their lives would be transformed by their participation in these wondrous happenings. The death and resurrection of Jesus constitute the basic events of the alteration of the human situation, that is, the reconciliation of the world with God. The ascension bespeaks the exaltation of Christ to the right hand of the Father, as well as the risen Lord's direct and active presence in the community of believers through his Spirit. We are now situated "between the times," the time of the community in the world, and the final phase that is still to come—the parousia at the end of the ages "when he comes again in the clouds of heaven with power and glory" (Matt. 24:30).

Karl Barth was a neo-orthodox theologian in that he reasserted the authority of a religious tradition that had receded into relative obscurity in Protestant circles after the Enlightenment.[36] After World War I the liberal theology of the nineteenth century had largely run its course and given way to a return of the classical, God-centered theology that had preceded it. The leader of this movement was none other than Barth. The Bible was for him the word of God pure and simple. Historical criticism and biblical critical apparatus were not major concerns for him after his student days. Revelation is a gift from above and does not emerge from our religious consciousness. Biblical faith is not only Christocentric but it also draws believers of necessity into the church. Without active church affiliation there is no genuine Christian life. Although there is no mistaking Barth for anyone other than a Reformed theologian in the tradition of John Calvin, his views on election and predestination are radically different from Calvin's. Barth teaches that all of humanity has been chosen by God in Christ. He maintains that salvation is available to everybody, for the "friendliness of God" as revealed in Christ knows no limits.[37] In spite of his enormous influence, especially during the years between World War I and World War II, after his death in 1968 there has been a decline of interest in the work of Karl Barth.

Wolfhart Pannenberg

After Karl Barth, no one has been more important to the development of Protestant dogmatic theology than Wolfhart Pannenberg (b. 1928). After completing his studies at Berlin, Göttingen, Basel, and Heidelberg, he spent a number of years as an instructor and then professor of systematics. In 1968 he was appointed professor of systematic theology on the Protestant theological faculty at the University of Munich, where he has remained for more than thirty years. Pannenberg's outstanding effort in Christology, *Jesus—God and Man*, was published in German in 1964 and translated into English in 1977.[38]

Pannenberg asserts that Jesus' unity with God was validated by his resurrection from the dead. His pre-Easter words and deeds pointed to the importance of his life and mission, but they could not unambiguously demonstrate that Jesus was the definitive bearer of God's salvation. Even the disciples could do no more than hope that his unique claim to authority, which was blasphemous to the Jews, would be verified and confirmed by God. Through his resurrection Jesus assumed the role of the Son of man who, as a heavenly being, would return at the end of the ages.

Although his initial overtures were directed to his fellow Jews, the inclusion of the Gentiles into the final salvation was inevitable as soon as the crucifixion was seen as Jesus' rejection by Israel. For Paul the resurrection means a new life with a new body (1 Cor. 15:35–56), a radical transformation. In the first century C.E. the hope of a general resurrection was rather widely held by the Jews. Pannenberg notes that even in our day human existence yearns and calls for some kind of continuance beyond the portal of death, and hence the expectation of resurrection does not appear to be an inappropriate expression of human destiny.

Pannenberg focuses on 1 Corinthians 15:3–8, where Paul formally enumerates the basic appearances of the risen Lord. This information must have come to Paul shortly after his conversion (33–35 C.E.) and probably no more than six to eight years after the occurrences. They are affirmed by Paul as historical events, even if we do not know the particulars. The appearance narratives and the tradition of the empty tomb are judged by Pannenberg to be historically very probable and should stand until contrary evidence surfaces (105). The affirmation of the resurrection cannot be justified if it is not assumed as a historical event that occurred at a certain time and place, even though we do not know anything more particular about it. The facticity of the event serves as a critical base for grounding our faith in the resurrection of Jesus. The unity of Jesus with God is certified by his resurrection from the dead. His pre-Easter words and deeds do not unambiguously demonstrate his unity with God, nor do they show that he was the bearer of God's definitive salvation.

Pannenberg points out that various approaches have been taken by theologians to express God's presence in Jesus. Paul's reference to Jesus, established as Son of God by the Spirit of holiness through his resurrection (Rom. 1:3), gave way to the Logos doctrine featured by John (1:14). This emphasis changed the focus from the presence of the Spirit in Jesus to the substantial presence of the preexistent Word in Christ, and the confession of Jesus as a divine person. His essential unity with God as Son was not a consequence of his resurrection. Rather, it was the resurrection that confirmed his pre-Easter claims to authority. If Jesus was recognized as Son of God in the resurrection, then he was always the divine Son. "The resurrection establishes retroactively that Jesus as a person is not to be separated from God in any way at any time" (141).

Paul presupposed the preexistence of the Son (Gal. 4:4) and portrayed his destiny as moving from heaven to earth and back to heaven (Phil. 2:6–11). Pannenberg attests that the notion of preexistence was developed from Jesus' resurrection as a logical consequence of his essential unity with God. The preexistent Son joined himself with the earthly corporeality of the man Jesus. The eternal sonship and Jesus' human existence are part of a single concrete life. Jesus' person cannot be separated from the divine essence because he is God's self-revelation. The distinction that Christ affirmed between himself and the Father in terms of submission and obedience is reflected in the divine essence. Although the Son is equal to God the Father (John 10:30), the Father is identified as greater than the Son (John 14:28) because of the distinction that Jesus reveals between the Son and the Father.

The Spirit also belongs to the event of God's revelation, and hence to the divinity of God, for what pertains to God's revelation belongs to the essence of God. Through Jesus the Spirit opens the way for the faithful to community with God. Inasmuch as the Father, Son, and Spirit are distinct moments in the unfolding of God's self-revelation, then they are such in God's eternal essence as well. Pannenberg defines salvation as the realization of the full and final destiny of man. Jesus' resurrection reveals the destiny of humanity and allows the faithful to anticipate a life of nearness to God. Future salvation is indeed foreshadowed in the words and deeds of the pre-Easter Jesus. His healings indicate that when the message of deliverance is fully accepted, salvation takes place. The nearness of God is expressed, for example, in the verses of the Lord's Prayer and in the parable of the prodigal son (Luke 15:11–32).

It is likely that Jesus had some idea of the possibility of his death when he made his way toward Jerusalem (Luke 20:28). What he thought of this, or how he explained it to himself, is difficult to say. Whether he saw himself as a just man who was to suffer for the sins of his people (Mark 10:45) is not clear. He was aware, however, of his claims to singular authority. The injunction, "But I say to you," repeated frequently in the Sermon on the Mount did equate his own authority with that of God. His acts of forgiving sins reflected authority that belongs only to God. The principal accusation leveled against Christ by the Jews was that he made himself equal to God (John 5:18). His willful activity in the temple (Matt. 11:15–17) astonished the chief priests and the scribes and led to the indictment that he placed himself above the law and claimed the authority of God himself. Because the Jews were not prepared to distinguish between the authority of God and the authority of the law, Jesus' behavior was viewed as blasphemy.

Pannenberg then turns his attention to the question of the divinity of Jesus in the Christian tradition. After Chalcedon (451) Christ appears as uniting two diverse substances in himself, and from this a whole series of questions has arisen. The Christology of Antioch struggled to keep the divine and human natures of Jesus distinct and integral, but it left unexplained how the human and the divine could be united in the one person, Jesus. This suggests a moral rather than an ontological unity. The Alexandrian Christology emphasized the unity of the natures so heavily that Christ's full humanity was threatened. As they portrayed him, Jesus seemed to possess no specific human individuality, and human nature without human individuality would be an anomaly. Although Chalcedon expressed the essential elements of truth affirmed by both schools, the attempt to force the acceptance of the Chalcedonian formula occasioned the first great confessional schism in which Syria, Palestine, and Egypt became largely monophysite.

Pannenberg asks whether the Incarnation could be more appropriately viewed as a process continuing through Jesus' entire earthly life, one that was completed only at the resurrection. In this scenario the unity of God with the man and of the man with God developed only gradually (306). In this fashion one would arrive at a theory that more effectively reflects the growth and development of the real humanity of Jesus.

Karl Barth failed to address adequately the question of the unity of God and man in Christ. His emphasis upon the humble condescension of God in the Incarnation did not provide an adequate explanation. The efforts of the kenotic theologians (who stress the self-emptying of the Word in becoming man) often diminish the full humanity of Jesus. Pannenberg notes that the unity of God and man in Christ can be decided only retroactively from the point of view of the resurrection. It is only in this culminating event that Christ's unity with God hidden to his contemporaries and even to Jesus himself becomes known. "The confirmation of Jesus' unity

with God in the retroactive power of his resurrection makes the
hiddenness of this unity during Jesus' earthly life comprehensible,
and thus makes room for the genuine humanity of this life" (322).
The issue of the nature of the union of the divine and human in
Christ, according to Pannenberg, remains an open question.

It seems certain that the pre-Easter Jesus did not identify himself
as Messiah or Son of God. Further, he did not welcome such con-
fessions from his contemporaries. Pannenberg asks how it could
be that Jesus would have known during his earthly life that he
was divine. Would not this have completely changed his human
self-consciousness and his human personality? Christ's lack of
knowledge must have extended to the question of his own personal identity. No doubt, in Jesus' self-consciousness there was an
awareness of his intimate and singular relationship with the Father. In Pannenberg's judgment, however, Jesus was not conscious
of a direct relationship with the Logos during his pre-Easter life.
His conscious union was with the Father. In and through the resurrection, he is revealed as the one who is obedient to the Father
in the fulfillment of his appointed mission. Through his dedicated
life and death, he is the revelation of the Father, and as such he is
one with God. In his total submission to the Father's will, Jesus reveals his divinity, and hence he belongs inseparably to the essence
of God.

Through his resurrection Christ completes his identity with the
eternal Son. It is only the resurrection that confirms the meaning
of Jesus' earthly life as total filial dedication to the Father. In this
manner Jesus shows himself to be identical with the eternal Son.
The dependence that grounded Christ's human dedication to God
the Father makes him identical with the person of the eternal Son.
Jesus' life of total dependence on the Father demonstrated that
he was one with the preexistent Son. Pannenberg attests, however, that Christ was a human individual only in consequence of
his union with the Logos, which reached its culmination in the
resurrection.

> Jesus' divinity is not a second "substance" in the man Jesus
> in addition to his humanity. Then precisely as this man, Jesus
> is the Son of God and thus himself God. Consequently, he
> is not to be thought of as a synthesis of the divine and the
> human.... Nor does something new, a third thing, result from

the mixture of the two. Nor is the humanity absorbed in the divinity so that it disappears. Precisely *in* this particular humanity, Jesus is the Son of God.... This historical uniqueness of Jesus' situation distinguishes him from all other men.... Thus, Jesus' identity with the Son of God is dialectical: the understanding of this man, in his humanity changed to its opposite, leads to the confession of his eternal divinity. (342–43)

The various elements of Christ's human existence were integrated into a whole by the person of the Son of God. This integration took place through the entire history of Jesus' earthly life as he moved more and more deeply into his role as the Father's obedient Son. Christ developed his personality through his singular relationship with the Father, and that personality was the personality of the eternal Son. As an individual man, only Jesus is the Son of God. Christians who participate in this filial relationship through the Spirit become adopted sons and daughters of God.

Contrary to the prevailing opinion, Wolfhart Pannenberg asserts that the resurrection of Jesus is a historical event that forms the basis for the affirmation of Christ's full divinity. The focal relationship for Jesus was his abiding openness to the Father. Christ's self-consciousness evolved throughout his life and was perfected in and through the resurrection. He was not aware of his divine sonship until the resurrection, when his relationship with the Father was finalized, and then his identification with the eternal Son was complete. Although Pannenberg affirms that his approach is a Christology from below, he wants us to understand and evaluate the words and actions of the earthly Jesus in the light of the resurrection that retroactively radiates its meaning on the entire life of the pre-Easter Jesus. His approach does not seem to coincide with the pattern followed by those who profess an ascending Christology.

With the publication of volume 2 of his highly regarded *Systematic Theology* in 1991, Professor Pannenberg returns to the subject of Christology.[39] He once again addresses the approach to the discipline that can be initiated from above or from below. Since the third century, Logos Christology emphasized the descending pattern that was predominant until the nineteenth century when the liberal Protestants popularized the approach from below. For

Pannenberg, the historical Jesus must be the starting point and the measure of all assertions regarding the person of Jesus. We can only know God himself through the words and deeds of Christ during his life on earth. The critical event, however, is his resurrection that validates his human life. Through the resurrection, he was acclaimed *Kyrios* (Phil. 2:9–11) and was appointed Son of God in power (Rom. 1:4). Only from the perspective of the resurrection is he the preexistent Son (283).

We are reminded, however, that the historicity of the resurrection event is crucial for the verification of the historical knowledge that serves as the basis of our confession of Christ. If we fail to affirm that the resurrection was a historical fact, the meaning of the life and work of the pre-Easter Jesus will not fully assert itself. A Christology from below does not need to rule out the classical Christology of the Incarnation, because it is indeed the eternal Son who became man. Nonetheless, the approach from below runs the risk of underplaying the divine in the drama of Christ.

Pannenberg notes that we humans possess an awareness that rises above the finite objects we encounter. In comprehending finite objects, we are simultaneously aware of the infinite that lies beyond them and that conditions our understanding of the finite. This theologian points to the Logos as the principle of differentiation among all creatures, and we humans participate in a special way in this function of the Logos. Behind this understanding is the overriding notion that the principle of all distinction in reality is the eternal Son who distinguishes himself from the Father. Moreover, it is the self-distinction from the Father that constitutes the sonship of Jesus. In his life of obedience, Jesus reverses the rebellion of Adam (Phil. 2:8) and accepts distinction from God in subordination to him.

The early church was not especially successful in reconciling the divine sonship of Jesus with his historical humanity as laid out in the gospels. Nor was the human distinctiveness of Christ sufficiently emphasized in the Middle Ages or in the Reformation period. Paul's portrayal of Jesus as the second Adam did not employ the notion of Messiah because he probably felt that the title was too closely tied to the special aspirations of Judaism. There is no doubt that Jesus was condemned as a messianic pretender and therefore as a rebel, although this was not true. The basic filial relationship with the Father that animated the life of Christ was prefigured in the image of the Judean kings (2 Sam. 7:14), and then with all the faithful members of the Jewish people (Deut. 14:1). This filial relationship is communicated by the Spirit (Rom. 8:14), who—in the case of Jesus—shaped and formed the character of the divine Son in the consciousness of Christ. In the resurrection Jesus was constituted as the eternal Son by the Spirit (Rom. 1:4).

It is the free self-distinction of the eternal Son from the Father that grounds the possibility of all created reality distinct from God. In this very self-distinction is an element of self-emptying that is the origin of the difference between creaturely existence and God. The eternal Son's self-distinction from the Father is expressed fully in the context of the creaturely existence of Jesus. And this subordination of the Son repairs the damage done by the arrogance of Adam, reconciling the world to God. It is the sending of the Son that brings about the restoration of the relationship between God and the world.

The assuming of human existence became the created medium for the expression of Jesus' self-distinction from the Father and the way of fulfilling his eternal sonship. The overriding message of his earthly proclamation was the imminence of the divine rule. He promised salvation to those who set their hopes completely in what Pannenberg calls "the future of God." The uniqueness of God calls for the uncompromising turning to God described in Deuteronomy 6:4–7. Those who respond to this dictate will participate in the fullness of eschatological salvation, foreshadowed in Jesus' table fellowship. This fellowship that was open to all— tax collectors and sinners as well—calls for personal participation in the movement of God's love into the world.

It would indeed have been difficult for Jesus to have identified himself as the Messiah because of the political overtones connected with that title in his day. This surely would have created great misunderstandings regarding his mission. The heart of his preaching, that is, the nearness of God's rule and the Father's abiding love, seemed to give Jesus a privileged role as the one bringing final salvation. Further, his table fellowship with sinners (Mark 2:16) and his claim to forgive sins (Mark 2:5) implied that God's definitive rule was already present, and this precipitated the charge of blasphemy. In the Gospel of John, there are recurring complaints that Jesus made himself equal to God (5:17–18, 8:53–59). His final condemnation by the Romans was based on his alleged mes-

sianic ambitions. The Easter community, however, pointed to the
resurrection as the confirmation of Jesus' claims. For Paul it was
quite clear that if there were no resurrection, there would be no
Christian faith (1 Cor. 15:17).

The early Christians saw the resurrection as the beginning of
the events of the endtime, and the pledge of the future resurrection of the dead. The appearances of the risen Lord and the empty
tomb provided the historical basis for their belief. The facticity of
these events, especially the appearances, give assurance that Jesus'
resurrection happened at a specific time and place. The title "Messiah," or Christ, became part of the name of Jesus but was viewed
as an expression of his suffering obedience. His institution into
sonship by the resurrection led Paul to affirm Jesus' preexistence
(Phil. 2:6–8; 1 Cor. 8:6, 10:4), and, given the preexistence, we
cannot think of the Father apart from the Son.

Pannenberg discusses the question of the inner basis of Christ's
divine sonship. The relation of the eternal Son to the Father, characterized by self-distinction from the majesty of the Father, took
historical form in the human relationship of Jesus to God (377). In
becoming man, he actively expressed his divine essence as the Son.
Throughout the entire history of Jesus, the eternal Son took shape
in him as the relationship to the Father deepened. Pannenberg admits, however, that in his *Jesus—God and Man* more emphasis
should have been placed on the eternal Son as the ground of the
earthly existence of Christ.[40] The indwelling of the Son in the humanity of Jesus and the lowliness communicated to the deity of
the Son precipitated an interchange that took place throughout
Christ's earthly life. In the death of Jesus, the Son reached the
extreme point of self-distinction from the Father.

Pannenberg insists that the person of Jesus is identical with the
eternal Son, but this does not mean that Jesus lacks his own personality, which was formed and shaped in the process of working
out his relationship with the Father. His human existence achieved
its personal identity in becoming even more deeply the Son of this
Father. The eternal Son took a creaturely form in order that the
future of God might be more intensely present in this world. To
extend God's rule among humankind, the Son needs the Spirit who
glorifies him (John 16:14). The Spirit of truth who proceeds from
the Father bears witness to Jesus (John 15:26) and leads believers
into the full range of truth (John 16:13). This same Spirit guar-

antees to the faithful the hope of resurrection and continues to communicate to them the richness of filial life.

Jürgen Moltmann

Coming out of the Protestant Reformed tradition, Jürgen Moltmann (b. 1926) received worldwide acclaim for his *Theology of Hope* (1964). After completing his studies at the University of Göttingen, he taught at Wuppertal and at Bonn before his appointment to the University of Tübingen in 1967, where he labored until his retirement as professor emeritus in 1994. Whereas his *Theology of Hope* develops the theme of the resurrection of Jesus as the ground for the final triumph over all evil and pain, his *The Crucified God* (1972; English translation 1991) focuses on the cross as the counterpoint of the resurrection.[41] He develops a trinitarian history of God that emphasizes the mutual involvement of God and the world.[42]

Although it is fair to say that the *Theology of Hope* can be considered as Moltmann's guiding light, he felt the need to turn his attention to the theology of the cross, which he judges to be the reverse side of the theology of hope. He paints a rather somber picture of the current ineffectiveness of the churches due to their blindness to reality and their insularity. Many have left the Christian ministry to engage in the service of the poor and the forsaken. Christ, he says, is to be found not in the churches, but in the ghettos and the slums. The church must direct its efforts to the liberation of humankind. We must never lose sight of the fact that Christ was a brother to the despised and the outcast, and was deeply identified with the sufferings of the poor and the misunderstood. These are the ones with whom Christians must bond if they hope to follow in the footsteps of Jesus. According to Moltmann it is imperative that our present bourgeois Christians embrace a theology of the cross.

He considers the cross an abiding symbol that should lead us to the oppressed. The more the churches conform themselves to the society and the culture around them, the more they leave the cross behind. The Christian cult of the sacrifice of the cross has abandoned the real meaning of the death of Jesus. Our cultic religion, which contributes to our isolation, must be replaced by the message of the cross. Our Eucharist should be celebrated with the unrighteous, just as Christ sat at table with tax collectors and sinners. However, his identification with the downtrodden is not driving the great majority of Christians today who instead adapt themselves to the lifestyle and the values of contemporary society.

Christ's proclamation of the righteousness of God to the rejected and the outcast prompted the opposition of the guardians of the law and eventually led to his death. His association with the marginalized made the scribes and the publicans uneasy and suspicious of him. He was a threat to their conventional understanding of Jewish faith and practice. Moltmann insists that following Jesus means that the poor must be helped now, because the church of the crucified is truly the church of the oppressed. Orthopraxis and suffering with the forgotten ones are the only authentic ways to engage in the imitation of Christ. The dialectic between crucifixion and resurrection must be lived out in the experience of each Christian.

Moltmann then raises the critical question about Jesus. Is he truly God? In the nineteenth century the liberal theologians insisted that he became the divine Son only after his human history had run its course. However, the Prologue of John clearly affirms that he was divine as the preexistent Word. It can be said that although in the order of human knowledge Christ was acclaimed Son of God after his resurrection, in the order of being he is the Son of God from eternity. The first question asked of him was, "Are you the one who is to come?" (Matt. 11:2–6). And his answer was that the blind are made to see, the lame walk, the deaf hear, and the poor have the good news preached to them. He proclaimed the arrival of the kingdom of God in his person. The messianic age had come and these were the signs of its appearance. There were questions about him because he was different from the figures whom his contemporaries remembered. He represented a departure from those who had contributed to Israel's salvation history and what the Jews thought they had been promised. Thus he was a scandal to them as well as a threat to the Jewish leaders.

The fact that he announced the kingdom of God to come in such a unique manner led eventually to his arrest and crucifixion. The six "But I say to you . . . " statements in the Sermon on the Mount (Matt. 5:22–45) assert his power over the Mosaic law. Also, his claim to forgive sin (Mark 2:5–12) caused the Jews to accuse him of blasphemy, for they said, "No one can forgive sins but God alone." Jesus had placed himself with sovereign authority above the law. He had in a sense deified himself, and as a relatively powerless human being there was a contradiction between his claims and his stature as one of the poor. His death was the consequence of his conflict with Jewish law and tradition. This contradiction between his claims and his human stature was ultimately resolved through the resurrection.

To the Hebrews he was a blasphemer, a false Messiah. To the Romans he was a rebel, guilty of the crime of sedition against the Roman state. The title placed above his cross points him out as an enemy of the authority of Rome. According to Moltmann, God the Father had identified himself with the crucified Jesus. Through the resurrection, Christ experienced a qualitatively new life that anticipates the general resurrection alluded to in the Book of Daniel (12:2–3) in the second century B.C.E. It is the resurrection that spotlights the cross as a saving event. Paul declares that Jesus died for our sins (Rom. 3:24–25) and that through his death there is new life for the unrighteous. His sacrifice brings hope to the hopeless. First the Jews and then the Gentiles were to share in his redemption.

One of Moltmann's most valuable contributions is his insistence that God the Father was himself active and suffered with Christ in his agony.[43] He cites 2 Corinthians 5:19, where Paul declares that God was reconciling the world to himself in Christ. The Father reveals himself in the passion and death of Jesus and becomes the Father of the godless and the godforsaken. The cross was truly an event between the Son and the Father wherein a change is revealed in God. The Son suffers and the Father suffers in a different way. The Father's suffering is a suffering of love, and through the exchange of suffering between the Father and the Son the cross makes possible the movement of the Spirit out toward humankind. According to this theologian, Martin Luther consistently emphasized a theology of the cross and pointed it toward the liberation of humankind enslaved under the compulsion of works (208).

Moltmann deals with the question of God's capability for suffering at some length. A God who cannot suffer is a being who cannot be involved, a loveless being. In the early ecumenical councils, God is portrayed as unchangeable and incapable of suffering. If he could not suffer, would he be capable of love? Moltmann thinks not. We cannot deprive God of the suffering that is grounded in love, for one who is capable of love is capable of suffering.

Moltmann describes the second person of the Trinity as the conscious center in the God-man, Christ. This human nature was assumed by the divine nature of the Son and is anhypostatically united to the divine person (231). Moltmann insists that the doctrine of the cross truly reveals the doctrine of the Trinity. While the Son undergoes death in his forsaken state, the Father who delivers him up suffers the death of the Son in the infinite grief of love.

> The suffering and dying of the Son, forsaken by the Father, is a different kind of suffering of the Father in the death of the Son. . . . To understand what happened between Jesus and his God and Father on the cross, it is necessary to talk in trinitarian terms. The Son suffers dying, the Father suffers the death of the Son. The grief of the Father here is just as important as the death of the Son. . . . [I]f God has constituted himself as Father of Jesus Christ, then he also suffers the death of his Fatherhood in the death of the Son. (243)

In the experience of the cross, the Father and the Son are most deeply separated and yet most inwardly one in their surrender. What results from this oneness is the procession of the Spirit from the Father and the Son. It is the Spirit who brings love and solace to the forsaken and forgotten ones. With regard to the relationship between the Father and the Son, the crucifixion is portrayed as a trinitarian event, although the role of the Spirit is less clearly delineated. For Moltmann this trinitarian emphasis in the context of the cross blurs the distinction between the immanent and the economic Trinity. God is no self-contained Triad confined to the heavens but is ever reaching out toward humankind and to all of creation.

God in the context of the crucifixion becomes the human God who suffers with us and intercedes for us, while humanity finds the power to embrace and extend this contagious love into the world. The Greek concept of the God who is incapable of suffering caused no little difficulty for Christology. Indeed it is only recently that theology has been able to confront this dilemma. If God is unchangeable and needs nothing, he then needs no friends. Moltmann cites Abraham Heschel, the renowned Jewish biblical scholar, who insists that God is no doubt affected by humankind. As a matter of fact, he takes humanity so seriously that he suffers under the actions of humans and can be injured by them. The apathetic God, so long a part even of Jewish theology in the Middle Ages, has been abandoned by Heschel and others. Heschel has developed a theology of divine pathos wherein God is indeed affected by human history. Moltmann returns again and again to the theme of Philippians 2:6–11, where God is portrayed in the person of the Son entering into the limited human condition and, through the cross, identifying with our God-forsakenness. God takes upon himself the death of the abandoned so that the forgotten souls can share a lasting communion with him (276).

In the third volume of his systematic theology, *The Way of Jesus Christ*, Moltmann revisits the subject of Christology and embellishes his earlier treatments with new and striking perspectives.[44] He sets his study within the context of Jewish messianic hope that arose out of the institution of kingship originating with Saul and David. The prophecy of Nathan (2 Sam. 7:3–16) addressed to King David reveals the promise of a lasting kingship. David was viewed as both a king and a priest, and his descendants were always obliged to defend the rights of the poor. After the political independence of the Northern Kingdom had ended (722–721 B.C.E.), the image of the Messiah began to take the place of the image of the king. Isaiah portrays the messianic figure as the one who will establish a kingdom of peace, and who defends the oppressed (Isa. 9:2–7). In the prophets Micah and Zechariah his dominion is described as extending from sea to sea, and it is he who will prepare the way for the coming of God himself.

After the exile (587–539 B.C.E.), the hope of the Messiah and the expectation of the Son of man gradually fused into a single vision of the future (13). The hope for the coming of the Messiah king began to fade, and the figure of the priest occupied the center of attention. In 2 Isaiah 40–55 the new servant of God is portrayed as exercising a redeeming function through his suffering, and his people are the poor of the land. When John the Baptist asks whether Jesus is the one who is to come, Christ responds by giving a recitation of his signs and wonders. The Jews, though, were not able to accept Jesus as the Messiah, although he was on the way to revealing his messiahship. God hardened their hearts until the full complement of the Gentiles will have come into the fold, and then all of Israel will indeed be saved (Rom. 11:25).

Moltmann envisions three stages in the development of Christology. Jesus is first recognized as the Christ of God. Then, God is professed to be the Father of Jesus and the one who raised him from the dead. Finally, the presence of Christ is experienced in the Spirit who is the giver of life. The salvation of Christ offers personal reconciliation and then looks out to the reconciliation of the cosmos, now threatened by nuclear catastrophe and ecological death. Our author describes the difference between an ascending and a descending approach to Christology and refers to the Incarnation as the movement in which the divine and human natures are united in the one person of the eternal Logos. This has been traditionally defined in terms of the nonpersonal human nature having been personalized by the eternal Son of God. Customarily Jesus' human nature is described as anhypostatic, in that the center that constitutes his personhood is the eternal Son himself. This humanity is thus considered as sinless and immortal, and is endowed with the excellence of soul and body that flows from his sinlessness.

Moltmann suggests that the nonpersonal human nature that he assumed when he came to earth would be difficult for us to identify with, because it would be so different from our own. He asserts that rather than dealing with the issue of the anhypostasia or enhypostasia of Christ's human nature vis-à-vis his divine nature, it is better to begin with Jesus' singular relationship to God the Father, in order to investigate on the basis of this mutual relationship, what in Christ is truly human and what is divine (53). The New Testament is not deeply concerned about the distinction between Jesus' human and divine natures. The concentration is rather on the intimate filial relationship between Christ and the Father. What Moltmann calls the triumphalistic Christology must give way to the Christology of history. Christologies from below, in Moltmann's view, originated in European Protestantism at the time of the Enlightenment. Especially in the nineteenth century, scholars emphasized the earthly Jesus who could be approached historically. The questions about essence gave way after Kant to questions about utility or functional usefulness. The approaches of theologians like Schleiermacher and Rahner focused on subjective salvation resulting from one's allegiance to Christ and did not emphasize the social and political dimensions of the redemptive effort of Jesus.

Moltmann insists that Christology must concern itself with the people who are living "on the other side." In our industrialized world it is the have-not nations of Africa, Asia, and South America that are shouldering the human costs of scientific advances. How can we of the First World consider ourselves Christian when we build our prosperity at the expense of the impoverished countries of the Third World? Who is Christ for us today, threatened as we are by nuclear extinction and the destruction of our natural environment? In this current context, the distinctions "from above" and "from below" seem rather unimportant. Moltmann urges that we study Jesus' humanity in order to understand his divinity and, similarly, contemplate his divinity so that we might best understand his humanity. The Christology that we must concentrate upon today must have an eschatological character. We must view Christ as being on the way to the future of God.

It is important, according to Moltmann, that we chart out a Spirit Christology so that we can appreciate the close relationship between the Spirit and Jesus during his earthly life. The Spirit directed him in all the critical moments of his human existence and now carries on the risen Lord's messianic commission. It was this ongoing messianic dimension that was neglected at Nicaea (325 C.E.), and that has become so significant in our day. The presence of the Holy Spirit in Christ was noted from the day of his baptism by John (Mark 1:10), while Luke affirms that he was actually conceived by the Spirit (Luke 1:35). Thus Christ's relationship with the Father and the Spirit was assumed from the beginning. Jesus enters the world in communion with the Father and the Spirit, and with him the Spirit comes to dwell in the world in the messianic Son, and then in the fellowship of believers. It was the Spirit who animated Jesus with his messianic consciousness. Whereas John the Baptist proclaimed the coming kingdom as judgment, Jesus announced the kingdom as grace and liberation for the poor and for sinners.

When the messengers of John the Baptist came to Jesus and asked whether he was the one who is to come, Jesus replied in effect that the messianic era had already arrived. For with him the sick are healed, the lame walk, and the poor have the gospel of salvation preached to them (Matt. 11:2–6). The natural enemies of the poor are the men and women of violence who enrich themselves at the expense of others. The Jesus movement was initially a gathering together of the poor of Galilee who found a new dignity in the message of Christ. According to Moltmann, it is only in communion with the poor that the kingdom of God is thrown open to others. When Jesus broke bread with sinners and tax collectors (Mark 2:15), he entered into a social conflict with the Pharisees and the priests which eventually led to his death. The ethics proclaimed by Christ is an ethics of community that serves as the ground for a "contrast" society. Just as the gospel is the messianic interpretation of the Torah for the Gentiles, the Sermon on the Mount is directed to all people and, according to our author, is indeed capable of fulfillment.

In the period before Constantine, the church saw itself as a people of peace who were conscious that they were living in the messianic era. In the fourth century the Roman empire was Christianized and the church in large part lost sight of itself as a contrast society. The implementation of the Sermon on the Mount was, then, in many respects postponed until the new life that follows after death. Jesus' choice of the twelve apostles was clearly a messianic act, for with them the final gathering of Israel had begun. This selection of the Twelve binds Jesus into a unity with his people that the gentile Christians do not in any way destroy. This symbol of the Twelve has a meaning for Israel alone.

Jesus neither affirmed nor denied that he was the Christ when questioned by his disciples (Luke 9:20–21) and responded by predicting his sufferings. He did not reject the title of Messiah but postponed a definitive response. His history will provide the answer. Moltmann asserts that Jesus seemed to grow into the messiahship, which he understood quite differently from his Jewish contemporaries. Although his messianic sonship can be grounded in his experience of the Spirit at his baptism, this does not yet signify a metaphysical or ontological identity of essence with God the Father (142). The exclusively mutual relationship referred to in Matthew 11:27 and John 14:10 seems to reveal, however, the preexistence of the Son. The rapport between the Son and the Father reflects a childlike relationship, as is evidenced in the Abba prayer. Moltmann holds that there are really three dimensions to the person of Jesus. His eschatological person identifies him as Israel's Messiah and the Son of man of the nations. His theological person reveals him as the child of God who lives in God and God in him. The final dimension is his social personhood that shows him to be the brother of the poor and the disenfranchised. Classical Christology emphasized the theological person of Jesus and rather neglected his role as Messiah. Also, his social relationships with his contemporaries were not considered as critical to his ontological identity.

With his prophecy regarding the destruction of the temple, Jesus set Israel within the context of the endtime. Further, the apocalyptic events that took place at the time of his death (Matt. 27:51–54) are seen as the foreshadowing of the end of days. When he brought his messianic message to Jerusalem with his prophecy about the temple, the priests had him arrested. In the context of the questioning by the high priest, he affirmed his claim to be the Messiah (Mark 14:61–62). As a result the Sanhedrin condemned him as a blasphemer. For the priests, Jesus put himself messianically on the level of God. They handed him over to the Romans because they were convinced that he wished to set himself up as king of the Jews. For the Romans this was sedition and warranted crucifixion because they considered him a political rebel.

Jesus died as a poor, powerless man. On the cross there was a mutual surrender between Father and Son, achieved through the Spirit who also bore the sufferings of Christ. Moltmann emphasizes that the cross serves as a privileged revelation of trinitarian life.

> In the suffering of the Son, the pain of the Father finds a voice. The self-emptying of the Son also expresses the self-emptying of the Father.... In the forsakenness of the Son the Father also forsakes himself.... For Jesus suffers dying and forsakenness.... But the Father who abandons him and delivers him up suffers the death of the Son in the infinite grief of love. (176–77)

It was Origen (ca. 185–ca. 254) who first affirmed that the whole Trinity is involved in this great movement of self-surrender. Through the suffering, crucified Christ, God reveals his solidarity with human pain and suffering.

The death of Christ brings about reconciliation, and his resurrection anticipates the new creation. Through the resurrection God opens up the future to everyone. Even the dead are offered fellowship and the power of the Spirit to free them from the last enemy, which is death (1 Peter 3:19–20). Jesus' liberating sovereignty will be fulfilled when he hands over the kingdom to the Father so that God will be all in all (1 Cor. 15:28). Through the exaltation of Christ, all of reality will be gathered together. This inspiring picture of the cosmic Christ is portrayed in the first chapters of Ephesians and Colossians.

The earliest testimony of the resurrection is recorded in 1 Corinthians 15:5–8. These experiences changed the lives of the people who saw the risen Christ—both men and women such as Magdalen and Paul. In this "seeing" they received their own call to the apostolate, and this transformed them. Moltmann asks whether an event such as Jesus' resurrection can be comprehended in historical terms. For Karl Barth the resurrection is simply an endorsement of the redemption achieved on the cross, with no saving power of its own. It is a new "vertical" act of God that endorses the redemptive work of Christ. Rudolf Bultmann, on the other hand, interprets the resurrection as an existential event that occurred in the lives of the apostles, generating their faith in Jesus as Lord. The cross becomes historically important when it touches individuals and generates faith in them.

Moltmann notes that the three Abrahamic religions—Judaism, Islam, and Christianity—are faiths played out in the arena of history and are straining toward the future. This directedness toward the future creates an atmosphere of expectation that affects both humankind and nature. It is the Holy Spirit who animates this forward thrust. Because Christ died in solidarity with all created things, his resurrection opens up a vision of the resurrection of all nature (Col. 1:20), laying the groundwork for a cosmic Christology. Moltmann asserts that through Christ's death all created things are reunited to God and have their own right to exist. The resurrection experience of Jesus creates a new destiny for all of reality—humans, animals, plants, stones, and all cosmic life systems (258). In this new destiny death will be no more. There could well be a new dependence of some sort between humankind and nature. This is not to be ruled out. It is only through the resurrection of nature that this horizon of expectation will be fully achieved.

In the judgment of Richard Bauckham, Moltmann insists that every individual creature that has ever lived will be resurrected in the new creation.[45] This seems to mean that death has the same significance for every type of creature. If for Moltmann all life seems to have equal value, Bauckham suggests that his theological basis is inadequate for the ethical distinctions that have to be made.

A Summary

Pius XII's encyclical of 1951, *Christ the Eternal King,* celebrating the fifteenth centenary of the Council of Chalcedon, leaves one with the impression that, apart from some further refinements regarding the humanity of Jesus, Christology is a theological discipline that had largely attained its final state of development. The work of theologians like Charles Boyer seems to be in accord with that assessment. The Jesuit found evidence for Christ's divinity in many verses of the New Testament, which are, however, disputed or rejected as demonstrations of divinity by scholars today.

Bernard Lonergan's use of the New Testament to demonstrate the divinity of Christ follows more closely the findings of contemporary biblical scholarship, and his approach to Jesus' humanity calls for a distinct human subjectivity which, he asserts, is required by Chalcedon. There were in Christ two consciousnesses and one psychological subject. Although Lonergan holds that Jesus possessed the beatific vision in his human intellect, he admits that there are quite a number of questions regarding the human knowledge of Jesus to which we as yet have no answers. In spite of the fact that Lonergan portrays the redemption as a ransom of sorts, he does allow for other options. For example, God could have freely forgiven humankind for its sinful ways without the need for the atoning passion of Christ. He does not agree with Paul Galtier that Christ possessed a separate human ego and was not aware of his divinity in his human mind. For Lonergan Jesus was indeed conscious as man of his divine personhood.

The Christology of Karl Rahner embodies a rather different and more engaging perspective. He is obviously concerned that in classical Christology Jesus might be viewed by many as a kind of mythological figure, and that Christology as popularly portrayed could well call forth a monophysitic understanding of Jesus. He is sensitive to the fact that Christology from above might not be enough for many believers today, and that the Christology from below, evident in the early chapters of Acts, might have a new relevance in our time. Although he teaches that the beatific vision was an indispensable emergent of the hypostatic union, it need not necessarily be beatifying. Rather, the immediate vision of God could well have been at the subjective pole of the earthly Christ's consciousness, rather than being the vision of an object.

Jesus' "abiding unreflexive consciousness of a radical closeness to God" deepened and expanded during his life on earth, and was consistent with his lack of knowledge of certain matters at various times.

Rahner argues for a genuine human self-consciousness, a distinct personal center, as absolutely necessary for Christ's role as mediator. He unabashedly encourages the development of a new statement of belief beyond the two natures/one person formula of Chalcedon. Although Rahner's Christology is of the descending variety, he attempts to give it a unique and challenging thrust by situating it in the context of a transcendental anthropology—God and creation coming together, with Christ as the high moment of that convergence. He holds for the preexistence of the Son since he is the absolute event of salvation; God offers himself and (at the same time) humanity freely responds. In this case, as the absolute saving event, the Son must be preexistent. Rahner succeeds more than his colleagues who affirm a classical Christology in defending and making a case for the distinct created humanity of Jesus.

Gerald O'Collins introduces his work with an extended treatment of the biblical data concerning Christ, and especially the passages dealing with the resurrection. He portrays Chalcedon as the virtual culmination of christological development in that it articulated the terms and the parameters that prevail even to the present. Considerable emphasis is placed on the work of Thomas Aquinas whose Christology from above remained normative in the schools for centuries. According to O'Collins Christ has to be formally proclaimed as being substantially divine. He is not the window revealing God, but God himself. Further, inasmuch as Jesus is described in the New Testament as possessing the qualities of genuine humanity, he is therefore authentically human.

Contrary to the findings of James D. G. Dunn who holds that only in John do we find a clear affirmation of the Son's preexistence, O'Collins claims that preexistence is unambiguously asserted not only in John but in 2 Corinthians 8:9, Philippians 2:6–8, Colossians 1:15–17, and Hebrews 1:1–3, 6; 9:26, and 10:5–10. Although this places him firmly in the Christology from above camp, he does allow for a distinct human consciousness in Christ which, however, is not set forth as well as it is in Rahner's work. O'Collins maintains that there are two consciousnesses in Christ with the ego of the Word operating through both. The earthly Jesus had a limited human understanding of his divine identity and no awareness of his preexistence. In the judgment of O'Collins, the earthly Jesus apparently did not enjoy the beatific vision since he is pictured in some detail as a man of faith—and faith rules out the possession of the immediate vision of God as beatifying. Apart from his somewhat singular stand on the beatific vision, O'Collins seems to be more content with his descending Christology than was Karl Rahner, who was continually searching for new approaches and alternatives to the Chalcedonian formula.

Karl Barth was unquestionably one of the most significant theologians of the twentieth century, although his popularity did wane after his death in 1968. For him all theology is christological. Everything begins and ends with Jesus. Barth's is clearly a Christology from above. The preexistent Son of God became flesh and "ventured into the far country." After his student days Barth was not especially concerned with biblical criticism and the latest refinements of New Testament scholars. For him Jesus was not a political reformer, nor did he identify with any religious group within Judaism. He did, however, feel free to criticize and correct them on various occasions when he felt that they misunderstood or misrepresented the Father's demands. According to Barth, the Son of God was human in a very different way from the rest of us. The redeemer suffered and satisfied the penalty of sin for us, while redemption in us consists in acknowledging that our sinfulness is truly dead. Barth is indeed a Reformed theologian in the tradition of John Calvin, but his views on the availability of salvation for all are very different from those of his sixteenth-century mentor. For Barth the "friendliness of God" knows no limits.

The resurrection of Jesus is affirmed by Wolfhart Pannenberg as a historical event, even though we are unsure of the particulars. If it is not a historical fact, the resurrection cannot serve as the ground of our Christian faith. The early two-stage Christology (Rom. 1:3) soon gave way to belief in the preexistent Son (Gal. 4:4; John 1:14), and this meant that the Son could not be separated from the divine essence for he is God's self-revelation. The Spirit also belongs to the event of God's revelation and therefore to the divinity of God, because what pertains to God's self-revelation belongs to the divine essence. Since the Father, Son, and Spirit are distinct moments in the unfolding of God's self-revelation, then they are such in God's eternal essence as well.

It is quite possible that Jesus realized the dangers as he made his final journey to Jerusalem (Luke 20:28). It was his repeated claim to divine authority over the Mosaic law and the forgiving of sins that brought down the accusation of blasphemy and eventually resulted in his crucifixion. Jesus' resurrection validated his claims and revealed him to his followers as the Messiah and the Son of God. In the reflected light of the resurrection, his total earthly life can be seen as a progressive revelation of his divinity through the total submission to the Father's will. This subordination of Jesus to the will of the Father repaired the damage done by the arrogance of Adam and reconciled the world to God. His consistent proclamation of the nearness of God and the imminence of God's rule gave Jesus a unique and privileged role as the bearer of God's final salvation.

In becoming man, the Son expressed his divine essence in terms of his self-distinction from the Father. Throughout the entire history of Jesus, the eternal Son took shape in him as Christ's relationship to the Father matured. His human existence achieved its personal identity in becoming even more deeply the Son of the Father.

In *The Crucified God*, Jürgen Moltmann concentrates on the cross as the counterpoint of the resurrection. He insists that the churches are relatively ineffective today because they fail to commit themselves to the service of the poor. It is the cross of Jesus that should inspire us to concentrate on the oppressed of our age. Orthopraxis is the only true way to follow in the footsteps of Christ. Because of his dedication to the outcasts and the marginalized of society, Jesus became a threat to the conventional Jews, and this eventually contributed to his death. The cross is to direct us to the authentic imitation of Christ. Moltmann holds that in the order of human knowledge Christ was professed as Son of God after his resurrection, whereas in the order of being he is the Son of God from eternity.

In his announcement of the kingdom of God, Jesus asserted his authority over the law of Moses. Then, in his practice of forgiving sins, the Jews found him guilty of blasphemy. They saw a contradiction between his claim to sovereign authority and his status as a human being. In the sufferings of the crucifixion, God the Father also suffered, for a God who cannot suffer is a being who cannot be involved. One who is capable of love is also capable of suffering. It is the second person of the Trinity who is identified as the conscious center of the God-man Christ. In the experience of the cross the Father and the Son are most deeply separated and yet are united in their surrender. Out of this oneness proceeds the Holy Spirit who brings love and comfort to the forsaken.

In the third volume of his masterful systematic theology, *The Way of Jesus Christ*, Moltmann revisits the subject of Christology. He concentrates on the messianic dimension of Jesus and affirms that rather than dealing with the ontological question of the union between his divine and human natures, it is more appropriate to begin with Jesus' singular relationship to God the Father. For it is preferable to search out what is truly human and what is divine in Christ within this context. On the cross there was a mutual surrender between Father and Son achieved through the Spirit, who also bore the suffering of Christ. By virtue of his resurrection Jesus anticipates the new creation. Because he died in solidarity with all created things, Christ's resurrection opens up the vision of the resurrection to all of creation (Col. 1:20).

This sampling of recent popular and widely respected Christologies reveals that Jesus' divinity is portrayed by these theologians in light of the preexistence of the eternal Son who appears on earth at a given time, bringing salvation to humankind, however that salvation is defined. The true challenge of descending Christology is to articulate and defend the full and genuine humanity of Jesus, so that he can be seen by us believers as truly man "in all things but sin." Questions concerning his human knowledge and its necessary limitations, his distinctly human subjectivity, the authentic character of his suffering, and his experience of desolation on the cross remain a constant challenge for these theologians. Unless we can identify a genuine humanity in Jesus, his role as mediator between God and humankind remains problematic.

Notes

1. Raymond E. Brown, *An Introduction to New Testament Christology* (Mahwah, N.J.: Paulist Press, 1994), 185–89. Brown lists those passages that imply Christ's divinity: Rom. 9:5; Titus 2:13; John 1:18; 1 John 5:20; 2 Peter 1:1 (178–84). He also insists that Phil. 5:5–6 and 2 Cor. 8:9 announce the divinity of Christ in preexistent categories (183). James D. G. Dunn asserts that it is only in the Gospel of John that we can speak of a full-blown doctrine of

the Incarnation of the Word of God. See his *Christology in the Making*, 2d ed. (Grand Rapids, Mich.: Eerdmans, 1989), 259.

2. Claudia Carlen Ihm, ed., *Papal Encyclicals*, vol. 4, *1939–58* (Ann Arbor, Mich.: Pierian Press, 1990), 203–4 (para. 3).

3. Ibid., 206 (para. 17).

4. Ibid., 207 (para. 23).

5. The early Monophysites maintained that there was only one nature in Christ, which was either divine or a blend of the divine and the human.

6. Ihm, ed., *Papal Encyclicals*, 208 (para. 29).

7. Ibid., 210 (para. 38).

8. Charles Boyer, *De Verbo Incarnato*, 2d ed. (Rome: Gregorian University, 1952).

9. Bernard Lonergan, *De Verbo Incarnato*, 2d ed. (Rome: Gregorian University, 1961).

10. H. Denzinger and A. Schönmetzer, *Enchiridion Symbolorum*, 32nd ed. (Freiburg: Herder, 1963), 1529.

11. Bernard Lonergan, *De Constitutione Christi Ontologica et Psychologica* (Rome: Gregorian University, 1964). The 1964 edition was a reprint of the 1956 publication.

12. Bernard Lonergan, "The Dehellenization of Dogma," in *A Second Collection*, ed. W. Ryan and B. Tyrrell (Philadelphia: Westminster Press, 1974), 25.

13. Bernard Lonergan, "Christology Today: Methodological Reflections," in *A Third Collection*, ed. Frederick Crowe (New York: Paulist Press, 1985), 91–94.

14. Herbert Vorgrimler, *Understanding Karl Rahner*, trans. John Bowden (New York: Crossroad, 1986), 88–91, 93.

15. Karl Rahner, *Theological Investigations*, vol. 1, trans. Cornelius Ernst (London: Darton, Longman and Todd, 1961), 149–200.

16. Karl Rahner, *Foundations of Christian Faith*, trans. William V. Dych (New York: Crossroad, 1986). This work was originally published in German in 1976.

17. David Tracy, *The Analogical Imagination* (New York: Crossroad, 1986), 184 n. 27.

18. See Karl Rahner, "Dogmatic Reflections on the Knowledge and Self-Consciousness of Christ," in *Theological Investigations*, vol. 5, trans. Karl-H. Kruger (London: Darton, Longman and Todd, 1966), 193–215.

19. *Papal Encyclicals*, 52 (para. 75).

20. Gerald O'Collins, *Christology* (New York: Oxford University Press, 1995).

21. Dunn, *Christology in the Making*, 259.

22. John Macquarrie, *Jesus Christ in Modern Thought* (London: SCM Press, 1990), 121, 390–92.

23. Roger Haight, "The Case for Spirit Christology," *Theological Studies* 53, no. 2 (June 1992): 257–87.

24. Aquinas, pars IIIa., q. 7, a. 3.

25. Edward Schillebeeckx, *Jesus: An Experiment in Christology*, trans. Hubert Hoskins (New York: Seabury Press, 1979), 554–56; Hans Küng, *Credo*, trans. J. Bowden (New York: Doubleday, 1993), 41–45.

26. Karl Barth, *The Humanity of God*, trans. J. N. Thomas and T. Wieser

(Louisville, Ky.: John Knox Press, 1960), 37–46. See also Barth's "Evangelical Theology in the Nineteenth Century," in the same volume, 11–33.

27. Karl Barth, *The Epistle to the Romans*, 6th ed., trans. E. C. Hoskyns (New York: Oxford University Press, 1968).

28. Ibid., 332–33.

29. For a brief summary of Barth's "Christology," see Karl Barth, *Church Dogmatics. A Selection*, comp. Helmut Gollwitzer, 1st Amer. ed., trans. and ed. G. W. Bromiley (Louisville, Ky.: Westminster/John Knox, 1994), 87–133.

30. Geoffrey W. Bromiley, *Introduction to the Theology of Karl Barth* (Grand Rapids, Mich.: Eerdmans, 1979), 198.

31. Karl Barth, *The Doctrine of the Word of God, Church Dogmatics*, vol. 1, part 1, trans. G. T. Thomson (New York: Scribner's, 1936), chap. 11, 465.

32. Ibid., chap. 11, 491.

33. Karl Barth, *The Doctrine of Reconciliation, Church Dogmatics*, vol. 4, part 1, trans. G. W. Bromiley and T. F. Torrance (Edinburgh: T & T Clark, 1956), chap. 59, 184.

34. Ibid., chap. 59, 202.

35. Ibid., chap. 59, 283–357.

36. Peter Berger, *The Heretical Imperative* (New York: Doubleday, 1979), 67–68.

37. Clifford Green, ed., *Karl Barth: Theologian of Freedom* (London: Collins Liturgical Publications, 1989), 31–32.

38. Wolfhart Pannenberg, *Jesus—God and Man*, 2d ed., trans. L. Wilkins and D. Priebe (Philadelphia: Westminster Press, 1977). Subsequent page references can be found in the text.

39. Wolfhart Pannenberg, *Systematic Theology*, vol. 2, trans. G. Bromiley (Grand Rapids, Mich.: Eerdmans, 1994). Subsequent page references can be found in the text.

40. Ibid., 384–85 n. 173.

41. Jürgen Moltmann, *The Crucified God*, trans. R. A. Wilson and J. Bowden (San Francisco: HarperCollins, 1991).

42. Richard Bauckham, *The Theology of Jürgen Moltmann* (Edinburgh: T & T Clark, 1995), 5–6.

43. Moltmann, *The Crucified God*, 190–94. Subsequent page references can be found in the text.

44. Jürgen Moltmann, *The Way of Jesus Christ*, trans. Margaret Kohl (London: SCM Press, 1990). The German edition was published in 1989. Subsequent page references can be found in the text.

45. Bauckham, *Theology of Jürgen Moltmann*, 210. This work of Bauckham is considered by many to be the first comprehensive study of Moltmann's full theology.

✳ *Chapter 2* ✳

Recent Protestant Efforts to Construct an Ascending Christology

Bultmann and His Disciples

According to Albert Schweitzer, it was Hermann Samuel Reimarus (1694–1768), a professor of Oriental languages at Hamburg, who initiated the first quest for the historical Jesus, which grounded the christological approach from below.[1] His work, entitled *The Aims of Jesus*, was published posthumously by Gotthold Lessing (1729–81), a German Enlightenment philosopher and playwright. According to Reimarus, Jesus identified with the messianic hopes of Judaism but insisted that the end was very near. He was accepted as Messiah and Son of God by his followers, but certainly not in an ontological sense. Although Jesus did preach a higher morality, he never intended to break with the Jewish law or the Jewish faith. His disciples, on the other hand, were forced out of Judaism, and this led them to establish a new religion. It was Reimarus's belief that Jesus was attempting to provoke a political uprising in order to free his people from bondage, but he was not successful.

Most students of nineteenth-century Protestant theology will agree that the father of liberal theology was Friedrich Schleiermacher (1768–1834), who taught at the Universities of Halle and Berlin. His masterpiece, *The Christian Faith*, appeared in 1821–22 and was revised in 1830.[2] For Schleiermacher, the uniqueness of Jesus consisted in his God-consciousness, which evolved in him in a singular and preeminent way. Although all of us possess a germ of this consciousness, Christ was different from all others in that his God-consciousness amounted to a veritable existence of God in him which was so powerful that it animated his every thought and action. Thus it could be said that the very existence

56

of God was present in the world through Jesus, who became the privileged mediator of God to creation. The unity of two natures, divine and human, in the one person of Christ was a complete anomaly for Schleiermacher. The patristic and scholastic explanations regarding the two natures and the one person in Jesus were for him no longer valid. It is the God-consciousness in Jesus—a continual, active presence—which constitutes the real existence of God in him, and from which all his words and actions proceed. Thus it can be said exclusively of him that in Christ, God became man. The perfect human soul of Jesus was inspired by this unique presence of God that permeated the soul of Christ in all its functions. This is how Schleiermacher describes the personal union between God and the man Jesus. The resurrection and the ascension are not essential components of the doctrine of Christ. A Christian can profess belief in them since they seem to be affirmed in the New Testament, but faith in Jesus as the privileged presence of God in the world and as redeemer does not depend on the resurrection events. Christ's redemptive activity consists in sharing his own God-consciousness with believers, thus taking us up into the fellowship of his life, which Schleiermacher defines as the state of grace.

The nineteenth century was literally overwhelmed by the scores of lives of Jesus that were published in Europe, especially in Germany. Perhaps the most controversial of these was the two-volume work by David Friedrich Strauss (1808–74) published in 1835–36, entitled *The Life of Jesus Critically Examined*. Strauss distinguishes between the Christ of faith and the Jesus of history, and he considers the Easter experiences as merely subjective visions shared by the disciples. He applies the notion of myth to Jesus' wondrous healings and acts throughout the gospels—coating almost all of his saving deeds with a layer of legend. It is very difficult to discern what Strauss actually thought of Jesus. Apparently he believed that Christ conceived of himself as the Messiah who would be taken up to heaven and, in time, return again to establish God's final kingdom. Strauss's life of Jesus created such a negative reaction among Europe's scholarly community that his prospects for a promising academic career were all but destroyed.

On the other hand, the life of Jesus written by Ernest Renan (1823–92) and published in 1863 was enthusiastically received by the European community. This scholar, a professor of Semitic languages at the Collège de France, portrays Jesus as a master teacher whose preaching was gentle and rich with allusions to his native country. After his rejection in Jerusalem, however, Jesus became something of a revolutionary and the mildness of his early preaching disappeared. He was forced to promote his cause by performing marvelous deeds. According to Renan, at the time of his last trip to Jerusalem, Christ was filled with disappointment at the failures he had experienced in his public life and longed for martyrdom. The work is shot through with sentimentality that softens somewhat his rather critical views concerning Jesus' divinity and his miracles. Renan's *Life of Jesus* went through many editions since his sympathetic portrait of Jesus attracted countless nineteenth-century readers.

Toward the end of the century, there appeared at the University of Berlin an outstanding scholar of early Christianity and one of the most convincing proponents of liberal theology. Adolf Harnack (1851–1930), whose *What Is Christianity?* is widely read even today, believed that the Reformation, which left many of the Christian dogmas intact, must continue on. Also the historical form of Christianity should never be absolutized, but should rather be allowed to change its structure in response to the needs of each age.[3] According to Harnack, Jesus believed that he knew God in a unique way and that his vocation was to share this knowledge of God by word and deed. We shall never comprehend how Jesus evolved from his awareness that he was the Son of God to the conviction that he was the promised Messiah. It is Harnack's position that Christ's message is remarkably simple. It has to do with the Father and not the Son. Jesus gradually began to become aware of the fact that he is the way to the Father. In Jesus the divine manifested itself as fully and completely as it can upon earth. His role was to extend the fatherhood of God and to invite all men and women to become God's sons and daughters. It was not Christ's intent to prefix his gospel with a christological creed. Harnack feels that it is not possible to make any clear and valid statements about Jesus' "divine nature." Faith in the Father, the Son, and the Holy Spirit should in his judgment be sufficient, and one must leave it to every Christian to determine how he or she might conceive of the person of Christ.

Rudolf Bultmann

Although liberal theology had its followers into the second and third decades of the twentieth century, the movement had lost much of its nineteenth-century élan. Just as Karl Barth broke from the liberal camp in 1914, Rudolf Bultmann (1884–1976) also became disenchanted with the nineteenth-century fixation on the historical Jesus. To him, the many biographical essays that portrayed Christ with this or that sort of special mission were not representative of good biblical scholarship. These lives of Jesus were nothing but nineteenth-century projections of ideals current at the time upon a little-known figure of the first century. The education that Bultmann received at Tübingen, Berlin, and Marburg pointed him more in the direction of the historical and critical analysis of the biblical texts, and the study of comparative religions such as Jewish apocalyptic, Hellenistic mystery religions, and Gnosticism. He became a professor at Marburg in 1921 and taught there until his retirement in 1951. In his important study, *Jesus*, published in 1926, Bultmann asserts that we can know very little indeed about the person and the life of Jesus, since the New Testament writings showed little interest in the details of his life and personality.[4] Although he considers this issue of minor importance, Bultmann's own view is that Jesus did not believe himself to be the Messiah. What is most important is Christ's teaching that confronts us with the question of how we should interpret our own existence. The scholar's initial effort was to get back to the earliest layers of the synoptic tradition to come to grips with the teaching of Jesus in its most primitive form. This message emphasized the coming of the kingdom of God (Luke 10:23–24) and the need for each individual to decide for the kingdom (Matt. 5:29–30), which involved, first of all, a call to repentance. For Jesus, the worth of a man or woman is determined by the decision he or she makes in the actual concrete circumstances of life to respond wholeheartedly to the will of God as it is revealed at that moment.

Bultmann considers Christ as a prophet largely because of the persistence of his eschatological message (Matt. 21:11; Luke 7:16), and a rabbi because of his characteristic teaching methods (Matt. 7:2; Luke 17:7–10). Jesus did not oppose Jewish religious practices such as prayer, fasting, and almsgiving, but he did condemn the exaggerated emphasis on ceremonial and ritual laws. Whereas the scribes treated all scriptural admonitions as equally binding, Jesus prioritized the more important prescriptions, that is, judgment and mercy and fidelity (Matt. 23:23–24). In the Sermon on the Mount (Matthew 5–7) he separated obedience from legalism. The will of God, rather than the minutiae of the law, is what is important. God demands the whole person rather than certain specific acts, and he leaves the concrete decision to the individual—for if one really loves, he or she knows what to do. It is sufficient for individuals to know that God has placed them under the need for decision in each and every particular circumstance of life.

Under the influence of Martin Heidegger (1889–1976), who taught at Marburg from 1923 to 1928, Bultmann became attracted to certain aspects of existentialist philosophy that had a lasting effect upon his own teachings. His emphasis on the "now" as the moment of decision allowed him to reinterpret the eschatological message of Jesus in such a way that absolutely everything depends on what we make of each moment of decision for the kingdom. According to Bultmann Christ's teaching concerning the fatherhood of God was not especially new, for this belief was current among the Jews of his day who saw themselves as God's chosen children because of the marvelous things he had done for them in the past. And finally, in the judgment of Bultmann, there is no evidence either in Jesus' sayings or in the records of the early Palestinian church of any statement concerning his metaphysical nature. The first Christians did believe him to be the Messiah, but they did not ascribe to him a particular metaphysical identity that added weight to his teachings. It was the Greek-speaking Christians who portrayed Christ as the Son of God and claimed for him a divine nature.

In an important essay that he wrote in 1941, Rudolf Bultmann takes aim at the prevalence of mythology in the New Testament.[5] He labels such notions as vicarious atonement, the preexistence of the Son, and our eventual transition into a heavenly realm as incredible and incomprehensible. He concludes that if the New Testament is to retain its validity it must be radically demythologized. The Christ event portrayed in the New Testament is overlaid with legend, for example, the virgin birth, the empty tomb, the resurrection, and the ascension. The only truly historical event is the Easter faith of the first believers who were touched by God's saving act in Christ, which is the ground of our hope. For Bultmann myth is the unworldly clothed in worldly garb and the transcendent when it appears as immanent.

Some years later, in his *Theology of the New Testament*, Bultmann reexamines the preaching of Jesus.[6] It is his judgment that in the Synoptics Jesus does not invite men to believe in his person, as is the case in John. Nor does Christ identify himself as Messiah. Rather, he points to someone else, that is, the Son of man who is to come. The oldest "Son of man" sayings refer to this figure in the third person. Christ's role is to call men and women to decision (Matt. 8:22), a decision of radical obedience to God. The will of God is summed up in the demand for love (Mark 12:28–34), which commandment carries with it few specifics. It merely invites us into the "now" of our encounter with our neighbor. Jesus' notion of God was about the same as that found among the devout Jews of his day, but for him God was very near at hand. The Lord's Prayer affirms that (Matt. 6:9–13). And the believer discovers what God wants of him or her in the encounter with one's neighbor.

In the initial Palestinian kerygma Jesus was proclaimed as prophet, teacher, and the coming Son of man, but not as divine. It was in the Hellenistic kerygma that Jesus was called the divine man. In the Palestinian church Christ was proclaimed as the one whom God had constituted as the Messiah through the resurrection, and they anticipated his return as the Son of man who, at the end of time, would return from heaven to judge and impart salvation. The title "Son of God" was, according to Romans 1:3, already used before Paul, but neither in Judaism nor among the first-generation Christians did it carry the ontological implication it had in Hellenistic Christianity. It was a regal title adopted by the earliest Christians as a result of Jesus' resurrection.

In February 1951 at a conference of Swiss liberal theologians, Rudolf Bultmann was invited to give his reaction to the christological confession of the first assembly of the World Council of Churches in Amsterdam in 1948, which proclaimed Jesus as God and Savior.[7] In Bultmann's view, John 20:28 is the only New Testament passage that clearly addresses Christ as God. There are no such references in the Synoptics, Acts, or in Paul. There are a few passages in the deutero-Pauline literature (e.g., Titus 2:13) but their meaning is doubtful. Bultmann teaches that it was only with the Apostolic Fathers (e.g., Ignatius of Antioch, ca. 110) that Jesus was unambiguously proclaimed as the only begotten Son of God (Ignatius to the Ephesians 7,2). The title *kurios*, when used in the New Testament, points out Christ as a divine figure, but certainly not God. He was superior to the angels (Heb. 1:4), and somehow enjoyed preexistence (Phil. 2:6). As the image of God (Col. 1:15) he was considered to be the agent of creation, but in Bultmann's judgment these passages only reveal Christ as a divine figure who is subordinate to God. Furthermore, Bultmann notes, such statements tell us about his significance rather than his nature. In Jesus' words and actions God speaks to us and acts on our behalf. We encounter God in Christ and only in him.

The New Testament adamantly professes the true humanity of Jesus against any and all gnostic and docetic tendencies. As the "true God and true man" dilemma presented itself to the early church, the solution was formulated in the Greek thought patterns of the Chalcedonian definition which, in Bultmann's judgment, are no longer comprehensible to us. When we say that Christ is God, we cannot understand this in any ontological or metaphysical sense. The statement can only be understood as the event of God's acting in Jesus. As a matter of fact, Bultmann urges us to avoid such formulations because they generate misunderstandings. We should rather confine ourselves to saying that Jesus is the Word of God. He concludes by asking whether the profession of the World Council of Churches, which acknowledges that Jesus is God and Savior, is in accord with the New Testament, and Bultmann's response is, "I do not know."

Ernst Käsemann

One of Bultmann's more prominent pupils was Ernst Käsemann (1906–98), whose teaching career took him to Mainz, Göttingen, and Tübingen. In a memorable lecture given to a group of former Marburg students in October 1953, Käsemann revived the quest for the historical Jesus that had been largely abandoned since the 1920s.[8] Karl Barth and his neo-orthodox colleagues were more concerned with the revival of the theology of the Reformation, while Bultmann was convinced that any pursuit of the historical Jesus was futile. His concern was to discover the primitive Christian proclamation (kerygma) in the earliest layers of the Synoptics. Although this contained a mixture of the preaching of Jesus and the kerygma of the first Christian communities, Bultmann was not especially interested in drawing clear lines between the former and the latter. For him the Jesus of history was no longer of decisive significance for Christian faith.

Käsemann asserts that Bultmann's radical stand was generating a reaction, prompting a return to the study of the historical Jesus. Biblical scholars recognized more and more that the synoptic gospels contain a great deal of authentic tradition, as do the passion and the Easter narratives. The neo-orthodox theology of scholars like Barth and Emil Brunner (1889–1966) has placed before us a stunning portrait of the "divine man" which is difficult for us to assimilate since it seems to require a considerable sacrifice of the intellect and does not strengthen our faith. Käsemann contends that the gospels alone present the message of Jesus within the context of his earthly life. The other New Testament writings generally focus on the passion, death, and resurrection as the only events of significance for the early Christian communities. The synoptic gospels, according to Käsemann, attempt to portray authentic traditions concerning the earthly Jesus, but John's gospel does not. He does not follow the synoptic patterns and is more concerned with depicting the risen and glorified Christ who is present among believers. It is not possible, however, to write a life of Christ even from the synoptic gospels, because the Jesus we encounter there is the Christ of the early faith communities. Nonetheless, it is only through the kerygma of primitive Christianity that we can come into contact with the life history of Jesus. Whereas Matthew's gospel envisions Jesus as a second Moses imparting the new law, Mark periodically reveals glimpses of the glorified Christ during his earthly life. Luke, as viewed by Käsemann, is the first Christian historian who maps out in his gospel and in the Acts the initial stages of salvation history, and Jesus is portrayed as the focal point of that early history.

The Synoptics connect the gospel narratives with the current situation of their readers, but at the same time they take pains to animate the passages with the flavor of the past. Although John, as seen by Käsemann, does not generally share the same concern, he does make it clear that the life of Jesus was situated and grounded in human history. All of the evangelists were of the mind that the earthly history of Jesus is the very bedrock of our faith. As soon as we lose touch with this truth, we are giving way to Docetism.

Since the gospels present us primarily with the primitive Christian kerygma, the individual words and actions of Jesus have to be extracted from it through the use of scientific methods such as form criticism (i.e., the study of individual texts or passages prior to their inclusion in larger sections of the gospels). It is through this kind of careful research that we can begin to open windows into what Jesus actually said and did, but the process is extremely painstaking and requires a great deal of patience and expertise. In the gospels we meet an astounding variety of portraits of Jesus which identify him as rabbi, prophet, teacher of wisdom, the Son of man, the Messiah. Which of these images will most surely take us back to the historical Jesus, or can all of them play a part in that adventure?

Though it is true that Jesus conducted himself as a rabbi and a prophet, it is Käsemann's judgment that the only title that does full justice to his claims is that of Messiah. It is not enough to say that Jesus merely made the demands of the Mosaic law more stringent. He did change the law. He was, according to Matthew, a new lawgiver. Jesus was aware that he was able to overturn the prescriptions of the old law, and this as much as anything brought him to his death. Rabbis derive their authority from Moses and would never oppose the Torah. Nor would the prophets ever take a stand against the law of Moses, for this would brand them as false prophets. The parables reveal Jesus as a teacher of wisdom, which also distinguishes him from the rabbis, as does his consistent assurance that in his utterances he is revealing the will of God.

Was Christ aware that he was the Messiah? According to Käsemann there is no way of knowing, since the messianic passages of the New Testament (even Mark 8:38) were formulated by the primitive Christian communities. If Jesus did not claim the title of Messiah, this would have been consonant with his character such as we know it. The first-generation Christians could well have given him the title based on their perception of the uniqueness of his message and mission.

Käsemann concludes his study by observing that we still cannot construct a life of Jesus based upon what we know about him. However, our continuing interest in his earthly life is not only valid but essential, since there are events and sayings of Jesus in the synoptic tradition which are widely recognized as authentic. Abandoning our fascination with the earthly Jesus would, in a sense, be taking a step toward Docetism. We must keep in mind that the primitive Christians always insisted upon the identity between Jesus of Nazareth and the glorified Lord. Thus Ernst Käsemann sets the stage for the resurgence of a new quest for the historical Jesus.

Günther Bornkamm

Bultmann's disciple, Günther Bornkamm (1905–90), taught at the Universities of Göttingen and Heidelberg for many years. His study, *Jesus of Nazareth* (1956), was the first book on the historical Jesus from the school of Bultmann since Bultmann's own *Jesus* (1926).[9] In chapter 3, Bornkamm describes the family of Jesus, that is, his parents, brothers (Mark 3:32), and sisters (Mark 6:3), and he considers the genealogies and the infancy narratives in Matthew and Luke to be in large part legendary. The author's approach can be clearly identified as originating from a Christology from below. After his baptism by John, which Bornkamm finds rather difficult to explain, Jesus begins in Galilee with his preaching and healing. He preferred the smaller towns and villages to the larger cities like Tiberias. People flocked to him because of his charisma, but the singular quality of his words and his demands did create enemies who spoke out against him. The turning point of his public life was his decision to go to Jerusalem where he would communicate his message within earshot of the Jewish leaders.

Jesus was identified as a prophet (Mark 8:28; Matt. 21:11), although he never spoke of his calling as did the other prophets before him. He was also considered a rabbi because wherever he went he discussed and commented on the prescriptions of the Jewish law. However, his followers, unlike those of the other rabbis, included women and children, tax collectors, and public sinners. Further, Jesus did not merely analyze and interpret the texts of the law as did the other rabbis. His teaching left his hearers with the impression that the very authority of God was present and active in and through his words. There was a directness and an immediacy about him that communicated a mysterious sense of sovereignty over the various situations he encountered. Bornkamm affirms that it is difficult to doubt that Jesus possessed miraculous powers to heal and cure, although the nature miracles (e.g., walking on water, calming the storm, and so forth) were probably legendary. He did, however, require faith, that is, a readiness to receive the miracle, to perform his wonders (Mark 6:1–6). Jesus was also able to read the thoughts of men. His authority was ultimately grounded in his genuine and total involvement with the persons and situations at hand. No one listened as he listened. His special gift was to make the very reality of God present and active.

Jesus' message centered on the coming of the kingdom (Mark 1:15) and the victory he promised over the powers of evil. He was not at all concerned with the revival of national political aspirations like the Zealots of his day. His preaching of the kingdom was always deeply related to everyday life and to the people who formed his audience. Parables were at the heart of his proclamation. He did not merely use them as examples of his message; they were the essence of his message, conveyed in simple, graphic language that all could understand. He compared his work to an insignificant mustard seed that would eventually grow into an impressive and stately bush where birds could nest in its branches (Matt. 13:31–32).

Although Jesus directed his mission to Israel, he was principally concerned with "the lost sheep" (Matt. 15:24), that is, those on the fringes of society like the tax collectors and sinners (Matt. 21:31) with whom the other rabbis refused to associate. He seemed to exercise a sovereignty over the Mosaic law regarding such issues as the Sabbath rest (Mark 2:27), the prescriptions for ritual cleanness (Mark 7:15), and even the rules governing divorce (Luke 16:18; Matt. 5:31–32, 19:8–9). Even though the rabbis often did not differentiate the many obligations of the law into what was more and what was less important, Jesus emphasized that the love of God and then the love of neighbor were really all that were necessary to inherit eternal life (Luke 10:25–28). Further, the Jewish tendency to deify the law actually resulted in the separation from God of many who thought themselves righteous because they simply obeyed the law. The parable of the Pharisee and the publican (Luke 18:9–14) vividly illustrates this. Love as the greatest commandment (Matt. 22:34–40) is graphically portrayed in the parable of the good Samaritan (Luke 10:29–37), and the interrelationship between the love of God and neighbor is movingly expressed in Matthew 5:23–24, where we are advised to be reconciled with our neighbor before presuming to offer our gift to God. Throughout the entire Sermon on the Mount (Matthew 5–7), Jesus clearly challenges us with a new message that carries with it a quantitatively and qualitatively higher set of demands.

Bornkamm reminds his readers that the identification of God as Father was initially evident in the Old Testament. God was addressed as Father by individual Jewish believers at least from the early second century B.C.E. (Sir. 4:10). Jesus, however, wanted his hearers to know that God is the Father of all, both the just and the unjust, as the parable of the prodigal son attests (Luke 15:11–32). After a certain number of months, or years, of the Galilean ministry, Jesus felt the need to go to Jerusalem since his gospel had to be delivered there. His entry into Jerusalem and the cleansing of the temple provoked the Jewish authorities, increasing the conflict between Jesus and his adversaries. The touching scene in the garden of Gethsemane poignantly revealed his complete humanity prostrate before his Father. And, before the Sanhedrin, in response to a question from the high priest, he seemed to confirm for the first time that he was indeed the Messiah (Mark 14:62).

For Bornkamm, however, the question of Jesus' messianic consciousness is still not clear. It seems that his close followers were convinced prior to his death that he was the Messiah (Luke 24:21), but according to this author there is no certainty that Jesus claimed for himself any of the messianic titles. His confession of messiahship before the Sanhedrin was in all likelihood the product of the primitive Christian community in Palestine. This is possibly true of the attribution of the title "Son of man" to him, although there is some evidence that Jesus applied that designation to himself. The messianic character of Christ, in Bornkamm's estimate, is revealed ultimately in his works and actions, and in the singular "unmediatedness" of his presence.

According to Bornkamm, the final historical fact concerning Jesus is the Easter faith of his first disciples (1 Cor. 15:3–8). The Easter experience consisted in the newborn awareness that Jesus lives, as that is dramatically reflected in the Emmaus story (Luke 24:13–35). In the resurrection God had intervened and liberated Jesus from the power of sin and death, constituting him as Lord of the world. Bornkamm echoes Bultmann when he says that Jesus has now become a part of the message, the kerygma. More than thirty years after the appearance of Bornkamm's *Jesus of Nazareth* in the German edition, biblical scholar James Charlesworth notes that this study is "the first and still the best post-Bultmannian attempt to write an account of Jesus' life and teaching."[10]

Bornkamm portrays Jesus as a man who was especially endowed by God to speak and act in his name. An undeniable messianic power radiated from him. To a great extent his authority came from the fact that he took everyone he encountered with utmost seriousness. This apparently was no small part of his healing presence. He truly paid attention to people and dealt with them as individuals. His unique relationship with the Father allowed him to discern the weaknesses and limitations in the religious practices of his people. Their fulfillment of the law generated self-righteousness, but this, in a sense, distanced them from God. As a matter of fact, for many the fulfillment of the law became their God. Jesus preached love of God and love of neighbor, and revealed what he meant in the parables, such as the Pharisee and the publican, the prodigal son, and the good Samaritan. He ultimately felt the need to confront the Jewish leadership in Jerusalem with his message, and this occasioned his arrest and his death. Bornkamm does not clarify what he means by the resurrection of Jesus, although he affirms that Christ's postresurrection sojourn on earth and the ascension were later developments supplied by the early Christians. Bornkamm does not explain clearly the manner in which, after the resurrection, Jesus was established as Lord of the world.

The very last saving act of God, the final historical fact concerning Jesus, was the generation of the Easter faith of his first disciples. Thus Bornkamm was the first of the Bultmannians to chart a life of Jesus, but his Christology is undeniably from below. Jesus of Nazareth, who was later proclaimed Messiah, Son of man, and Son of God by the early Christian communities whom he inspired, was a messianic figure who was especially close to God and revealed in a singular way the presence of God, but Bornkamm does not attribute divinity to him. The man of Nazareth was a miracle worker who, unlike the rabbis of his time, felt called on to challenge a number of the prescriptions of the Mosaic law which were actually leading the Jews away from God. He asserted a sovereign power over the Sabbath regulations, the many laws of ritual purification, and indeed, over the divorce regulations of his own people. Bornkamm attests that Jesus became an integral part of the kerygma, but his identity in and after the resurrection remains for him a mystery that he does not attempt to penetrate.

British and American Attempts
to Reshape the Mystery

John Knox

The American Anglican theologian John Knox (b. 1900) produced a very influential book in 1967, *The Humanity and Divinity of Christ*.[11] Although the study came to only a little more than one hundred pages, it has been frequently quoted by those who have felt the need to put a more modern face on the study of Christology. Knox's purpose is to discern the pattern of development of the christological message within the New Testament and to chart its evolution. The author asks about the place of the humanity of Jesus in the primitive Christian story. He concludes that Jesus' humanity was not a problem for the earliest Christians. It was simply taken for granted. The first few chapters of Acts clearly assume that Jesus was a human being in the full sense of the term. The differences begin with the interpretations of the resurrection in the early speeches of Peter in Acts (2:14–36, 3:12–26, 4:8–12, 5:29–32, and 10:34–43), which declare that God not only raised Jesus from the dead but actually constituted him as both Lord and Messiah (Acts 2:36).

This raising of Jesus "in power," his exaltation to a place of lordship at God's right hand, occurred in and after the resurrection according to these early Petrine sermons in Acts. Knox refers to this earliest Christology as *adoptionism*. This first stage of theological development was bound to undergo revisions inasmuch as a rewriting of his earthly life was certain to take place. If Jesus was indeed the Christ, God must have known him as such beforehand, and therefore the assertion of Christ's preexistence was inevitable. Paul talks about Christ's preexistence (Phil. 2:5–6) and assumes that this notion is familiar to his readers. According to Knox, this knowledge was already widely accepted in the primitive church when Paul's major letters were written (ca. 54–60). It was reflection upon the resurrected Christ that led the early Christians to the confession of his preexistence. This affirmation did not initially bring about modifications in the original narratives concerning his earthly life.

The adoptionist phase reflected in Acts 2:36 soon gave way to what Knox terms the *kenosis phase* found in Philippians 2:5–11. Both the adoptionist and the kenosis stages were quite simple in structure and apparently antedated the composition of the New Testament writings. The assertion of Christ's preexistence seemed to provide the background necessary for the declaration of faith in his resurrection from the dead. It did, though, create new difficulties for the early Christians. For example, how could a heavenly being actually become a fully human being such as they remembered him? It was very likely out of this dilemma that Docetism arose. Jesus, said the Docetists, was not really human but only seemed to be. His humanity was merely apparent. He was a heavenly being who made himself appear like a man. The primitive church was unable to accept this docetist interpretation since it eliminated certain indispensable elements of the early Christians' recollection of Jesus. Hence, there arose a third stage of interpretation that Knox calls *incarnationalism*, which fused together certain elements of the adoptionist and the kenotic models.

Knox holds that Paul's incarnationalism was very close to the pure kenotic model, that is, preexistence, a perfectly human life, resurrection, and return to heavenly existence. On the other hand, the Fourth Gospel, according to Knox, comes closest to approaching Docetism, for the Jesus of John's account seems to be more of a heavenly being than a full-fledged member of the human condition. For Paul, Jesus seemed to be subjected to roughly the same limitations as the rest of humankind. Paul did not use the "Son of man" title, although he did describe Jesus as the second man, the new Adam (e.g., Rom. 5:12–19). Jesus was also identified by the apostle as the Wisdom of God (1 Cor. 10:1–4), and as the one through whom all things were created (1 Cor. 8:6). And yet for Paul, Christ could be said to be truly one of us.

Knox teaches that in the synoptic gospels, from the time of his baptism in the Jordan, Jesus knew that he was the divine Son of man, and in Matthew and Luke his messiahship was more widely recognized by his followers. John's rendition goes much farther. Jesus always knew that he had come from God and was returning to the Father. His sovereignty over persons and events is more complete. However, in spite of this, the Fourth Gospel does portray Jesus as a genuine human being (John 1:14), but John did clothe him in divine radiance as much as he could. The Gnostics were, like the Docetists, of the mind that it was not critical that Jesus be identified as fully human. It was sufficient that he should have appeared to be human. The Gnostics were convinced that

Jesus came to impart a higher knowledge, but only to those who were capable of comprehending it. Knox feels that there was an emphasis in John upon the knowledge of Jesus that in some slight fashion resembled the gnostic position. Knox even asks whether there might have been some vestige of Gnosticism even in Paul, since he occasionally referred to Jesus as coming "in the likeness of men" (Phil. 2:7).

Knox then addresses the Christology in the Letter to the Hebrews, and finds traces of adoptionism in certain early passages (e.g., 2:9, 5:5, 6:20). The exaltation of Jesus is described as occurring after his death (8:1–6), while on earth he was a man like all of us, in spite of his preexistence. Knox is puzzled by the fact that the earthly life of Jesus was portrayed by Paul and by Hebrews as a normal human existence despite the fact of his preexistence. In Hebrews the earthly life of Christ is described as an indispensable phase of his preparation for the high priesthood (2:17–18). He was like us in every way so that he might be our high priest before God. As a matter of fact, he was tested in every fashion, yet was not guilty of sin (4:15). His priesthood is perfect and everlasting because of the ineffable sacrifice that he offered only once (7:27–28). In Knox's estimate, Hebrews comes very close to a pure kenoticism, that is, the portrayal of a preexistent divine being who became like us in all things but sin in order to establish his priesthood, and who was then after death returned to his exalted position on high.

Adoptionism, according to Knox, can be considered the minimally basic Christology that might even be adequate in some respects—and for some Christians—today. At the outset, in the Palestinian Christian community all attention was centered on the event of salvation in Christ and not on the person of Jesus. If that state of things had not changed, the creedal confession of Acts 2:36 ("God has constituted Lord and Christ this Jesus whom you crucified") would have remained satisfactory, since it attests to his true humanity as well as to his divine lordship through the resurrection. Further, it announces the truth that God was truly operative in the Christ event. Knox notes that possibly we would not have felt the need to say any more if we had received this earliest creed directly from the Palestinian Christian community.

As the attention shifted from the significance of the saving event to the nature of the person who brought salvation, the issue of

Christ's preexistence was raised. If this person was now established by God as Lord and Messiah, what was he before his earthly existence? If he is Lord now, he must somehow have been Lord then. In Knox's judgment it is logical and unavoidable that Christ should soon have become identified with divine Wisdom or the Logos, and therefore be considered as sharing in the divinity of God. Once this step had been taken, a definite strain was placed on the assertion of Jesus' true humanity.

The Gospel of John reveals this tension in a very special way. On the one hand, Jesus is declared to be genuinely human, and on the other his divinity shines through and colors nearly everything he does and says. The theologians of the Antiochian school retained a special sensitivity for the humanity of Christ but, as Knox sees it, they did not prevail against the Alexandrian school in the articulation of the ontological reality of Jesus in the early ecumenical councils. For Knox Jesus must have had the same kind of self-consciousness that we have and must have known anxiety, frustration, and loneliness just as humankind does. Human goodness and character are forged in the struggle with evil and inevitably bear the scars of conflict. Knox asks if Christ's goodness is a genuinely human goodness if it is without weaknesses or flaws. Is only God good in that way (Mark 10:18)?

After the identification of Jesus with the preexistent Logos, Christ's humanity was under severe pressure. The New Testament declares his humanity beyond question. And the more primitive the New Testament source, the clearer is the picture of his simple and natural humanity. In spite of the consistent portrayal of his eminent and singular personality, the genuineness of his humanity is never lost. It was the resurrection—which, according to Knox, is undeniably affirmed in the New Testament as an objective occurrence—that elevated Christ to the level of living Lord. However, this never altered the fact that the earliest Christians continued to remember him as an authentically human being. Without this firm and vivid recollection, the primitive Christians would not have been able to affirm him as their Lord. It was because of this that the church rejected any explicit Docetism.

Christ's mission required that something be accomplished for the human race that could only be realized by a true human being. It was critical that Jesus participate in our actual existence in order that he might transform it into a new humanity. In Christ God created this new humanity (Rom. 5:12–21). According to Knox, Christ could not be the "new man" if he were not one of us in every way. To invoke the ancient patristic principle: what he did not share in, he was not able to redeem. How then could a human being like us have redeemed us? It is the action of God in Christ that brought about our salvation, and this intimate collaboration was what triggered the abiding concentration upon the nature, the reality of Jesus.

Knox reviews his findings as follows. The original Christology was adoptionist. Jesus, a man like us, was elevated through the resurrection to the status of Messiah and Lord. The next development was virtually inevitable, that is, the predicating of preexistence to Jesus. At that juncture there were two alternatives—kenoticism or Docetism. There could be no middle ground. Since Docetism was unacceptable to the earliest Christians, kenoticism was the alternative—some sort of divine preexistence, a completely human earthly life for Jesus in every respect, and then full restoration to the divine status in the resurrection. This is the scenario revealed in Philippians 2:6–11 that Professor Knox finds incredible. He reviews the options available to the first-century church. They could reject the kenotic story as false, which they were not able to do, or they could reinterpret its intent and meaning, which was hardly feasible. Their only option therefore was to soften the abruptness of the kenotic scenario, as was done in the more recent layers of the New Testament. Especially in John and the early Fathers of the church, the kenotic story was modified, the sharp edges smoothed, into the incarnational Christology that was defined at Chalcedon (451). This model involved three stages, that is, the divine preexistence of the Son, the manifestation of both the humanity and the divinity in the earthly Jesus, and the exaltation of Christ to the right hand of the Father through the resurrection.

It is Knox's view that Chalcedonian Christology is not fully credible today, or even intelligible, leaving countless Christians confused and hesitant about their faith. In his judgment we can assert the full humanity of Jesus without affirming his preexistence, or we can affirm his preexistence without insisting on his full humanity—but we cannot have both. His conclusion is that we must retain the kenotic and the incarnational models as an integral part of our Christian tradition and interpret them as best we can. Knox explains his understanding of the preexistence of Jesus as follows.

God the Father was involved in and was active through the entire human life of Jesus, who was destined for his indispensable mission by the Father from the beginning. What was preexistent was the eternal Word of God who was enfleshed in Jesus and fully expressed in Jesus' true humanity. For Knox, Jesus' divinity consisted in the total involvement of his human life in the redeeming activity of God and the abiding presence of God's saving action in and through Christ's human existence. It was through this man that God created a new and redeemed humanity. It is Knox's conviction that we Christians may well differ in terms of our vision of "the story," but we are united regarding the reality which "the story" is attempting to express.

John Knox's approach to Jesus clearly falls into the Christology from below camp. The divine plan envisioned the redemptive activity of Jesus from the beginning, but when the author states that the Word of God was enfleshed in Jesus, Knox is not thinking of the hypostatic union. Although he affirms some sort of belief in the Father, the Son, and the Holy Spirit, these for him are three personal "modes of being," indicating some kind of complexity in God. But he does not identify Jesus with one of the persons of the Trinity. The divinity of Jesus consists in his redeemed and redemptive humanity. In this man, God revealed himself in an absolutely unique and singular way. The mediation of Christ consists not only in his new manhood that he opens out to us, but also in the fact that we believers cannot think of Christ without thinking of God.

John A. T. Robinson

During an extended period of convalescence in 1962, the British bishop John Robinson (1919–83) wrote an engaging little piece that was published in March 1963, entitled *Honest to God*.[12] In chapter 4, "The Man for Others," he addresses the question of the humanity and the divinity of Christ and asks how one person can be identified as both God and man. It is his idea that the response formulated at the Council of Chalcedon (451) was more a statement of the problem than a solution. No doubt Chalcedon's declarations will always have a defining value for Christians, but the council set the stage for a largely docetic christological development. Today's challenge is to paint a more humanist picture of Jesus, the most God-like man who ever walked the earth.

Robinson contends that the nineteenth-century liberal theologians assisted countless believers to hold on to their Christian faith as the traditional supernaturalistic model became more and more unbelievable.

This supernaturalistic view of Christ, in Robinson's judgment, cannot be demonstrated from the New Testament, which affirms Jesus as the Word of God and the Son of God but does not unambiguously declare that Jesus is God. The author is quick to assert that when one saw and heard Jesus, one saw God (John 14:9). In him, his followers witnessed God acting and bringing life and salvation to humankind (2 Cor. 5:19). It is not clear what titles Jesus claimed for himself (Mark 10:18). Perhaps he preferred to be called "Son of man," but scholars are not in total agreement even with that. It is evident that in the resurrection God set his seal upon Jesus as both Lord and Christ (Acts 2:36). His self-surrender was so complete and his oneness with the Ground of his being so total that John's gospel could say of him, "I and the Father are one" (John 10:30). As Jesus empties himself of any desire to direct attention to himself, he reveals God in a most transparent way. It is therefore the kenotic theory of Christology—which emphasizes the total self-emptying of Jesus—that offers the best hope of reconciling with some adequacy the divine and the human in Christ.

Robinson is fond of referring to Jesus as "the man for others"— which is reminiscent of the language in Dietrich Bonhoeffer's "Outline for a Book."[13] Christ was totally open to the Ground of his being and to other men and women, and it is at this point of unbounded love that we encounter God who is love. The life of God is enfleshed without limitation in the life of this man, who in truth can be called perfect man and perfect God, that is, the fullest embodiment of the beyond in our midst. Robinson concludes his chapter 4 by suggesting that we must also demythologize our understanding of Christ's atonement, and he quotes those moving passages in Paul Tillich's sermon, "You Are Accepted," where the essence of atonement consists in accepting the truth that we have indeed been accepted by God in Christ, and thus experience grace and the love whereby we are brought into union with the very Ground of our being. This will enable us to overcome all the estrangement and the alienation that surrounds us in our world.[14]

Ten years after the publication of his extremely popular *Hon-*

est to God, Bishop Robinson completed a fuller treatment of his views on Christology, *The Human Face of God.*[15] Each generation attempts to give its response to Jesus' question, "Who do men say that I am?" (Mark 8:27). Jesus did not seem to be entirely pleased with the term *Messiah* and apparently felt more comfortable with "Son of man," although we are not sure that he applied the latter to himself. We should not make Jesus into our own image, for that is what so many of the "life of Jesus" people did in the nineteenth century with only questionable success. We must try to comprehend what the New Testament writers and the early Fathers wanted to say about Jesus' humanity and divinity, and we may well have to formulate language different from theirs to express in our day what they were trying to say in theirs.

The shift from the mythological scenario or model was necessary because the language of myth—once so critical to humankind for expressing the deeper levels of human experience—no longer speaks to us with any effectiveness. Myth can no longer be used as a vehicle to communicate how things are in reality. The same can be said, according to Robinson, regarding the use of metaphysical language that in our time, at least for many, is confusing and troublesome. He feels that great numbers today have lost touch with the supernaturalistic ontology in which Christian truths have been clothed for so long. He urges us to move from an ontological to a functional mode of thought with which so many modern minds can more readily identify. When we turn in the direction of the functional, Robinson warns that any contemporary Christology will seem to be reductionist when compared with the categories of classical Christology. Any approach that begins with a full, frank, and open consideration of his humanity will probably be considered reductionist by the proponents of a more traditional classical theology.

Once the notion of preexistence entered into the Jesus narrative, questions arose concerning the genuineness of his humanity. This explains why Docetism was the first heresy that the early Christians had to confront. Was he so different from us that he could not be considered as human in the full sense? Robinson states that the doctrine of Christ's "impersonal humanity" (an-hypostasia) raises a question concerning the authenticity of his personhood and erodes his solidarity with the rest of humankind. (*Anhypostasia* is the theological term used to express that Christ's human nature, although complete, does not subsist on its own as a human person.)[16] The bishop also has serious difficulties with the doctrine of the virgin birth since it seems to remove Jesus from the living stream of humanity and to throw doubt on the very authenticity of Christ's human nature.

Was it essential that Jesus be identified as the absolutely perfect man? We know that his knowledge was in some respects limited and on occasion reflective of the inadequate and erroneous notions of his time.[17] Why did he have to be considered as unqualifiedly perfect? Is it not sufficient to say that although he was limited, he was perfectly true to himself in every way? The Letter to the Hebrews reveals that he learned obedience from his sufferings, and thus he was made perfect (Heb. 5:7–9). He was tested in every way but remained without sin (Heb. 4:15). Robinson does not choose to describe Christ as utterly incapable of sinning, but rather that his sinlessness was the result of his genuine and steadfast human freedom.

The question of Christ's divinity was the next issue for consideration by Bishop Robinson. To affirm that Jesus is the Christ is already to declare divine qualities concerning him. Although this man does reflect to us the reality of what God is, how can what is divine about him not completely overshadow his humanity? The Council of Nicaea (325) set the parameters of the discussion, affirming that Christ was of one substance with the Father. He was made man and then suffered and died for our salvation.[18] For both the Alexandrians and the Antiochians, Christ was a divine person—the person of the Logos—but in Robinson's judgment, at least for the Alexandrians he was not a human personality in the contemporary sense, that is, a distinct human center of conscious selfhood. What they really meant was that Christ's humanity constituted a permanent mode of being of the person of the Word. The fourth- and fifth-century Fathers of the church generally theologized out of a clear preference for the divine in Christ. Even Pope Leo I's *Tome to Flavian* against the monophysite Eutyches, which was much praised at Chalcedon, along with Cyril of Alexandria's second letter to Nestorius and his letter to John of Antioch, failed to do justice to the full and integral humanity of Jesus. Robinson considers as astonishing the doctrine of anhypostasia that affirms that Jesus assumed a human nature but not a distinct human personhood. It seems that those who hold fast to this position must maintain that although Christ was, and is, a singular subject with two distinct modes of consciousness, he was able to switch off one or the other at will.

The words and deeds of Jesus reveal for Robinson not so much his own divine nature, but rather what a human being can do who is totally and completely open to the power of God operating through him. Jesus is, in fact, the very presence of God in our midst. He is God for us in human flesh. The author refers again to the virgin birth story that he says is primarily intended to affirm that the advent of Jesus was first and foremost a divine initiative. His human existence and his activity constituted a definitive breakthrough into human history (Mark 1:27). His hearers were amazed at his teaching and his charisma: "No one has ever spoken like this before!" (John 7:46).

Turning to the resurrection, Bishop Robinson maintains that in the days after Christ's death, genuine shared experiences on the part of his followers served as the ground for the faith that grew into the new community of love that had such striking attributes and qualities that they could only be explained through God's creative intervention. The new community from the outset radiated the same love, forgiveness, and other-directedness that Jesus himself revealed, and hence this community of believers constituted a presence of Christ himself, just as Jesus had been while he was physically with them. Robinson manifests a certain curiosity regarding the narrative of the empty tomb, which he admits is based upon a very early tradition, but he does not hazard an explanation for the tradition. He only adds that the old was not the material out of which the new was born. For this author, neither a supernatural entrance nor a supernatural exit is required by our faith in Christ.

The question of preexistence surfaces again as Robinson attempts to reconcile the positions of Paul, John, and Hebrews. Whereas Paul showed little interest in the earthly Jesus, and John was inclined at times to paint him with something of a docetic brush, the Letter to the Hebrews emphasized the striking polarity between the humanity and the divinity of Christ more graphically and in greater detail than any other New Testament writing. However, neither Paul nor John nor the author of Hebrews has left us with a rationale with which to coordinate the human and the divine in Christ. Robinson is not certain that the New Testament carried the notion of preexistence to the point where it necessarily involved an individual heavenly person who at a moment in time assumed a human nature. The New Testament use of the wisdom literature of the Old Testament (e.g., Prov. 8:22–31; Wis. 7:22–8:1) brought forward the notion of a personified Wisdom as God's agent in creation. In the Old Testament this Wisdom came to dwell in certain holy persons, designating them as special friends and messengers of God. However, this was in no way seen as a threat to their humanity.

Jesus was singularly designated at his baptism (Mark 1:11) as the beloved Son who would stand in the place of Israel as the representative of God to the world. In the Letter to the Hebrews he is identified not as an angelic being, but as a man (Heb. 1:1–3) who became the Christ in something of an adoptionist fashion (Heb. 2:10, 3:2). Paul, too, has reflected a strain of that adoptionist thought when he states that Jesus was designated Son of God through the resurrection (Rom. 1:4). Robinson interprets the hymn in Philippians 2:5–11 as referring not to Jesus' divine nature but rather to an original image of God that he always possessed. Jesus is portrayed as the authentic Son of God whom Adam was initially destined to be. Adam would have continued to share in a divine glory that he proceeded to lose for himself and his progeny through the fall. Jesus lowered himself to the state of fallen humankind—not even sharing in the glory that Adam had originally been given but lost—and he took the form of a slave, being obedient unto death. Therefore, God exalted him and raised him above everyone, making him Lord. Robinson notes that Philippians 2:5–11 embodies not only the notion of preexistence, but an adoptionist strain as well.

In the Gospel of John, there is no suggestion of adoptionism, but neither is there a hint of any contradiction between Christ's preexistence and his genuine humanity. In discussions with the Jews he claims divine sonship (10:34–36), which should have been their inheritance, but morally they have renounced their claim (8:42–47). In Robinson's estimate, only Jesus can affirm that he can see God, and this prerogative, according to the author, seems to be based on moral rather than metaphysical grounds (6:45–46). Further, because Jesus is the totally obedient man, he is able to say, "He who sees me sees the Father" (12:45). The complete other-directedness of his humanity left him so transparent that it could be said of him that he was God's man, or that God was in Christ, or that he was God for us.

It is Robinson's contention that just as the mythological model of late Judaism and early Christianity gave way to the ontological model of Nicaea and Chalcedon, which translated the more symbolic expressions of the New Testament into metaphysical ones, so now there is a need to transpose the ontological patterns into functional language. The emphasis should shift from Christ as the divine hypostasis in human flesh to Christ as the one who does for us what God does, who represents God in a singular way and acts on our behalf. Jesus has to be identified as the man who "lived" God. His absolutely unique relationship to God is emphatically stated in Matthew 11:27, and in the parable of the evil tenants (Mark 12:1–12) who killed even the son sent to them by the gracious landowner. In Robinson's judgment Jesus was on the same metaphysical level as every other son and daughter of God. Further, the Gospel of John declares that he is functionally unique because only he acts in a manner that is always pleasing to the Father (John 10:34–38, 8:29). Thus he and the Father are one (John 10:30) inasmuch as he is speaking and acting like the Father. Robinson holds that there is no affirmation in John that makes the sonship of Jesus into a second superhuman nature. Further, he argues that the titles that Jesus allegedly claimed for himself (i.e., Son of God, Christ, Son of man) are very uncertain and highly debatable even today.

There is little doubt, however, that in changing the obligations of the law (Matt. 5:21–48), in forgiving sins (Mark 2:1–12), and in exercising control over the evil powers (Mark 1:21–27), Jesus moved into the realm that is properly God's. There is no doubt that Jesus acted in God's name and on his behalf with absolute and total confidence. The early church, however, was not satisfied with what could be described as a functional understanding of Christ's sonship but moved beyond that at Nicaea (325) and Chalcedon (451) to an ontological model—Christ is the divine Son who is *omooúsios*, that is, of the same substance as the Father. Robinson feels that this metaphysical model makes Christ less (rather than more) real for many believers today. How, he asks, can we express this union of the human and the divine in Jesus? Can it be achieved most convincingly by predicating two natures that are hypostatically united in the person of the Word, or can we assert what we want to assert by affirming that God, in an absolutely unique and mysterious fashion, acted in and through this man?

The conflict between the Alexandrians and the Antiochians in the fourth and fifth centuries and beyond was focused precisely upon what model best expressed the union of the human and the divine in Christ. The Alexandrians failed to give adequate treatment to the humanity of Christ, while the Antiochians were unable to arrive at a meaningful articulation of the unity in Jesus. Even Karl Barth in our time was so afraid of having Christ appear as one man among many that he held to the view of anhypostasia, which deprives Jesus of a distinctly human personal existence, since the *esse* of Jesus is the *esse* of the Word of God. Bishop Robinson expresses a preference for the model provided by process thought (which will be dealt with in chapter 4). According to this model, the Word is viewed as being active in and through the entire cosmic process of growth and evolution from the very beginning. Then, at a given point in time, the Word broke through and expressed itself in Jesus, who is the decisive event and the high point of human development, setting the pattern for what should follow. This event of Jesus is not discontinuous or an insertion from the outside. Rather it is a progressive development from within cosmic and human history, and at the same time a "given," but a given from within the process. For Robinson Jesus is different from us in degree rather than in kind, since a difference in kind would jeopardize his solidarity with the rest of the human race. In the New Testament Jesus appears as a person who is more independent, more profoundly obedient to the Father, and more evidently excelling in goodness than the rest of us. Moreover, the key to his singular appeal is the result of his absolutely unique relationship with the One whom he calls Father. For these reasons he was charged with a destiny to which no one else was called.

The final section of Robinson's Christology deals with the continuing presence of Christ in the world. This presence is brought about by the Holy Spirit who animates the Christian community of believers whose task it is to keep the world focused on God. If the world is to believe in the God of Jesus, they must see Jesus reflected in the life of the community of Christian believers, as they saw God revealed in the words and deeds of Jesus himself. Although for the Christian Christ represents the definitive revelation of God, there may be other ways to salvation for those who are not acquainted with Christ. Also, the nature and the conduct of the Christian churches could well be an obstacle to the growth of Christian faith, inasmuch as the values of Christ are often not reflected in a very transparent manner out of their institutional life. Christ for us today, according to Robinson, is the one who comes unrecognized into our presence, revealing himself first as the generous neighbor before he can be acknowledged as Lord (Luke 24:13–35; John 21:1–14). The presence of Christ in our day is really the embodiment of the transcendent in our midst. We are Christians to the extent that we can discern the divinity that reveals itself out of the men and women around us.

John Macquarrie

In 1966 John Macquarrie (b. 1919), a Scottish-born theologian, published an engaging summary of Christian thought, *Principles of Christian Theology*, which was issued in a second edition in 1977.[19] It is clear from the outset that he prefers the approach of Christology from below. Macquarrie espouses a transcendental anthropology similar to Karl Rahner's, in which Christ represents the ultimate convergence of the human and the divine, and the goal toward which all created being tends. As humankind manifests self-giving and love, it shows forth the divine. This self-giving was uniquely revealed in Jesus and becomes complete in his acceptance of death, at which time there is a coming together, a union of the human and the divine in one person. Indeed, it can be said that the fullness of the divinity dwells bodily in him (Col. 2:9). Jesus constitutes the very definition of the nature of God and the nature of man.

Macquarrie struggles with the question of preexistence since it seems to tempt us into Docetism. He resolves the matter for himself by asserting that from the outset of the creative process the Logos had been on the way to self-expression in Jesus. As a result, Christ was active in creation from the beginning and was its very aim or goal. Macquarrie observes that from Schleiermacher (1768–1834) to the present there has been a consistent emphasis in christological thought upon the humanity of Jesus, through whom human nature attained its ultimate perfection.

The saving work of Christ was exquisitely portrayed in the parable of the prodigal son (Luke 15:11–32). Macquarrie does not favor the notion that Jesus suffered in our place, since for him it is not a satisfactory explanation of the mission of Jesus. He recommends that we find a new model. Perhaps the point of departure should be the self-giving of Jesus that has brought God's other-directedness into the world in a totally unique fashion. This self-giving is to engage humankind and enable it to turn from the self-centered course it has taken into a new path of graciousness and concern for others. This work identifies Jesus especially in his passion and death, and this is what must animate his followers, inspiring and enabling them to carry on the universal reconciling enterprise of God throughout creation.

In 1990 John Macquarrie published what could be called his definitive treatment of Christology in *Jesus Christ in Modern Thought*.[20] About three-fourths of the study is taken up with a thorough review of the field from the New Testament to the present. Then he gives his own rendering of the humanity, the divinity, and the mission of Christ in the last hundred or so pages. At the beginning the author reminds his readers that efforts to spell out in extended detail the specifics of the person of Christ have over the centuries often generated more confusion than light. He feels that in so doing we can rather easily get out of our depth.

After this extended survey of the development of christological thought in the West, John Macquarrie's own presentation opens with a preliminary discussion of several historical questions. He affirms that there is no longer any serious debate over the existence and the human earthly presence of Jesus and he raises the issue of Christ's messianic consciousness. It is Macquarrie's judgment that Christ possibly believed that another individual would appear at some time in the future to bring the messianic epoch to full term. Jesus was convinced that he was called by God to proclaim the kingdom, and he conceived of himself as the Son of God, though not in the technical sense of Nicaea and Chalcedon. He spoke of God as Father and shared an abiding and intimate personal relationship with him. Although volumes have been written since the nineteenth century concerning Jesus' self-understanding, the question is still very debatable. After a certain period of public ministry in Galilee, Jesus determined to go to Jerusalem but we are not really sure why. Macquarrie is hesitant about saying that Jesus went to Jerusalem to die, in spite of the fact that in the New Testament he predicts his death in that context. Rather, he may have made the journey to enter into discussion with the forces opposed to him and his ministry, realizing that this exposure could possibly lead to his death.

Macquarrie asserts that Jesus differs from all other humans in degree, but not in kind, and that any contemporary Christology must certainly begin with a full and detailed profession of the complete humanity of Jesus. He then proceeds to adopt the approach of transcendental anthropology popularized by Rahner and others. According to this model, human nature has the capacity to cross many new boundaries and move from one horizon to the next, almost without limit. It is the infinite that beckons and draws humankind ever onward and, in the process, humankind extends itself and grows. For Macquarrie, to call Christ the God-man is to affirm that in him this process of human transcendence has reached the point where he has become so closely conjoined with God that his human existence can be said to have become "deified." This Macquarrie calls an ascending Christology, which must initially admit the possibility of this kind of convergence and then affirm that it has taken place in an absolutely unique and once-and-for-all manner in Jesus Christ. For Macquarrie Paul attests to this in Philippians 2:6–11. Moreover, it is this kind of dynamic upward thrust to which Irenaeus (ca. 140–ca. 200) refers as the progressive development of the image of God in man.

The point of departure for the consideration of the divinity of Christ is precisely this concept of humanity that has the potential for indefinite development upward. If God is depicted as "wholly other" and totally separated from humankind, then the notion of Incarnation seems almost impossible. Macquarrie feels that the Old Testament doctrine of God was not particularly open to the possibility of Incarnation. With the new approach to God revealed in Jesus, the situation is very different. Christians could not conceive of God without thinking of Christ (1 Cor. 8:6). Further, it is the knowledge of the possibility of an ever-expanding human transcendence and a capacity for reaching out to God that allows us to posit such a capacity in Jesus. Similarly, the belief that God continually makes himself present and known in and through creation serves as the ground for our faith recognition that he became present and known in an absolutely singular manner in Christ.

The traditional formulas of Chalcedon remain normative for Macquarrie, but some of the words and expressions have become almost unintelligible to us. It is extremely difficult if not impossible for us to identify with the fifth-century concepts of *ousia* (being), *physis* (nature), and *hypostasis* (substance?), whose meanings were ambiguous at best even then. The use of the terms by the fourth- and fifth-century Fathers was anything but uniform. As a matter of fact, a good many of the misunderstandings that surfaced in the first five ecumenical councils were due in no small part to imprecise language and confusion regarding the meaning of terms. What is to be preserved from the deliberations of Chalcedon is the "governing intention," though the terminology employed may no longer be adequate for us.

Then, as he did earlier in *Principles of Christian Theology*, Macquarrie concludes his Christology with a summary of "about a dozen happenings" or mysteries in the life of Jesus. Regarding the first mystery, the question of preexistence, Macquarrie holds that in spite of the affirmations in John and Hebrews, and perhaps some traces in 1 Peter, Ephesians, and Revelation, there is no rock-solid case for the affirmation of preexistence as an indispensable element in Christology. The only kind of preexistence that Macquarrie can accept without question is Jesus' preexistence in the divine plan of God, which, he says, would constitute a very high degree of reality indeed.

The Incarnation and the nativity of Jesus can be explained as the culmination of the self-manifestation of the Logos into the world, while the virgin birth has to be reviewed very critically since this would dramatically separate Jesus from the rest of humanity. The baptism of Christ by John is viewed by Macquarrie as a focal event, a kind of messianic anointing, although Jesus might not have fully understood this at the time. After this he dedicated himself to the preaching of the kingdom. Both Matthew (4:1–11) and Luke (4:1–13) expand upon Mark's reference (1:13) to the temptations of Jesus by Satan. According to Macquarrie's reading of the New Testament, we are taught that Jesus, as a matter of fact, did not rather than could not sin. The transfiguration accounts in Matthew, Mark, and Luke are puzzling to Macquarrie. Do they reflect a postresurrection experience, or are they legendary anticipations of the resurrection?

Christ's passion and death were undeniably historical events that were proclaimed as having a profound redemptive effect for all of humanity. His punishing death came to be understood as atonement, which was explained by Anselm as necessary satisfaction demanded by God for the sins of humankind, or by Calvin as Christ's substitution as victim for humankind, to endure the wrath of an angry God. Unfortunately, Macquarrie does not provide his readers with a particularly convincing explanation of the Christian notion of atonement. He does, however, give two rather diverse interpretations for the resurrection. The first, which he labels "the happy ending," affirms that certain powerful experiences, for example, the empty tomb and the postresurrection appearances, led the disciples to believe that God had intervened in a special manner in the case of Jesus, allowing his followers to encounter him in a new way. What was raised up was a spiritual body that they experienced, and they articulated this experience in the words, "Jesus lives!" After a certain period the risen Lord *ascended* in glory to the Father, and we await *his return* to inaugurate the new age.

Macquarrie then very briefly outlines a second scenario that he terms "the austere ending." What if we were to close the narrative at Jesus' death upon the cross? Would that destroy everything? Would the message of salvation in Christ be rendered meaningless thereby? Macquarrie does not think so, since the two central revelations that are distinctively Christian would still stand, that is, that God is love and that God is uniquely revealed in Jesus. The selfless love that he manifested throughout his life and especially in his passion and death constituted a stunning victory over evil that would stand, even if there were no resurrection. In the Gospel of John, Christ's death on the cross is portrayed as his exaltation (12:32–33). Rudolf Bultmann is the one whose theology comes closest to espousing this more stark conclusion, whereas Macquarrie himself leaves to the reader the choice between the happy ending and the austere one.

In 1998 Macquarrie published a small volume, *Christology Revisited*, that confirms his preference for enhypostasia because of the essential affinity between the divine and the human, which allows the two to coalesce, giving the human a completion and a perfection it could achieve in no other way.[21] The Incarnation did not consist in the hypostasis of the divine Logos displacing the human hypostasis, but rather, the human hypostasis was transfigured by a "constant immersion" in the divine. That constant immersion is the "something more" in Jesus. Macquarrie repeats his belief that the resurrection experience on the part of the disciples was the result of their continuing sense of the presence of

Christ, along with meditation on such events of his life as the transfiguration and his death on Calvary. This brought them to a belief that in Jesus they had indeed experienced the glory of the Father. Regarding the preexistence of Christ, Macquarrie asserts again that Jesus the incarnate Word was there "in the counsels of God" from the very beginning.

A Summary

Out of the Enlightenment came a movement away from the traditional supernaturalist theology that had been the mainstay of Christians since at least the fourth century. Rudolf Bultmann, although a product of the nineteenth-century school of liberal theology, committed his life to a rigorous study of the New Testament based on the use of the recently developed scientific tools of biblical criticism. As a result of his exposure to the existentialist thought of Martin Heidegger, Bultmann developed a rather unique approach to Jesus and to the message of the New Testament. From his biblical research, he was convinced that very little could be known about the historical Jesus. What is really important is the kerygma—the message concerning the coming of the kingdom. Each believer must hear the word of Jesus in the moments of personal decision, and when we accept and acknowledge the word of Jesus as the very word of God, then at that moment Christ reveals himself to us as divine.

Bultmann did not hold to any kind of ontological explanation of the divine in Jesus. The earliest Christians believed him to be the Messiah but did not attribute to him any ontological divinity. The Greek-speaking Christians proclaimed Jesus as Son of God and attested to his divine nature. The task of demythologizing the New Testament was indeed a central mission for Bultmann. Such notions as the preexistence of the Son, the virgin birth, vicarious atonement, the resurrection, the empty tomb, and the ascension had to be jettisoned so that the essential message of the kerygma could be clearly heard. After the death of Jesus the one truly historical event that is to be proclaimed is the Easter faith of the first believers who were touched by God's saving act in Christ.

The role of Jesus' call to decision remains the same now as it was during his earthly life, that is, to summon men and women to a decision of radical obedience to God. The believer discovers what God wants in the encounter with his or her neighbor. The terminology and the thought patterns of Chalcedon are no longer meaningful to us. When we say that Christ is God we can only mean that God acts in an unparalleled manner in Jesus. As a matter of fact, Bultmann urges us to avoid such statements inasmuch as they generate misunderstanding. Rather, we should confine ourselves to professing that Jesus is the Word of God.

In 1953 it was Ernst Käsemann, a disciple of Bultmann, who reversed the trend emphasized by his mentor and revived the search for the historical Jesus. Biblical scholars were becoming more and more convinced that there is a great deal of authentic tradition concerning Jesus in the synoptic gospels, and in the passion and Easter narratives. Although the Gospel of John does not follow the synoptic models, all four of the evangelists acted on the assumption that it is the earthly history of Jesus that grounds our faith. The words and deeds of Jesus must be lifted out of the primitive Christian kerygma through the use of modern scientific methods in order to discover more accurately the actual sayings and deeds of Jesus.

It is Käsemann's judgment that although Christ presented himself as a rabbi and a prophet, the only title that can do full justice to his claims is that of Messiah. Käsemann teaches that it is not possible to determine whether or not Jesus knew that he was the Messiah. The first-generation Christians awarded him this title based on the singular character of his mission. Though we are not able to write a life of Jesus from the information available in the New Testament, there is a good deal that we can know about the acts and the words of Christ from a careful, critical study of the gospels. Käsemann is convinced that if we abandoned the quest for the historical Jesus, we would be moving in the direction of Docetism.

Another of Bultmann's disciples, Günther Bornkamm, published an outstanding study of Jesus in 1956. The author describes in some detail the human family of Jesus, discounting any reference to his supernatural origin. After his baptism by John, Christ began his mission of preaching and healing in Galilee and met with considerable success, although opposition began to rise up against him. Bornkamm identifies Jesus as a prophet and a rabbi whose followers included women, tax collectors, and public sinners. He healed many of their infirmities but did require faith from those whom he cured. The power that Jesus demonstrated over people, according to Bornkamm, seemed to grow out of his complete openness and availability to the persons and the situations at hand, and it was this genuine and undivided attention that constituted his authority and made the reality of God present and alive through him.

Jesus seemed to be especially attentive to those on the margin of society, unlike the rabbis of his day. There is little doubt that his journey to Jerusalem aggravated the conflict between him and the Jewish authorities and led to his arrest and execution. It seems that prior to his death his followers believed Jesus to be the Messiah, although it is not certain that he claimed that title for himself. For Bornkamm the disciples' Easter experience consisted in their new awareness that Jesus still lives and is active among them. His messianic character is revealed in the quality of his words and actions, and in the unspeakable power of his presence. It is not clear how Bornkamm interprets the resurrection, but he does maintain that the final saving act of God was the generation of the Easter faith among the disciples of Jesus, which served as the ground of the Christian movement. Christ was a messianic figure who enjoyed an unparalleled closeness to God and revealed the presence of God in a unique and definitive manner. However, for Bornkamm, he was not divine. The identity of Jesus after the resurrection remains a mystery that the author does not attempt to explain.

The work of John Knox has influenced a good number of scholars in the past generation or more. His 1967 study charts a pattern of development in the Christology of the New Testament. The early speeches of Peter in Acts reveal an adoptionist approach that probably represented the most primitive christological reflection. Knox is of the opinion that if the emphasis had remained upon the deeds of Christ, this adoptionist Christology would probably have continued to occupy a significant place in the creedal tradition of Christians. However, the concentration soon switched from his works to the person of Jesus, and that inevitably brought with it an assertion of his preexistence.

The second development was what Knox terms the kenotic model, found, for example, in Paul's Letter to the Philippians (2:5–11). A divine being, at a given point in time, assumed a human nature, lived a fully human life, and was recognized by all as a man. After his death on the cross, he rose again and ascended into heaven in glory, thereby assuming his place at the right hand of the

Father. The third stage Knox describes as the incarnational model. In this scenario, which is most dramatically evidenced in the Gospel of John, the earthly life of Jesus reflects both his divine and his human dimensions, so that the transition from preexistence to his human life is less abrupt, inasmuch as both his divine nature and his human nature are clearly operative during his earthly sojourn.

John's portrait of Jesus almost makes him out to be more divine than human, and this is probably what gave rise to Docetism and, to some extent, Gnosticism. There is no question that after the identification of Jesus with the preexistent divine Logos, his humanity was under severe pressure. However, the fact that the earliest Christians distinctly remembered him as a genuinely human being allowed them to rule Docetism out of hand. For Knox it is essential that Christ be acknowledged as a fully human being in order that he might transform our nature into a new humanity. According to Knox, Chalcedonian Christology is not really credible today, for we can assert the full humanity of Jesus without affirming his preexistence, or we can affirm his preexistence without insisting on his full humanity—but we cannot have both. In Christ, God has revealed himself in an absolutely unique way, such that we Christians cannot think of Christ without thinking of God.

No Christian theologian exerted a greater influence in the 1960s than John A. T. Robinson through the publication in 1963 of his *Honest to God*. He is convinced that the declarations of Chalcedon set the stage for a christological development that has been for the most part docetic. Such a supernaturalist view of Christ is not evident in the New Testament, which does not unambiguously declare that Jesus is God, although his disciples witnessed God speaking and acting through him. We are not certain what titles Christ claimed for himself, but it is clear that in the resurrection God designated him as both Lord and Christ (Acts 2:36). Robinson prefers to call Jesus "the man for others," since his total self-emptying not only characterized his earthly life, but this other-directedness revealed God in a most convincing and transparent manner. He was indeed the perfect embodiment of the beyond in our midst.

In his 1973 study Robinson presents a fuller treatment of his Christology. He urges that we move away from the metaphysical language of Chalcedon and adopt a functional mode of thought that will be more understandable to Christians today. He warns, however, that the turn to functional language will seem by many to be reductionist when compared with the thought patterns of classical Christology. We must begin with a full and candid discussion of Christ's humanity—which approach will also be considered by many as reductionist. Further, Robinson is convinced that the failure to acknowledge a distinct human personhood in Jesus erodes his solidarity with the rest of humankind.

Jesus' divinity is described not so much in metaphysical terms but as the power of God operating in and through him. Jesus is the very presence of God in our midst. He is God for us in human flesh. Christ is on the same metaphysical level as every other human being, but he is functionally unique because only he acts in a manner always pleasing to the Father (John 10:34–38). Thus he and the Father are one (John 10:30). Robinson is not sure that the New Testament evidence necessarily involves the need to posit the notion of preexistence in terms of an individual heavenly person who at a given time assumed a human nature.

Although there is need for us to shift from Christ as the divine hypostasis in human flesh to Christ as the one who does what God does, we must also proclaim in no uncertain terms that in changing the obligations of the law, forgiving sins, and controlling the evil powers, Jesus moved into the realm that is properly God's. Robinson chooses to affirm that Jesus is different from us in degree rather than in kind, since this deepens his solidarity with the human race.

John Macquarrie did not produce his definitive treatment of Christology until 1990, when his *Jesus Christ in Modern Thought* was published. Most of this study consists of a valuable historical summary of the subject from New Testament times to the present. It is only in the last quarter of the book that he presents his own personal reflections on the topic.

Macquarrie is doubtful about the question of Christ's messianic consciousness. Perhaps Jesus anticipated that there would be another individual who would appear in the future and bring the messianic age to full term. He did, however, see himself as Son of God, although not in the technical sense of Nicaea and Chalcedon. It is Macquarrie's judgment that any contemporary Christology must of necessity begin with a full and forthright presentation of the humanity of Jesus. He adopts Rahner's approach of transcendental anthropology, which sees human nature endowed with a capacity to cross many new boundaries and move from one horizon to the next, almost without limit. To call Christ the God-man is to affirm that in him this process of human transcendence has reached a point where he has become so closely united with God that his human existence can be said to have become "deified."

Christ's resurrection, he maintains, allows for two rather different interpretations. The first scenario, which he terms "the happy ending," asserts that certain powerful experiences (e.g., the post-resurrection appearances) led the disciples to believe that God had intervened in a special manner, allowing his followers to encounter Jesus in a new way. After a time Christ ascended to his Father in glory, and we anticipate his return on the last day. The second scenario is the one Macquarrie terms "the austere ending," where the narrative comes to a close with Jesus' death on the cross. Would that render the message of Christianity meaningless? This theologian does not think so since the two central revelations that God is love and that he is singularly revealed in Jesus would still stand as valid and meaningful. Macquarrie leaves to the readers the choice between the happy and the austere ending.

Notes

1. Albert Schweitzer, *The Quest of the Historical Jesus*, trans. W. Montgomery (New York: Macmillan, 1968), 13–26.

2. Friedrich Schleiermacher, *The Christian Faith*, trans. from 2d German ed. of 1830, ed. H. R. MacKintosh and J. S. Stewart (Edinburgh: T & T Clark, 1986).

3. Adolf Harnack, *What Is Christianity?* trans. Thomas Bailey Saunders (Philadelphia: Fortress Press, 1986).

4. Rudolf Bultmann, *Jesus and the Word*, trans. Louise P. Smith and Erminie H. Lantero (New York: Scribner's, 1958). This is a translation of the 1926 study, *Jesus*.

5. Rudolf Bultmann, "The New Testament and Mythology," in *New Testament and Mythology and Other Basic Writings*, ed. and trans. by Schubert Ogden (Philadelphia: Fortress Press, 1984).

6. Rudolf Bultmann, *Theology of the New Testament*, vol. 1, trans. Kendrick Grobel (London: SCM Press, 1952), 3–53. This is a translation of the first German edition of 1948.

7. Rudolf Bultmann, *Essays Philosophical and Theological*, trans. James C. G. Grieg (London: SCM Press, 1955), 273–90.

8. Ernst Käsemann, "The Problem of the Historical Jesus," in *Essays on New Testament Themes*, trans. W. J. Montague (London: SCM Press, 1964), 15–47.

9. Günther Bornkamm, *Jesus of Nazareth*, trans. of 3d ed. by Irene and Fraser McLuskey with James M. Robinson (New York: Harper and Row, 1960). See also James M. Robinson, *A New Quest of the Historical Jesus* (London: SCM Press, 1959).

10. James Charlesworth, *Jesus Within Judaism* (New York: Doubleday, 1988), 225.

11. John Knox, *The Humanity and Divinity of Christ* (1967; reprint, Cambridge: University of Cambridge, 1992).

12. John A. T. Robinson, *Honest to God* (Philadelphia: Westminster Press, 1963).

13. Dietrich Bonhoeffer, *Letters and Papers from Prison*, ed. E. Bethge (New York: Collier Books, 1972), 380–83.

14. Paul Tillich, *The Shaking of the Foundations* (New York: Scribner's, 1948), 153–63.

15. John A. T. Robinson, *The Human Face of God* (Philadelphia: Westminster Press, 1973).

16. Gerald O'Collins and Edward G. Farrugia, *A Concise Dictionary of Theology* (New York: Paulist Press, 1991), 11.

17. Raymond E. Brown, *Jesus—God and Man* (New York: Macmillan, 1967), 54.

18. Denzinger and Schönmetzer, *Enchiridion Symbolorum*, 125.

19. John Macquarrie, *Principles of Christian Theology*, 2d ed. (New York: Scribner's, 1977).

20. Macquarrie, *Jesus Christ in Modern Thought*.

21. John Macquarrie, *Christology Revisited* (Harrisburg, Pa.: Trinity Press International, 1998).

✳ *Chapter 3* ✳

Contemporary Catholic Approaches to an Ascending Christology

God's Singular Presence in Jesus

The attempts to design an ascending Christology on the part of Catholic thinkers have been relatively recent compared with the work of Protestant theologians. In 1969 Robert North prepared a booklet titled *In Search of the Human Jesus.* This brief study summarizes the early work of three Dutch Catholic theologians, Ansfried Hulsbosch, Piet Schoonenberg, and Edward Schille-beeckx. At the heart of their effort is the thesis that the divinity of Jesus consists in the perfection of his humanity. North's pamphlet received a considerable amount of attention in the United States in the early 1970s.[1] These three Dutch scholars were attempting to take Catholic Christology in a new direction in response to the growing disaffection of many of the faithful regarding the classical Christology taught in the schools. North was convinced that the implausibility of certain theological positions reduces their credibility and erodes the faith. Thus it is the task of every age to review the models and the language of our dogmatic statements to make certain that the formulas continue to reflect—with as much clarity as possible—the normative faith of the New Testament.

Hulsbosch opens his presentation by asking how the Jesus whom we know as man and proclaim as God can really be both at once. If his divinity is a separate reality that is somehow contained in or placed in conjunction with his humanity, how can this Jesus be the definitive revelation of God for us? We profess that Jesus is God's most transparent revelation to humankind, and, there-fore, Hulsbosch reasons, his divinity can only be perceived as a dimension of his humanity. Hence, he concludes, the divinity of Christ must consist in the perfection of his humanity. The author is favorably impressed by Teilhard de Chardin, who taught that our spiritual or conscious activities are attributable to an evolutionally organized "inner face" of matter itself. Hulsbosch feels that the same kind of approach should be taken regarding the unity of the divine and the human in Christ. It was Teilhard's conviction that our spiritual activities are due to an inherent quality in matter itself. Continuous quantitative input effects, at certain stages or levels, qualitative change in beings. Jesus is the one who represents the full and total realization of the evolution of matter. Hence, in Hulsbosch's judgment, we need not posit in him a separate divine principle to explain his unique and unparalleled prerogatives, for the divinity of Jesus consists precisely in the singular character of his humanity. In his response Schillebeeckx has reservations regarding Hulsbosch's refusal to find a place for the two natures/one person formula. Furthermore, he questions whether Hulsbosch's position grasps the essence of the dogma of the hypostatic union. Although Schoonenberg praises Hulsbosch's efforts, he is not prepared to concede that duality in Christ can be evaded simply by making his divinity an aspect of the Father's own divinity.

In Hulsbosch's estimate, the human is the measure in which the divine appears. If he is God (and he professes that he is), we know this only out of his mode of being man. The unlimited God can appear in the limited livery of the human. The proper subjectivity of Jesus is a human subjectivity in which God manifests himself personally. The divine value of Jesus is evident in the fact that he, as a human, reveals the Father (John 14:9). The single reality of Christ can be seen from two viewpoints—the created and the divine dimension. The distinctiveness of his person is to be found in his singular human subjectivity, rather than in his preexistence as a divine person. Since the divine dimension of Jesus is indeed genuinely divine, it is therefore in that sense eternal. Hulsbosch is unwilling, however, to make the personal subjectivity of Christ a preexistent divine reality distinct from anything human. The subsistence of the Son, independent of the Incarnation, implies the two-natures pattern that Hulsbosch repudiates. Schoonenberg is almost prepared to agree with him, but with certain reservations. For Schoonenberg, there is no person of the Son independent of the Incarnation. The true basis for Jesus' preexistence is the divine wisdom present with God from or before the moment of creation (Prov. 8:22–31). Although there are intimations of preexistence in the New Testament (e.g., 1 Cor. 8:6; Col. 1:15; Eph. 1:4; John 17:5), these can be understood as references to the divine wisdom operating with God from the beginning.

Apparently it was Novatian (a prominent Roman theologian of the mid-third century) who first affirmed in the West that the Son was born of the Father before all time. Origen (ca. 185–ca. 254) in the East taught the preexistence of the Logos, but also affirmed that all created spirits preexisted before the material creation. The profession of the preexistence of the Son was attached as an appendage to the Nicene Creed in 325, and became a part of the creed of Constantinople I (381).[2] These formulas, however, leave open the slight possibility that the Son's preexistence is affirmed with an eye toward the unfolding divine plan of the Incarnation.

Both Hulsbosch and Schoonenberg formulate a new approach to Christology beginning with a reappraisal of preexistence. Schillebeeckx, however, expresses doubts as to whether the personal unity of Christ is sufficiently preserved and maintained in Hulsbosch's scheme. Jesus' unique way of making God present was achieved by his being the man that he was. The dogma of the hypostatic union was shaped over time to express the reality that Jesus is essentially the human way of being God. If we disregard the hypostatic union, it is the judgment of Schillebeeckx that Jesus' human uniqueness will be destroyed. Hulsbosch discards the hypostatic union formula, but insists that he has retained the heart of the mystery by declaring that Jesus enjoys an experience of God that is essentially unique and different from that of other humans.

The three Dutch theologians seem to agree on the following propositions:

> The Council of Chalcedon employed the word *person* without affirming that the term includes the notion of a separate and distinct cognitive self-awareness. This concept of person is incompatible with modern psychology.
>
> The divine nature of Jesus is to be explained in terms of its being an absolutely unique elevation of his human nature.
>
> Preexistence—which is intimated in certain New Testament passages—can very likely trace its origin back to the nonhypostatic Wisdom of Proverbs 8:22–31.

The formal teaching concerning the preexistence of Christ derives primarily from Origen, who held that all rational souls were preexistent as well.

Piet Schoonenberg

About three years after the appearance of the three aforementioned articles in the Dutch journal, *Tijdschrift voor Theologie*, which Robert North summarized for English readers, Piet Schoonenberg (b. 1911) published his own study on Christology in 1969, titled *The Christ*. The English translation was made available in 1971.[3] At the outset, the author raises the issue of the two natures in Christ. What loyalty does our faith demand regarding this traditional teaching? He affirms that the notion is being questioned more and more in our day, and suggests that perhaps a reformulation is called for. He notes that after the Council of Constantinople I (381) the preexistence of the Son literally controlled christological thought and belief. After that event, Alexandrian Christology seemed vulnerable to Monophysitism, while Antiochian Christology was open to the dangers of Nestorianism.

The Council of Chalcedon was, according to Schoonenberg, unable to reconcile these two positions except by declaring that there are two natures and one person in Christ. The Council of Constantinople III (680–81), with its pronouncement on the existence of two wills in Christ, almost resulted in the acknowledgment of two distinct subjects in Jesus. The two key questions for Schoonenberg are these:

Does Christ have a human personhood?

Does his humanity have a divine character?

Schoonenberg holds that the absence of human personhood would make Jesus' human nature completely unreal, since he would be depersonalized as a man. The New Testament data seems to affirm that there is but one subject in Christ. There is no evidence of dialogue within Jesus, between his divine and his human nature. His dialogue—throughout his life—is with the Father. Schoonenberg questions how Christ's human act-center could stand outside his ontological person. If Apollinaris of Laodicea (ca. 310–ca. 390) was condemned because he taught that Jesus did not have a human soul inasmuch as the Logos took its place, how then can we deny him a created act of being? For without a created act of being, Christ would no longer seemingly be a human being. Would this not amount to a more significant mutilation than that proposed by Apollinaris?

In Schoonenberg's judgment, anhypostasia (Christ's human nature subsisting in the act of being of the Word) would deprive Jesus of an essential dimension of manhood. God's self-communication does not as a rule exclude the operations and perfections of being of his creatures. Rather, he leaves them intact and respects their integrity as much as possible. These reasons militate against the loss of individual human personhood and the absence of an individual human act of being in Christ. Since so much speaks against the denial of Jesus' individual human personhood, and since one person cannot have two acts of being, how is this dilemma resolved?

Because Christ is a human person in Schoonenberg's estimate, is there a sense in which he can also be considered a divine person? The primary dialogue in Jesus is between Christ and the Father. Hence it is not possible to posit a divine person in Jesus because this would obscure the primary dialogue. According to the Thomistic doctrine of the Trinity, the divine persons share in a relative way the consciousness and the freedom proper to the divine nature. Therefore, consciousness and freedom are not called for as specific and inalienable attributes in the trinitarian concept of person. Therefore, reasons Schoonenberg, if the Son does not possess individual and distinct consciousness and freedom as a divine person, and Jesus does possess these attributes as a human person, then there are not two subjects in Christ that are "person" in the same manner.

Schoonenberg proposes a different approach to the personhood of Jesus. Initially he asserts that Christ is a human person and, then, through the identification of God's very being with this human person, a new person is brought about in God himself, that is, the Son of God. According to Schoonenberg, there is no point in asking whether or not the Word existed before the Incarnation, for there is no time in God. The Word's preexistence is bound up with the prehistory of Jesus. This christological stance reversed the traditional understanding of enhypostasia proposed by Leontius of Byzantium (ca. 480–543) to explain the Chalcedonian two natures/one person doctrine. In Schoonenberg's judgment, Leontius affirmed that Christ's human nature became a person by being assumed in the divine hypostasis of the Word.[4] Schoonenberg's thesis runs in the other direction. The very being of God is identified with this human person, Jesus. In this manner, God becomes in Christ a historical personality, that is, the Word becomes flesh. Indeed, "in him [Jesus] dwells all the fullness of the divinity bodily" (Col. 2:9). This indwelling was realized in Christ from the very moment of his conception. Thus, according to Schoonenberg, the dilemma of the two natures in one person is addressed by means of a unique and unparalleled presence of God in this human person. Schoonenberg terms his stance a Christology without duality, that is, a Christology of God's complete presence in the whole man.

Schoonenberg teaches that Jesus differed from the rest of humankind only accidentally and not essentially. Nonetheless, he is the absolute culmination of human nature, God's complete and definitive Word in human flesh. One of the most unique features of Jesus is his relationship to the Father. His attitude at prayer allows us to catch a glimpse into the consciousness that he had of God. His approach to the Father is marked by clarity, simplicity, and immediacy. One is left with the impression that during his earthly life Jesus was utterly open to the Father. He sensed that the Father was constantly at work in him, and Jesus' aim was to share this immediacy with others. Christ's mandate of love (Matt. 5:44) was considerably more demanding than the Old Testament injunctions that extended fairly exclusively to fellow countrymen and neighbors. The parable of the good Samaritan (Luke 10:29–37) broadens the obligation of love to all men, even to one's enemies.

Although there was sinfulness among Jesus' ancestors (Matt. 1:1–17), Schoonenberg affirms that Jesus was not personally subject to sin. The question of his human knowledge, although widely discussed and debated by theologians, would in the judgment of Schoonenberg be much easier to address if we were to replace the divine person in Christ with God's total presence in Jesus. The issue of the beatific vision has been much more openly treated by theologians recently, and in many cases without protest by the magisterium. The affirmation in the encyclical *Mystici Corporis* (1943) that Christ possessed the beatific vision from the womb does not currently enjoy a great deal of favor.[5] All of the official statements on the question issued since Pius X's time, notes Schoonenberg, had been made with the two natures/one person scheme as a backdrop, and if we are justified in lifting up an alternative, then these declarations would have to be given a different interpretation.

Jesus' statements regarding the future were probably based on his own presentiments concerning what might occur. He most likely saw that his passion and death were a real possibility, given the growing opposition against him on the part of certain official elements in Judea. Likewise, he could have suspected that the political turmoil between Rome and those continually advocating insurrection would soon escalate into a genuine crisis for Jerusalem. Moreover, these intuitions of Jesus were undoubtedly embellished by the primitive church and by the evangelists in the decades after his death. Schoonenberg is of the mind that it was difficult for Jesus to express the consciousness of his identity and mission through some kind of title. During Jesus' life, the term *Messiah* could easily have been misunderstood by many of his hearers as having a political connotation. Jesus probably employed the "Son of man" designation, but it is not always clear whether he was referring to himself or to someone else. The people certainly saw him as a prophet (Mark 6:15; Luke 7:16), and Jesus understood his mission as such (Luke 13:33; Matt. 13:57). A good many theologians in recent times have been prepared to recognize that there was a development in Christ's awareness of his mission during the course of his public life. His role was always to proclaim the kingdom of God, rather than to proclaim himself.

The question of the integrity of Christ's human decisions under the two natures scenario raises difficulties for Schoonenberg. The third Council of Constantinople declared that the human will of Jesus was "subjected to his divine and mighty will."[6] To take human freedom seriously, we have to assume that there is a human will in Christ that fully subjects itself to the Father. This is, after all, what the New Testament evidence strongly indicates. Again, the issue of the Chalcedonian two natures/one person model has created difficulties for believers. The alternative scenario of God's complete presence in the human person Jesus, who enjoys his own free human will and actions, would allow us to rise above many of the issues raised by the Chalcedonian formula.

The assertion of the scholastic theologians that Christ could not sin is rather difficult to reconcile with his perfect freedom. The New Testament tells us that Jesus did not sin (Heb. 4:15; John 8:46), but it does not assert that it was impossible for him to do so. Schoonenberg is of the opinion that an incapacity for sin would place Jesus outside of the human condition. The temptation references in the gospels (Mark 1:13; Matt. 4:1–11; Luke 4:1–13) were something of a prelude to the conflict he experienced in the garden of Gethsemane (Matt. 26:36–46), where the temptation was to abandon his mission and thus free himself from what he perceived to be inevitable. His response was the absolute rejection of the temptation to flee and the total surrender to his Father.

Schoonenberg's study places a great deal of emphasis on the resurrection of Jesus. He stresses at the outset that without the resurrection our faith in Christ is empty and vain, since we would still be under the judgment of sin (1 Cor. 15:17). Schoonenberg notes that through the influence of Rudolf Bultmann and others, there is less talk these days about eternal life and a corresponding resurgence of interest in our present earthly life. In Schoonenberg's book, a great deal of attention is paid to the work of the German biblicist Willi Marxsen, who questioned the resurrection and published an influential piece on the subject in 1968.[7]

Schoonenberg's interpretation of Marxsen, although nuanced somewhat, makes clear that the German biblicist failed to reflect the full reality of Christ's resurrection. The resurrected Lord can be present as person both for the first witnesses and for us today without being merely called up by our memory. Jesus lives now in his glorified state and also in us. What is more, the declarations of the New Testament (e.g., 1 Cor. 15:3–8; Luke 24) afford us a wider and deeper hope than the promise of God's salvation merely within this earthly life. They testify to Jesus, not just as a remembrance, but as a living person, risen from the dead, who is active and who in no way can be reduced to projections of our memory. Furthermore, faith in eternal life is unambiguously affirmed in the New Testament. We should not forget, however, about our Christian obligation in the here and now to contribute actively to the expansion of God's kingdom on earth (Matt. 25:31–46).

In the profession of faith against the Albigensians and the Cathars, Lateran Council IV (1215) affirmed that the dead will rise with the same bodies that they now have.[8] Nothing of what is proper to us will disappear, in Schoonenberg's judgment. We will likely rise with corporeality and with earthly associations, just as Jesus did. We shall rise with our own bodies that have been made pure or impure during our personal histories. John the Evangelist has affirmed that the risen Lord showed his wounds to his apostles (20:20). The risen body of Christ is the expression of the person that he was during his earthly life, and it is conceivable that he lives in our world, among us today. Christ in his completion still works for the future, which is his completion in us.

In his conclusion, Schoonenberg expresses the hope that he did not in any way diminish or distort the divinity of Jesus by his questions regarding the preexistent divine person. Christology today, for the most part, runs the risk of undermining the humanity of Jesus by continuing to extol his divinity. For this theologian, the Word is enhypostatic in the man who is Christ.

The Pontifical Biblical Commission's 1984 document on Christology, *The Bible and Christology*, refers to Schoonenberg's work in the context of updating the formulations of the Council of Chalcedon. The formulas must continually be renewed, notes the document, in order that they might more perfectly reflect the object of the definitions.[9] The commission speaks specifically of Schoonenberg's reference to the "human person" of Christ, and they suggest that it would perhaps be better to speak of his "human personality" rather than his human person.[10] However, they do not accuse Schoonenberg of heretical teaching.

Bernard Lonergan is more pointed in his criticism of *The Christ*.[11] He writes that Schoonenberg fails to do justice to the christological dogmas.[12] Although he credits the Dutch scholar for grounding his efforts upon two unassailable premises (i.e., Jesus was a man; Jesus was a person.), his conclusion that Jesus was a human person is based upon a "mystifying" exegesis of scripture and the conciliar enactments. If Schoonenberg means that Jesus was only a man and not the preexistent divine person, then, according to Lonergan, he would have fallen into the heresy of the Ebionites (those who believed that Jesus was merely a human person, the son of Joseph and Mary, upon whom the Spirit descended at his baptism).[13] Lonergan concludes by saying that in his judgment Schoonenberg has not confronted the issues "fairly and squarely."

In an article published about a decade later, Schoonenberg again addresses the question of the divine and the human in Christ.[14] He holds that the two natures mutually permeate each other. Jesus is human in a divine way and divine in a human way. Therefore, he is human in the fullest sense. In him, humanity's divinization and God's humanization are perfectly achieved. The Logos truly became flesh. Both natures complement each other with their respective differences. Jesus is to be conceived of as a "God-man" person. The two natures are so related that what Schoonenberg calls a reciprocal personhood is realized. He refutes the charge made by his critics that Jesus' personhood is exclusively human. Rather, both the divine and the human realities make up his person. He is not half divine and half human. Both natures enhypostasize each other. The Logos perfects the humanity and is determined in a new way. The Word's openness to the role of mediator between God and the world is brought to fulfillment in his being one person with Jesus' humanity. Christ now is truly Son, the only begotten of the Father.

Hans Küng

The theological training of Hans Küng (b. 1928) began in the fall of 1951 at the Gregorian University in Rome. In 1957 he completed his doctoral studies at the Institut Catholique in Paris and soon joined the theological faculty at Tübingen where he has worked ever since. His Christology is set out in his 1974 publication, *Christ Sein*, which appeared in English in 1976 under the title *On Being a Christian*.[15] The author begins with the observation that the Chalcedonian two natures/one person doctrine is simply not intelligible today, nor is it identical with the New Testament proclamation. All christological thought must commence with the humanity of Jesus before it attempts to describe the relationship of Jesus to God. Christ is to be portrayed initially as a genuine human being whose hometown was Nazareth in Galilee. He was born no later than 4 B.C.E., began his public life in 28 or 29 C.E., and was put to death in about 30 C.E. According to the Gospel of John, Jesus' public ministry spanned three Passover celebrations, whereas in the Synoptics it seems that he witnessed only one Passover during his public life.

Küng holds that the essence of Christ's proclamation, his behavior, and his fate can be reconstructed quite reliably from the gospel narratives. It is apparent that his name, his family, and his background were thoroughly Jewish. Even his prayers as reflected in the gospels reveal his Jewish origins. It is equally clear that he was not a member of the Jewish establishment. He was related neither to the priests in Jerusalem, nor to the scribes in Galilee, nor to any of the affluent or aristocratic families. Jesus was not a Sadducee, nor was he recognized as a Jewish theologian. He could be more accurately described as a villager and a public storyteller. It can be said, however, that he was animated all through his public ministry by an intense anticipation of the end, when whatever is anti-God and pro-Satan will finally be destroyed. The apocalyptic movement that became active in Israel in the second century B.C.E. colored Jesus' thinking and hopes very profoundly indeed. The opening pronouncements of his public preaching were punctuated by his forecasts of the imminent coming of the kingdom (Mark 1:15). According to Küng Jesus could well have become aware of his mission on the occasion of his baptism in the Jordan (Mark 1:9–11).

Although it is true that Galilee was the home of the revolutionary Zealots, Judea was also populated with bands of Zealot brigands who were in the habit of triggering insurrections especially on the occasion of the major religious feasts. Their aim was the freeing of Israel from political bondage, and they were hoping for a liberator who would appear in their midst as an apocalyptic figure (e.g., the Son of man). Jesus avoided the title Messiah, no doubt because of its widely accepted political connotations. He was not a social revolutionary or a political agitator. Rather he was a carpenter's son (Matt. 13:55) who in all likelihood plied the carpenter's trade himself (Mark 6:3), and lived the life of a wandering preacher. He was supported by friends and a group of women who saw him as a prophet and the bearer of good news.

The religious group that Jesus encountered most frequently as he traveled through the small towns and villages of Galilee were the Pharisees. Principally craftsmen and tradesmen, they were quite sincere and devout people who were not at all close to the priestly establishment in Jerusalem. The scribes who studiously applied the 613 regulations of the Old Testament to every detail of daily life were their spiritual mentors. The Pharisees tithed, fasted, gave alms to the needy, and engaged faithfully in regular habits of prayer (Luke 18:11–12). They believed that if the weight of their sins was balanced by the weight of their good deeds, they would be counted as pleasing to God. They separated themselves from those who did not follow the law, and somehow survived after the destruction of 70 C.E., holding on to the scribes as their religious leaders.

The parable of the Pharisee and the publican (Luke 18:9–14) rather dramatically reveals the differences between Jesus and the Pharisees. For him, the various regulations concerning ritual purity had very little meaning, nor was he particularly bound by the Sabbath regulations, since he felt that the Sabbath was made for man and not vice versa (Mark 2:27). The approaching kingdom of God provided the horizon for his message and mission. Jesus' genuine conviction that the kingdom of God and the final consummation were coming very soon is abundantly confirmed in his parables, and in this regard he was not correct. The end of the world did not materialize, but his message did not lose its meaning. God is still out ahead of us and the final consummation will come through God's action. However and whenever that will occur, the hour of personal decision is now at hand.

Küng treats the question of Jesus' miracles at some length, since they evidently belong to the gospel tradition, and wondrous works were reasonably familiar phenomena in New Testament times. Küng is more inclined to give the miracles of Jesus a figurative rather than a literal interpretation where he can. There must have been physical cures of various sorts that called for faith on the part of the subjects (Mark 5:25–34). Also, Jesus was able to heal various personality disorders and cases of mental illness that were attributed to the devil (Mark 9:14–29). However, the nature miracles (e.g., walking on water, quieting the storm, raising Lazarus from the dead) are viewed as embellishments intended to picture Jesus as Lord of life and death. These incidents are more appropriately spoken of as signs, indicating that the power of God is breaking through. Jesus was intervening forcefully and convincingly in the areas of human weakness and injustice.

It is evident that Christ set himself above the Jewish law, the Torah. His lack of appreciation for the cultic purity regulations, the prescriptions concerning fasting, and the rules governing conduct on the Sabbath created a great deal of hostility with the Pharisees. He attacked the basic pharisaical premise that by following all of the hundreds of religious regulations, one would thereby be considered righteous. His Sermon on the Mount (Matthew 5–7) proposed a very different sort of ethic, making unconditional appeals and leaving it to others to apply his norms to particular situations. Jesus demanded nothing short of a *metanoia*, a conversion to a completely different set of values involving service to one's fellow man over service to the law (Luke 10:29–37). Although he did seem to restrict his saving work to the Jewish people, his command to love even one's enemies opened the door to a more universalist mission (Matt. 5:43–48). His affinity for the weak, the handicapped, the poor, and his frequent association with tax collectors (Luke 19:1–10), sinners (John 7:53–8:11), and those on the fringe of society had the effect of extending his call to everyone. It is true that Jesus claimed to be sent only to the house of Israel (Mark 7:27), and yet he foretold that many would come from the East and the West to partake of the banquet in the kingdom of heaven (Matt. 8:11).

Opposition to Christ developed early on, not only as a result of his sovereign attitude toward the Jewish law, but particularly in regard to his assertion of the power to forgive sin (Mark 2:7). It is probably true that he spurned the title of Messiah, but Küng notes that he did make frequent use of the "Son of man" epithet inasmuch as it is recorded as coming from his lips eighty-two times in the gospels. The meaning of this latter title is much disputed today, but if the *Similitudes of Enoch* (*1 Enoch* 37–71) are in any way a reflection of the meaning of the term at the time of Christ, then it is at least possible that "Son of man" could refer to a preexistent heavenly individual, a chosen one, an anointed one, who was to play a messianic role in the salvation of Israel. Although the relationship between *1 Enoch* and the gospels is quite doubtful, the concept of the "Son of man" as a savior figure could have had some vague currency in the first century C.E.[16] Further, Küng notes that although Jesus in all likelihood did not apply the term *Messiah* to himself, his very actions and words asserted a clear claim to messiahship.

Christ's approach to God was characterized by an attitude of exceptional closeness and familiarity. He was not the first to address God as Father, for that had become somewhat more widespread in later Judaism (Wis. 2:16–18; Sir. 4:10). However his reference to God as "my Father" and his use of "Abba" as applied to God were extraordinary. The portrait that he painted of a God who is concerned about every single sparrow (Matt. 10:29), and who knows our needs before we even make our requests to him (Matt. 6:8), does show forth a face of God that was new in Israel. Especially is that true of the revelation of the Father in the parable of the prodigal son (Luke 15:11–32). Küng considers the "Our Father" as absolutely unique in its brevity and precision. Finally Christ's long hours spent in prayerful solitude confirm his unusual intimacy with the Father, although in the Synoptics he never identified himself with God.

Christ's decision to go up to Jerusalem was fraught with danger and constituted the turning point of his life. However, he knew that if he wanted to announce his message to the whole nation, he would have to make his presence felt in Jerusalem. Though his predictions during his public life concerning his passion and death were probably injected into the narratives by the primitive Christian community, Jesus must have known that his enemies were many, and that the pressures mounting against him were life-threatening. His entry into Jerusalem and the cleansing of the temple occasioned his arrest by the guards of the high priest and led to his trial before the Sanhedrin and before the Roman procurator, Pilate. The religious charges against him were that he assumed an unwarranted sovereignty over the Jewish law and the temple cult, and that he presumed to forgive sins—a prerogative belonging to God alone. The civil charge was that he identified himself as a political Messiah–king of the Jews. As a result of the hasty and rather confused legal proceedings against him, he was condemned as a political revolutionary.

Unlike his portrayal of the virgin birth, the ascension, and the miracles, Hans Küng describes the resurrection of Jesus as an unambiguously supernatural event. He describes it as a real event, though not a historical one. The explanation of the resurrection as simply the survival of Christ's "cause" is not acceptable to Küng. Jesus does not merely live on through the faith of the disciples. His personal identity survives in a new mode of being, a wholly different and imperishable life. Among the Pharisees, life after death was something they prayerfully anticipated. The Book of Daniel, written during the persecution of the vicious Seleucid king Antiochus IV (167–164 B.C.E.), apparently represented the first expression within Judaism of hope in the resurrection, both for the righteous and for the wicked (Dan. 12:1–13). Although the Sadducees and their followers did not accept this belief because it was not evident in the Torah, the Pharisees embraced it as a matter of faith. Jesus and his followers were also attuned to this tradition.

According to the oldest Easter testimony (1 Cor. 15:4–8) the disciples acquired their faith as a result of their encounters with the risen Christ. The reason for the change in the apostles was their experience of the risen Lord, which brought them to faith and to their sense of mission. Although Küng was fascinated by the notion that the apostolic faith originated in the prayerful reflections of the followers of Jesus, he concluded that the appearances of the living person himself were indeed a supernatural intervention that generated the faith of his first followers. It is this faith of the foundational witnesses that serves as the ground of our belief.

Küng reviews the various titles applied to Jesus in the New Testament, for example, "Son of man," "Christ," "Lord," "Son of God," in terms of their origin and connotation in the apostolic period. He concurs with a number of other scholars who hold that the title "Son of God" was originally understood in a functional sense and did not initially identify Jesus as a divine being. As a matter of fact, the term was at first attributed to him as a result of the resurrection (Rom. 1:3–4) and then gradually found its way back to his baptism (Matt. 3:17), his birth (Luke 1:35), and finally he is called Son of God from eternity (John 3:16–17). The evolution from the functional connotation of Son of God to a metaphysical or ontological meaning took place under the influence of Greek thought. Küng reminds us that we must translate these more important New Testament titles into our own language and thought patterns so that they might have greater significance for us today.

Turning to the notion of redemption, Küng notes that the explanation of Anselm is not especially helpful today. The implication of this thesis, which has been normative for almost ten centuries, is that Christ came only to die. Is God so cruel that he insisted on the agonizing death of his beloved Jesus to pay for the debt of human sin? Küng opts for a reinterpretation of the notion of sacrifice as applied to Christ. Apart from the Letter to the Hebrews and an occasional observation in the gospels (Mark 10:45), the theme of an expiating sacrifice is, for Küng, not of central importance to the New Testament message. Notions such as liberation and reconciliation could be developed as alternatives to the concept of vicarious sacrifice that might well create greater meaning for contemporary believers and make the actions and the words of Jesus more efficacious in our age.

The issue of preexistence is raised as a prelude to Küng's treatment of the humanity and divinity of Christ. Ontological sonship (i.e., Jesus as a divine being), rather than functional sonship, creates automatically the demand for the Son's preexistence. Incarnation Christology calls for preexistence, whereas exaltation Christology does not. It was with the ontological explanation of Christ's sonship—especially from the time of Ignatius of Antioch, ca. 110 C.E.—that the problem of reconciling monotheism with divine filiation became troublesome, precipitating factions and schisms that tore away at the fabric of the church for centuries. Küng affirms that while preexistence is difficult to grasp today, it was "in the air" at that time. If as Son Christ is now with God, how, they reasoned, could he not be with him from eternity? God's Word and God's Son together with God in eternity must have seemed plausible to first- and second-century Christians.

In the New Testament, Jesus' divinity is set forth primarily in the functional way and not metaphysically. Because no other conceptual system was available, a functional Christology became an ontological Christology that was given final form in the Councils of Nicaea (325), Ephesus (431), and Chalcedon (451). For Küng, when we say that Christ is truly God, we mean that God is present and at work in Jesus. All the affirmations concerning divine sonship, preexistence, Incarnation, and so forth, are intended to assert and confirm the uniqueness and the once-and-for-all character of God's call revealed in and with Jesus. His humanity must be unambiguously declared as the ultimate and definitive standard of human existence. Christ's capacity for suffering, fear, loneliness, insecurity, temptation, doubts, possibility of error—all of these must be affirmed without hesitation as part of his authentic humanity that he shares with us.

Concerning the question of the virgin birth, Küng outlines the rather late development of the doctrine from patristic times to the Middle Ages. He notes that apart from an infrequent correction (e.g., Luke 3:23), the two human parents of Jesus are routinely mentioned in the gospels (e.g., Luke 4:22; John 6:42). There are also references to his brothers and sisters (e.g., Mark 3:31–34, 6:3) which, according to Küng, should not without an adequate reason be simply interpreted to mean "cousins." James, the brother of Jesus (Mark 6:3; Gal. 1:19), exercised a leading role in the Jerusalem church (Acts 12:17, 15:13) before his martyrdom in 62 C.E. Küng asks how these kinds of insertions in the narrative would have been possible if there had been any thought of a virgin birth at that time. For Küng, the virgin birth was a striking symbol for the Church Fathers and the medieval theologians that in Jesus God had made an entirely new beginning.

Küng adds several observations regarding Jesus and the Holy Spirit. At the time of Christ, the Spirit was thought to have ceased being active in Judaism with the death of the last of the prophets but was expected to return at the endtime (Joel 2:25–3:1). In the Acts of the Apostles, the Spirit appears quite frequently, and it was Paul who reflected deeply on the nature and operations of the Holy Spirit. The Council of Constantinople I (381) expanded the role of the Spirit in the Nicene Creed. For Küng the Spirit can best be understood as the Spirit of Jesus (e.g., 2 Cor. 3:18; Gal. 4:6), for Jesus has become the life-giving Spirit (1 Cor. 15:45). The encounter with God, or Lord, or Spirit, is for the believer the same encounter (2 Cor. 13:13). In Küng's judgment the Spirit is none other than God himself as gracious love gaining control over the minds and hearts of men and women of faith. The Spirit is actually God's personal closeness and intimacy with humankind.

On Being a Christian was enormously popular especially in Europe and the United States. It was translated into many different languages and sold hundreds of thousands of copies. The German Bishops' Conference took exception to certain statements in the book shortly after its publication. Discussions with Küng over the nature of his Christology went on for several years. The bishops requested a number of clarifications and Küng attempted a written response to their inquiries in the final section of his *Existiert Gott?* published in Germany in 1978 and in the United States in the same year under the title *Does God Exist?*[17]

Küng opens with a discussion of the resurrection that he describes as life that escapes through the limits of time and space into God's invisible and incomprehensible realm. God did not abandon Jesus at the moment of death but exalted him, and this grounds our confidence that if we live like Jesus, we too shall be taken up into God. Küng then addresses what he means when he says that Jesus is the Son of God. In all his words and actions, Jesus was expressing God with such transparency that it has been difficult since to speak of God without speaking of Jesus. Some today are fearful that the classical formulas are no longer comprehensible to a great many believers, while others balk at the abandonment of the old, time-honored statements.

After reviewing several of the titles applied to Christ, Küng makes it clear that "Son of God" has a power that no other title has. He affirms that what is meant here is not a physical sonship, as was the case with the pagan sons of the gods, but an election and designation by God as God's delegate, spokesperson, representative, God's very expression. Was Jesus as Son with God from eternity? Küng responds that there has never been any other God but the one who revealed himself in Christ, and thus Jesus has a universal and eternal significance. Jesus is the authentic and unique revelation of the one true God, and therefore he is his Word. God encounters us in a simple and definitive way in the actions, the words, and the person of Jesus, who reveals the face of God that was still hidden in the Old Testament.

No doubt a great many still prefer the Greek terminology to articulate their faith understanding (e.g., person, hypostasis, nature, substance, essence). Today, however, many wish to express the same reality in a different fashion. The consubstantiality between the Father and the Son defined at Nicaea simply made it clear that Christ was not a second God, and that the one true God is fully present and active in him. Chalcedon's affirmation of the true humanity and divinity of Jesus announced that God himself is actually present and has spoken in Christ. God has definitively revealed himself in this man, and Jesus has shown us the authentic way to live and die in order to gain eternal life with God.

Hans Küng's difficulties with the German bishops and with the Vatican were by no means over. As a matter of fact, on December 15, 1979, the Congregation for the Doctrine of the Faith issued a declaration stating that Küng could no longer be considered a Catholic theologian or function as such in a teaching role.[18] The Congregation referred to its previous declaration against Küng, issued in 1975, in which some of his opinions were judged to be opposed "in different degrees" to certain church teachings that must be held by all the faithful. His views on the doctrine of infallibility and the question he raised concerning the possibility of a nonordained person celebrating the Eucharist in case of an emergency were specifically cited. The 1979 document noted that Küng has not changed his opinion on these issues and, furthermore, has more recently set forth positions on the consubstantiality of Christ and the Father, and also on the Virgin Mary, which differ from those taught by the church. Judging that Küng was not about to abandon these opinions, the Congregation declared that he could no longer be considered a Catholic theologian. Küng's short response to the declaration notes that he certainly does not intend to show contempt for the magisterium by his subsequent treatment of the subject of infallibility. Rather, his purpose is to encourage further scholarly discussion on the issue. Regarding the references in the 1979 declaration to differences in the areas of Christology and Mariology, he observes that these topics were never, to his knowledge, part of the Roman discussion and procedure against him. Because the areas of difference were never clarified or put to rest since 1979, the ban against Küng remains in force to this day.

The German scholar revisited the subject of Christology briefly in his recent volume issued in the United States in 1995, *Christianity: Essence, History, and Future*.[19] Küng describes what he calls the gentile Christian Hellenistic paradigm, initiated by Paul and brought to term by Origen (ca. 185–ca. 254). The center of Christian theology for Origen was no longer the cross and resurrection, but the relation existing among the three hypostases (i.e., Father, Son, and Holy Spirit) in the one Godhead. Origen was satisfied that he had decoded the revelation of the New Testament and given it its true meaning. Justin the Apologist (ca. 100–165) had taken the Johannine notion of Logos and fused it with the Greek metaphysics of the Logos, and hence, according to Küng, shifted the christological emphasis from the earthly and risen Christ to the preexistent Christ. Through the contributions of such Christian Fathers as Origen and Justin, the focus changed to a more static consideration of God in himself and the relation among the three divine figures. Küng observes that if the theological deliberations had remained closer to the data of the New Testament, they would have avoided the difficulties arising from the speculations concerning the one nature and the three persons in the divinity.

Origen interpreted the three divine figures as three hypostases who are distinct from one another. The Father is God in the fullest sense, while the Son, although begotten by God, only participates in the Father's divinity. The same can be said of the Spirit. The three hypostases, for Origen, are at different levels from one another. Küng then touches upon the adoptionist Christology of Paul of Samosata, a third-century bishop of Antioch, who taught that Jesus was an ordinary human being who was adopted by God at some point during his earthly life. Also, the modalism of Sabellius, who taught in Rome in the early third century, is briefly described as a doctrine that affirms that the Father, the Son, and the Holy Spirit are simply different manifestations of the one God. This position was condemned by Pope Callistus (217–22) who excommunicated Sabellius as a heretic.

The next christological crisis described by Küng was generated by the Alexandrian presbyter Arius (ca. 250–336), who taught that there were three hypostases in God that were subordinated one to the other. The Son is not of one substance with the Father and is not eternal. The Council of Nicaea, convened by Emperor Constantine, condemned Arius, asserting that the Son was indeed of one substance with the Father. After this, according to Küng, the shift to the early church Hellenistic paradigm was achieved. It then became difficult to think of Christ's distinction from God and his unity with God at the same time. Therefore, an appeal had to be made, in the judgment of Küng, to a conceptual mystery that was not evident in the preaching of Jesus nor in that of the apostles. The rather simple baptismal formula found, for example, in Matthew 28:19 had given way to something far more complicated.

The second ecumenical council, Constantinople I, repeated the condemnation of the Arians and the semi-Arians, and affirmed the identity of being of the Holy Spirit with God, so that after 381 we can speak more clearly of the dogma of the Trinity. This dogma was being enunciated and embellished by the Cappadocians, Basil the Great (ca. 330–79), Basil's friend Gregory of Nazianzus (ca. 330–89), and Basil's younger brother, Gregory of Nyssa (d. 395). Meanwhile, the relationship between the divine and the human in Christ was under serious discussion, especially in the East. Apollinaris (ca. 310–ca. 390), the bishop of Laodicea, taught that although the divine Logos took human flesh, he did not assume a human soul, which was replaced by the Logos. (Apollinaris's teaching was condemned by several eastern synods.)

The Alexandrian school emphasized the divinity of Christ to such an extent that his human nature seemed to be submerged in the divine nature. On the other hand, the Antiochian school maintained such a firm distinction between the two natures that the unity of Christ seemed in jeopardy. At the Council of Ephesus, Cyril (ca. 375–444), the leader of the Alexandrian school, had the Antiochian position condemned before Nestorius (d. 451), the Antiochian spokesman, arrived to take part in the deliberations.

At Chalcedon, the Christology of Pope Leo I and Cyril of Alexandria served as the base for the christological formula—truly God and truly man, two natures and one person—which would prevail. The one Christ exists in two natures unconfusedly, unchangeably (vs. the Alexandrian extremists), and indivisibly and inseparably (vs. Nestorius). This formula was to be accepted as a mystery that could not be penetrated by human reason. Christological disputes after Chalcedon continued for centuries and resulted in the separation of Christians into Chalcedonians, Monophysites, and Nestorians, divisions that persist today.

Edward Schillebeeckx

Edward Schillebeeckx (b. 1914) published the first volume of his highly respected study on Christology in 1974 in Holland. It became available in English in 1979 as *Jesus: An Experiment in Christology*.[20] The author sets the scene by depicting the situation in Palestine from the time of the Maccabean Revolt (175–135 B.C.E.) against the intolerable regime of the Seleucid kings, who attempted to deprive the Jews even of their religious heritage. During those generations before the birth of Jesus, the Jews were under the heel of the Greek kingdom of Syria, and later under Roman domination. It was a time of enormous frustration. The feeling was that the world must be transformed and the oppressors must be overcome. A mood of expectancy was apparent throughout the land. A celestial Son of man (cf. Daniel 7) who would overcome Israel's enemies and signal the approaching endtime was anticipated by many. It is into this troubled milieu that Jesus was born.

Schillebeeckx's first volume traces Jesus' steps from the beginning of his public life to his death, and to the solemn profession on the part of the apostles that he is risen and is truly the Son of God. Schillebeeckx's ultimate objective is to discover and explain what belief in Jesus can mean to us today. Some of the titles applied to Christ during his life and in the generation or two after his death have now lost much of their meaning. For example, the epithet "Son of man," which was so popular in the Greco-Palestinian and Judeo-Christian local congregations, acquired little currency in the Christian communities outside of Palestine. Although our knowledge of Jesus' own self-awareness is quite limited, a considerable amount can be learned about him by studying what he has

said regarding the coming of the kingdom, for he was its person-
ification and embodiment. Schillebeeckx attests that a good deal
of information can be gleaned from the gospels concerning Jesus'
message, his view of life, and his conduct.

As reflected in the New Testament writings, various Christian
communities stressed different aspects of Jesus' life and mission.
The gospels in particular reveal an interaction of divergent Christologies. Each gospel expresses its point of view initially through
the selection and arrangement of its materials. Schillebeeckx explains the importance of the "Q source" for the writing of the
Gospels of Matthew and Luke. According to Raymond Brown Q
is a hypothetical collection of sayings and some parables of Jesus
(comprising some two hundred or more verses) that was as old
as Mark (the 60s c.e.), and used along with Mark as a probable
source for the Gospels of Matthew and Luke. Strangely enough,
however, the materials in the Q collection contain no reference
to the crucifixion or the resurrection of Jesus. Since it is assumed
that Matthew and Luke were not acquainted with each other's
work, the material that was common to both of them—and not in
Mark—is widely assumed to have come from a common source
that has been termed Q.[21]

Jesus' baptism by John was the starting point of Christ's public ministry. Since the Maccabean period, a number of baptismal
movements in Palestine had an apocalyptic emphasis. Conditions
for the Jews were intolerable, and the hope of a historical remedy
had all but vanished. It was now up to some form of divine intervention to release them from their awful plight. During this period
many Jews began to hold out hope for the possibility of eternal
happiness in an afterlife beyond the portal of death. They sensed
that the end of the world was approaching, but before that, they
believed that they would be given one more divine offer of conversion, a final opportunity for a change of heart, that would come
to them through the presence in their midst of someone whom
Schillebeeckx terms the "eschatological prophet."

Jesus saw a similarity between the work of John the Baptist and
his own ministry. He could identify with John's appeal for conversion in light of God's approaching judgment. "The Kingdom of
God is near, therefore do penance and come to believe in the gospel" (Mark 1:15). Christ does not explain the nature of God's rule
as the kingdom draws near, but that rule is clarified in his parables.

In spite of the fact that there was a great deal of sectarianism and divisiveness in Israel in Jesus' time, his message ran in the opposite direction. Love your enemies (Matt. 5:44) and assist the stranger in need (Luke 10:29–37). His mission was to Israel, but there was a latent universalism in his message. It is doing good to one's fellow humans, neighbors and strangers alike, that will contribute most effectively to the coming of the kingdom.

It is difficult for us today to understand the significance of parables in a storytelling culture such as existed in Palestine in the first century after Christ. They are, however, extremely effective instruments in that they cause us to go on thinking about them and applying them to our lives long after we have encountered them. The listener is confronted with a choice and a challenge. Shall he/she identify with the good Samaritan or with the Levite in the parable (Luke 10:29–37)? The God of the parables is revealed as merciful (Luke 18:10–14), comforting (Luke 16:19–31), and magnanimous (Matt. 18:21–35). Salvation is portrayed as a gift rather than as a reward for a given level of achievement in life (Matt. 20:1–16). The parable of the talents is a perennial reminder of our obligation to make optimal use of our time and our abilities, regardless of how much or how little we have received (Matt. 25:14–30). The parable of the lost sheep remains a poignant revelation of Christ's own heart that searches out the lost and the forgotten (Luke 15:1–7). In the parable of the vineyard—which probably was told by Jesus almost as it appears today—the Lord reveals himself as the eschatological prophet who will be put to death by his own people (Mark 12:1–9). The gospels in all likelihood relate more parables than Jesus ever told because the primitive church was so struck by the power of this teaching tool as employed by Jesus.

Schillebeeckx affirms that miracles in Christ's time were understood very differently from the way in which we understand them today. In the gospels the historical and the legendary elements are blended together, creating a kerygmatic effect. They identify Jesus as the eschatological prophet who brings God's final offer of salvation to humankind. They vividly portray God's victory over the forces of evil. Without the miracle stories, the resurrection of Christ would stand in solitary isolation. Mark narrated sixteen separate miracle stories that were substantially taken over by Matthew and Luke, although Luke had recourse to another source(s) as well. The curing of the sick and the driving out of demons seemed to require the existence of faith in those who were healed (Mark 5:25–34, 10:46–52). Schillebeeckx teaches that the nature miracles (e.g., calming the storm, walking on water, and so forth) were legendary, affirming the need for absolute fidelity and trust in Jesus.

The cleansing of the temple is considered by our author as a difficult narrative. Its importance is underlined by the fact that all four gospels relate the event in some detail. The incident emphasized the exercise of authority by Jesus within the temple precincts, which aroused the wrath of the priests and elevated his conflict with the Jewish religious authorities to another level. According to Schillebeeckx, Christ acted in this instance as the eschatological prophet, protesting the gulf between Jewish theory and practice. His intervention was a prophetic act directed ultimately toward the conversion of Israel. There is little doubt that Jesus' action here was one of the causes of his ultimate arrest, because his attitude toward the law, the temple, and the Sabbath constituted a clear threat to the Jewish religious establishment. This action may well have made Jesus quite popular among those who were opposed to the temple priests, but it did create unrest and anger among the religious authorities. The Dutch theologian is inclined to locate the event neither at the beginning of Christ's public life (John) nor at the end (the Synoptics), but somewhere in the middle of his ministry.

Schillebeeckx presents a rather intriguing explanation regarding the grounds for Jesus' execution. According to Deuteronomy 17:12, anyone refusing to obey or listen to the formal requests of the officiating temple priest shall be punished by death. Jesus' refusal to answer the high priest's questions before the Sanhedrin constituted, for some, legal grounds for condemning him. The injunction of Deuteronomy 17:12 was applied because Christ refused to submit his teaching and his activity to the court. His action was considered to be a gesture of contempt against the priestly authority. However, since doubts remained in the minds of some as to the applicability of Deuteronomy 17:12 in this case, the issue was remanded to the judgment of Pontius Pilate.

Although the event of the resurrection of Christ is never directly described in the gospels, Schillebeeckx insists that some sort of gracious self-manifestation of the Lord after his death led the disciples to affirm that he is alive. The empty tomb alone would not have been sufficient to demonstrate the resurrection (John 20:9). It was a negative symbol that expressed the Jerusalem tradition of venerating Christ's burial place. The tradition of the tomb was more recent than the tradition of the appearances.

In 1 Thessalonians (1:10, 4:14) we encounter chronologically the first affirmation in the New Testament concerning the resurrection of Christ (50–51 C.E.). Several years later Paul declared that Jesus "made himself seen," first to Peter, then to the Twelve, and later to more than five hundred of the faithful. After that he appeared to James, then to all the apostles, and finally to Paul (1 Cor. 15:5–8). The sequence of events outlined in 1 Corinthians is as follows: Jesus died, was buried, was raised from the dead, and then he made himself seen. These appearances were not merely projections from the mind and the imagination of the disciples. They were events precipitated by the initiative of the risen Christ himself. In Schillebeeckx's judgment, only Luke and John contain accounts of appearances in the strict sense, because only they speak of the form and the manner of these manifestations. In these appearances, it was the risen Christ who was recognized as the living Jesus of Nazareth. Schillebeeckx asserts that the Easter experience was an objective event and not a purely subjective experience on the part of the disciples. Christ's resurrection vaulted him into a completely new mode of existence. The assurance of his followers that "Christ is risen" came from God alone. How that conviction was generated and how his risen presence took historical form can be discussed and debated endlessly.

Jesus' Abba experience is especially noted by Schillebeeckx. Through this singular access to the Father, he reveals an absolutely available and approachable God. Christ's unaffected, natural simplicity in relation to the Father as Abba has had a profound and lasting effect upon the church and its understanding of God. Because of the unprecedented depth of Jesus' experience of himself in the presence of the Father, the faith of the church called him the Son, thus defining Christ's creaturely relation to God. Schillebeeckx holds that this sublime union of a man with God can never result in the loss of man's proper being-as-man. Indeed, it is God's own creative action that constitutes man in his full humanity and integrity as man. Hence, he maintains that we can never speak of two components in Christ, but only of two aspects, that is, a real humanity in which the very being of God is realized.

Schillebeeckx insists that Jesus must be referred to as a human person, inasmuch as apart from a personally human mode of being, no one can be considered truly human. The man Jesus is this person, as a human being, because of his constitutive relationship with the Father. This relation to the Father makes him, in his humanity, the Son of God. For this theologian, it cannot be maintained that Christ is anhypostatic (that he is without a human person). Rather, he is enhypostatic (the human person of Jesus is incorporated into the person of the Word).[22] Schillebeeckx prefers not to use the term *hypostatic union* but employs instead the words "hypostatic identification." The implication of the Abba experience is that the unique turning of Jesus to the Father was preceded by the unique turning of the Father to Jesus. By virtue of this intimacy, he is called Son.

The man Jesus, within the confines of his personally human mode of being, is truly, at the same time, the Son, that is, the second person of the Trinity. The second person—coming into human self-consciousness in Jesus—brings about an identity of a finite personally human mode of being and an infinite divine mode of being. For Schillebeeckx this involves no contradiction. By virtue of this hypostatic identification, the Word of God, the second person of the Trinity, became a human person without there being any "opposite" between this man Jesus and the Son of God. However, the author adds, how the man Jesus can be for us the form and aspect of a divine person, that is, the Son, remains an inscrutable mystery.

Before proceeding to Schillebeeckx's second book, something should be said regarding the exchanges he had with the Congregation for the Doctrine of the Faith between 1976 and 1980 over some of the positions espoused in his *Jesus: An Experiment in Christology*.[23] In October 1976 the Congregation addressed a series of questions to Father Schillebeeckx concerning his historical and exegetical methodology, his treatment of the historical Jesus, and finally his approach to Christology and trinitarian theology. About six months later the theologian responded in writing to the inquiries in the order in which they were presented. After reviewing the responses, the Congregation gave a critique that, for the most part, opened up further questions in the same areas that were originally deemed problematic in their letter of October 1976.

At this point a "conversation" was suggested and scheduled between the author and several representatives of the Congregation. This colloquium was held in Rome on December 13–15, 1979. Apparently the Vatican officials were satisfied with several of Schillebeeckx's responses, but a number of the areas discussed still remained problematic for them. Through Cardinal Seper the Prefect, the Congregation informed Schillebeeckx of their conclusions and suggestions in November 1980. To clear up the ambiguities still remaining as a result of *Jesus*, Schillebeeckx was advised to publish clarifications so that those who might have been misled by some of the assertions made in the study might be brought back to the positions traditionally taught by the magisterium. The Schillebeeckx case was, to my knowledge, never officially brought to closure.

The chief points reiterated in the responses of Schillebeeckx to the Vatican inquiries were the following:

1. Jesus is initially identified as a human person, and this is the starting point of the author's historical investigation. Later, Christ is referred to as "personally human," that is, a humanly conscious center of action and freedom, a complete, independent, self-subsistent existence.

2. The theologian is opposed to anhypostasis because it would make Jesus an incomplete human being. He prefers the term *enhypostasis*, which implies a mutual identification between the Word and the full humanity of Jesus. It is Schillebeeckx's position that Chalcedon does not exclude the idea of a person or hypostasis proper to the humanity of Christ. The humanity of Jesus is personalized by the Word and, in turn, personalizes the Word. In Christ there is something of an identification between the hypostasis (person) of the Word and the humanity of Jesus which does not lack a hypostasis of its own.[24]

3. In response to the Congregation's questions concerning the relationship between the Easter faith of the apostles and Jesus' postresurrection appearances, the author affirms that the visual elements are not the ground of our faith in the resurrection. The appearances may have been the medium through which this revelation came to the apostles and the others enumerated in 1 Corinthians 15:5–8, but it is the divine revelation itself that serves as the basis for the apostolic faith. The revelation that Jesus is alive with God is, in a sense, independent of both traditions, that is, the empty tomb and the postresurrection appearances.

Schillebeeckx's second christological volume, *Christ: The Ex-*

perience of Jesus as Lord, was published in Dutch in 1977 and appeared in English in 1980.[25] His announced purpose in this work was to set forth the Christologies of Paul, John, the Pastoral and Catholic Epistles, and Hebrews. As it turns out, the study moves across a wide range of subjects, such as grace, justification, and redemption, which lie outside our focus. The study could be more correctly categorized as an extended treatment of soteriology rather than a presentation of New Testament Christology. Our concentration shall be focused upon what certain New Testament authors have to say about their faith in Jesus, and especially their affirmations concerning his divinity. Although certain passages in Paul have been interpreted as affirming the divinity of Christ (e.g., Rom. 9:5), the meaning is not especially clear. Regarding Philippians 2:6–11, Schillebeeckx asserts that there is considerable dispute over the interpretation of this passage. There is, in a sense, an affirmation here of Christ's preexistence with God, and yet he seems to see the heavenly character of Jesus in eschatological terms. The exaltation of Christ after his death is viewed as an eschatological gift, preexistent with God and ready for the time to come. In Colossians 1:15 this theologian sees an author of the Pauline school at work here. Christ is identified as the very image of God, the first-born of creation, and the one in whom God reveals himself. The preexistence in this case is eschatological. Christ is the eschatological salvation prepared by God from eternity to be revealed at the appointed time. The Letter of Titus, although not Pauline, is an extension of Paul's teaching. In Titus 2:13 the author speaks of "our great God and Savior, Jesus Christ." In Schillebeeckx's judgment, the unity of God and Christ is emphasized more strongly here than was customary for Paul. Christ is apparently identified in this passage as "the great God and Savior." In 2 Thessalonians 1:12 (which may or may not have been written by Paul) the author speaks of "the grace of our God and Lord Jesus Christ." This verse—largely due to obscurity in syntax—does not appear to be a clear affirmation of the divinity of Jesus. Although one or two of the authors of the Pauline school seem to affirm his divinity, Paul himself does not speak of Jesus as God in unambiguous terms.

The author of Hebrews, however, is more explicit in applying the word *God* to Christ (e.g., Heb. 1:8–9). According to Schillebeeckx, Hebrews explains more clearly than any other New Testament work the manner in which Jesus is the expression or character of God himself. Christ is both the visible image of God and the brother of humankind. In the humanity of Jesus we can actually see who God is. The salvation from God in Christ is then described in priestly terms. Jesus is not an angel, but a man who is superior to the angels. In fact, the risen and exalted Lord must be worshipped by all the angels. The apostolic tradition is interpreted in the Letter to the Hebrews in terms of a priestly and messianic Christology. Jesus is portrayed as the eschatological high priest. By virtue of his ascension, he has been raised through all the various spheres of the heavens into the very presence of God the Father. In this manner he has made access to God available to all his followers. Second Peter, probably the latest of the New Testament writings, speaks in the greeting of "the justice of our God and Savior, Jesus Christ" (2 Pet. 1:1). The naming of Christ as God in this verse—although disputed by some—is regarded by our author as a reasonably clear affirmation of the divinity of Jesus.

Schillebeeckx sees the Gospel of John as a critical source of revelation concerning the relationship between Christ and the Father. In the Prologue, Jesus is identified as the Word of God. The coming of Jesus (i.e., the Word) to earth is portrayed in the first eighteen verses of John. This Jesus is preexistent with God and the origin of all created reality. A great deal is made of the seven "I am" sayings in John, which are to be found in chapters 6–15 of the gospel.[26] Christ is not the Father, but he is the complete and final revelation of God and was sent to earth for that very purpose. In fact, he is the privileged access to the Father. As in the Synoptics, Jesus also addressed the Father as "Abba" in John (e.g., John 11:41, 12:27). Schillebeeckx asserts that the Father completely filled Jesus' consciousness. And because he was so totally aware of God as Father, we can understand how he considered himself to be the Son of this Father. The confession of Christ as Son of God the Father on the part of the apostolic church in all likelihood has its foundation in Jesus' self-awareness during his public life that he is the Son of God. The Son Christology evident, for example, in Matthew (11:27) and Luke (10:22) was no doubt a very early development in the Christian interpretation of Jesus. It was by no means an invention of John.

Schillebeeckx views the relationship between Jesus and God in primarily functional terms (e.g., John 10:34–38). Jesus is truly man but lives in an absolutely unique and singular relationship with God. Anyone who genuinely knows Jesus knows the Father (John 8:19), and anyone who sees Jesus through the eyes of faith sees the Father (John 14:9). What Jesus says and does reveals the mystery of his unity of life with the Father. In a very true sense, Christ reveals God the Father by revealing himself. However, in spite of this unity of the two intimately connected persons, in John's judgment, the Father remains the greater (14:28).

Because of the many critiques of *Jesus* and *Christ,* Schillebeeckx responded in 1978 with what he called *The Interim Report,* whose purpose was to clarify the methods he used and to respond to the objections that had been raised by various exegetes and theologians.[27] In this work he emphasizes again that the transmission of dead or obsolescent traditions is wrong because it leads to a loss of faith on the part of great numbers of believers. We have reached the point when Christianity can no longer be accepted simply on the authority of other teaching figures. There must be an internal credibility and cogency in the presentation of the kerygma, or it will not be welcomed today.

The Christian phenomenon goes back to the original experience that was refused by some (i.e., the scribes) and accepted by others (i.e., the disciples). Those who embraced the gospel of Jesus felt that they had been reborn, accepted, and understood by the Master. The revelation of the good news was initially received in joyous faith by the followers of Christ, and then later set forth in writing, constituting the first articulations of a Christology. These early statements of belief in Jesus as Lord—which varied somewhat from community to community—were embodied in several cognitive models that complemented one another. These models were woven into the fabric of the gospels. There is indeed a clear continuity between the Jesus of history and the Christ of the New Testament. Schillebeeckx insists that the earliest portraits of Jesus are found in Mark and the Q tradition, both of which precede the writing of Matthew, Luke, and John. Although there is no resurrection theology in Q, this tradition does possess a reasonably well-developed parousia Christology, highlighting the return of the Lord in glory at the end of history.

The diversity of Christian traditions suggests that the earliest believing communities had distinct Christologies, and we know precious little about some of them, for example, East Syrian and Egyptian Christianity. The gains made in the study of Christian origins have expanded our comprehension and broadened our approach to Christology. It is not merely a question of what the Jerusalem community taught about Jesus. Many diverse strains from elsewhere found their way into the New Testament writings. Just as a variety of models were used in the primitive church, so too we must not be afraid of complementary approaches and formulations today. Jesus' good news of salvation involves the offer of a new kind of seeing, healing, enabling—leading to an inner renewal, a *metanoia*—which then must spill out into an absolutely new approach to those around us and to the world in which we live. The uniqueness of Jesus consists in the fact that he not only taught us an entirely new and superior mode of thinking and acting, but he lived out that gospel throughout every moment of his human existence, up to and including his death. He is thus the eschatological prophet of the coming kingdom of God.

Schillebeeckx maintains that this was the very first interpretation of Jesus, prior to any of the New Testament writings. He cites Deuteronomy 18:15, "The Lord will raise up a prophet for you—a prophet like me [i.e., Moses]—and you must listen to him." The suffering servant image from 2 Isaiah (42:1, 49:1–9) was joined, for example in Q, to the Deuteronomic picture to describe the eschatological prophet who is to bring the final and definitive message of salvation to all humankind. Our author notes a growing consensus among scholars concerning the existence of an original Palestinian prophet Christology that served as the base for a number of other approaches, for example, a maranatha Christology (where Christ is portrayed as Lord of the future), a Jesus wonder-worker Christology, a Wisdom Christology (Jesus as Wisdom sent by God), and an Easter Christology (with Jesus' death and resurrection as central). In the parable of the vineyard (Mark 12:1–9) the last messenger sent by God was his beloved Son, the eschatological prophet greater than all the others, even Moses. The amply documented special Abba experiences of God on the part of Jesus make it difficult to deny that he was aware of being the Son of this Father in a very singular manner. The special experience of God shared by Moses (Exod. 33:10–23), along with the promise of Deuteronomy 18:15 that a greater prophet was to come, was realized in Jesus, who also shared a unique and intimate experience of God.

Schillebeeckx returns to the Easter experiences, which he says cannot be grounded in the empty tomb or the appearances alone. Faith in the resurrection is the result of a revelation, a grace from God that becomes effective in and through the human experiences, for example, of the appearances. These appearances are not merely the result of a reflection by the disciples on the pre-Easter Jesus. Although the risen Christ appeared only to believers (John 14:19), our author affirms that the resurrection appearances were by no means merely a subjective insight on the part of the apostles. Two factors were operating here: (1) the revelation granted by God to them that Jesus is risen, and (2) the experiences in their midst of Christ's new saving presence. The former could have been infused into the disciples on the occasion of the postresurrection appearances, but the two elements are distinct and complementary.

Schillebeeckx reminds us that the kingdom of God has made its appearance in Jesus (Matt. 12:28), who inaugurates a new relationship between God and humankind. Christ has revealed a God who liberates and does not enslave. In Jesus God confronts us with his own being and, therefore, Jesus is God's Word. Chalcedon attempted to express this by declaring that Christ is truly God and truly man. Jesus can be defined only in terms of his absolutely unique relationship with God and with humankind. Inasmuch as Christ is the decisive and definitive revelation of God, and because we cannot separate God's nature and his revelation, the man Jesus is indeed connected with the very nature of God. Schillebeeckx states that it is difficult to know whether we need to, or if we can make this theoretically more precise. There have been those who have understated the identity between God and Jesus, for example, the Arians and the Nestorians, and those who have overstated it, for example, the Monophysites. Is it possible for us to further refine the Chalcedonian model to make it more credible and acceptable to believers today? It is Schillebeeckx's view that further refinements will not help. Therefore, it is time to search out a new model from the original experience, to listen once again to the original story, and to participate in faith in the originating experience.

In the epilogue of *The Interim Report* Schillebeeckx describes again the relationship between Jesus and the Father. Jesus' deepest being lies in his utterly personal bond with the Father. Our author insists that God is part of the definition of who the man Jesus is. Moreover, God can only be most precisely defined in terms of the human life and activity of Christ. And yet, in spite of the union between Father and Son, the Father is still greater than his self-revelation in Jesus (John 14:28).

The Revival of Spirit Christology

According to several of the earliest versions of Spirit Christology that appeared in the first centuries, it was frequently the divine Spirit and not the eternal Son who took up his dwelling in Jesus. Thus Jesus was portrayed by a number of these early theologians as teaching and healing as an exemplary man who was animated by the Spirit. This type of Spirit Christology located Jesus among the prophets and, indeed, the last and most perfect of them. My review of Walter Kasper and Roger Haight will be limited to their rather different treatments of Spirit Christology, which has experienced a significant revival since the nineteenth century.

Walter Kasper

Walter Kasper (b. 1933), formerly a professor of dogmatics and bishop of Ruttenburg-Stuttgart in Germany, was appointed Roman cardinal on January 21, 2001, and, shortly thereafter, president of the Pontifical Council for Promoting Christian Unity. In 1974 he published an influential christological treatise, *Jesus der Christus*, which appeared in English in 1976.[28] He affirms that the initial task of the theologian is to address the historical questions concerning the life of Jesus and to study with great care the earliest christological formulations. Further, it is important to blend Christology (the study of the divine and the human in Christ) with soteriology (the evaluation of his mission and his work).

After analyzing Jesus' baptism, his message, his relationships to the scribes and Pharisees, his miracles, the various designations referring to Jesus, his death and resurrection, and early conciliar pronouncements concerning his identity, Kasper delves into what he means by Spirit Christology. He cites the eleventh provincial Council of Toledo (675), which affirmed that we must give credence to the fact that the Incarnation of the Son involves the activity of the whole Trinity, because the (external) works of the Trinity cannot be apportioned (*quia inseparabilia sunt opera Trinitatis*).[29] Scholastic theology did not give sufficient attention to the distinctive operation of the Holy Spirit in the Incarnation, perhaps because of its emphasis on the unity of the external operations of God. The author points out that the Incarnation took place in the Holy Spirit (Luke 1:35), and that Jesus was installed in his messianic office by the Spirit (Mark 1:10). Indeed, Matthew reveals that Jesus acts in the power of the Spirit (Matt. 12:28). It was through the Spirit that he was raised from the dead (Rom. 1:4), and Paul notes that the risen Lord, the last Adam, in fact became a life-giving Spirit (1 Cor. 15:45). The Spirit in this context is described as the personal bond of freedom and love between the Father and the Son. The Father communicates himself in love to the Son, and the Spirit is the surplus and the outpouring of the love between Father and Son.

In the Old Testament the Messiah is portrayed as the bearer of the Spirit and the one on whom the Spirit shall rest (Isa. 11:2). In the final days it is written that God will pour out his Spirit on all humankind and make them all prophets (Joel 3:1; Acts 2:17). All of Christ's activity was animated by the Spirit (Luke 4:14, 18), and in the Spirit he surrendered himself on the cross (Heb. 9:14). Jesus was raised from the dead in the power of the Spirit (Rom. 1:4) and, as risen Lord, became a life-giving Spirit (1 Cor. 15:45). As a matter of fact, Paul identifies the *kurios* and the *pneuma* (2 Cor. 3:17), and he informs us that no one can confess Jesus as Lord except in the Spirit (1 Cor. 12:3). In Christ the Spirit has fully realized his goal of initiating and animating the new creation. And now the Spirit has the task of integrating all of reality into that new creation. Actually, Christians are defined by Paul as those who are led by the Holy Spirit (Rom. 8:14).

At the Council of Constantinople I, it was defined that the Holy Spirit is not merely an impersonal force or a reality subordinate to Christ. Rather, he proceeds from the Father (and the Son) and is adored along with the Father and the Son. Indeed it was he who spoke through the prophets.[30] In Kasper's judgment, although the East and the West take somewhat different approaches to the theology of the Spirit in that the East teaches that the Spirit proceeds from the Father *through* the Son, while in the West the Spirit proceeds from the Father *and* the Son, these two creedal formulas are not very far apart. However, it must be added that the theology of the Spirit has a much richer tradition in the East than in the West.

Kasper's emphasis upon Spirit Christology is an example of the effort on the part of a number of theologians today to supplant or at least supplement the Logos model that they deem to be no longer completely adequate as the controlling pattern for Christology. As a matter of fact, the framework of the New Testament seems to favor a more Spirit-centered approach to christological studies.[31] The Old Testament stress on the Spirit of Yahweh, along with the New Testament accent on the Holy Spirit as the Spirit of Jesus, seems to provide a broad base for greater emphasis on the intimate relationship between Christ and the Spirit. However, according to Philip Rosato, there is some danger of adoptionism in this approach, for Christ could be considered as simply a human being who was possessed by the Spirit in a singular fashion, and then "adopted" at some point by God as his Son.[32] The Ebionites of the first and second centuries espoused a Spirit Christology of this sort and thereby reduced Jesus to the status of a mere man who was adopted by God as his Son on the occasion of his baptism when the Spirit descended upon him. This type of Spirit Christology denies the ontological sonship of Jesus and runs directly counter to the definitions of Nicaea and Chalcedon. Kasper's Spirit Christology, however, remains open to the preexistence of the Son, and to ontological statements about the consubstantiality between the Father and the Son.

Several of the earliest Christologies viewed Jesus as standing in the tradition of the Spirit-filled figures of Judaism. Christ is seen as a bearer of the Spirit (Isa. 11:2), and as anointed by the Spirit (Luke 4:21), who became a life-giving Spirit (1 Cor. 15:44–45). The identity of Jesus can almost be defined in terms of his unique relationship to the Holy Spirit. Actually, it is the role of Jesus to send the Spirit into all humankind. It has to be conceded that Logos Christology had become somewhat divorced from the sweep of salvation history and grounded itself in ontology that was largely distanced from the grand design of salvation history.

In the Old Testament the Spirit is portrayed as the life-giving power of God, the agent who leads the course of history to its completion. It is the Spirit who is God's openness to history and the divine principle of the self-communication of God to humankind. According to Orthodox theology, emphasis is placed more on the Holy Spirit as the outward thrust of the Father and the Son into the human community rather than on the expression of the inward love between Father and Son. The work of Christ and the church can be described as the mission of enabling others to enter into the inner life of God through the Holy Spirit who permeated the historical existence of Jesus.[33] Being in Christ, therefore, and living in the Spirit can be viewed as one and the same thing.

Roger Haight

Another less conventional approach has been taken to Spirit Christology by Roger Haight, a professor of systematic theology at the Weston School of Theology in Massachusetts. He affirms that our present-day hermeneutical tools are extremely helpful in discerning the meanings of the biblical texts, so that they can be brought forward into the present, having been unloosed from the limitations of the past. It is only in this fashion that Jesus' words and deeds can be rendered more meaningful to us in the present. The fundamental christological challenges, however, remain the same. Who was Jesus? How do we describe his relation to the Father? What is the character and scope of his mission? Is a Logos Christology more adequate for our purposes than a Spirit Christology? These fundamental questions must be addressed in our day with the tools available to us. At the heart of the message of Jesus is the kingdom of God, which looks to the endtime that for Jesus was imminent. His words and deeds rendered the kingdom present. It is crucial that we find some meaning for God's kingdom in our world, and it is primarily the parables that reveal its significance.[34]

Spirit Christology, according to Haight, explains how God is present and active in Jesus and thus discloses the divinity of Jesus through the use of the biblical symbol of God as Spirit, and not the symbol Logos. Haight suggests that this is quite possibly a more effective paradigm for our age that is so centered on the humanity of Jesus. The traditional issue with Logos Christology is that it makes the assertion of the full and integral humanity of Jesus more problematic.[35] Our current christological enterprise must set forth the identity of Christ so that present-day Christians can more readily discover their salvation in him. It must be faithful to the biblical language concerning Jesus, and faithful to Nicaea and Chalcedon, which are universally accepted in the mainline Christian denominations. Finally, our Christology must be placed in correlation with our contemporary world that seems to be calling for certain reformulations of our traditional beliefs.

A Spirit Christology has as its principal symbol God as Spirit, who is active outside of the divine being in the world of God's creation. The Spirit is the creative power of God who is active in the world. During his life on earth, Jesus was animated throughout by the presence and the dynamism of God as Spirit. According to Haight, after the resurrection the Spirit is experienced as the outpouring of eschatological salvation through Jesus. The risen Christ becomes God's life-giving Spirit (1 Cor. 15:45). In Haight's judgment the Spirit is God's very own self, operating in and through Jesus, unlike other symbols such as Word and Wisdom, which tend to connote something less than God. He adds that the subordinationism that frustrated christological development from the second through the fourth centuries was, to a notable extent, the outgrowth of the Logos symbol itself, when it became objectified in the discourse of that period.

Haight then sets out his argument favoring a Spirit Christology. He asks whether or not such a christological approach conforms with Nicaea. His response is that the notion of *Spirit* more clearly reflects the consubstantiality of the Son with the Father than does the term *Logos*. Haight's paraphrase of the definition of Nicaea can be stated as follows: not less than God was present and active in Jesus. He notes that the symbol *Spirit* can convey this truth even more effectively than the symbol *Logos*. Regarding the Chalcedonian definition of one person and two natures in Christ (451), Haight argues that the Spirit symbol is just as appropriate here too. Today we spontaneously accept Jesus as a fully human person, and his divinity can be identified as God present and at work in Jesus.

This theologian steps into rather controversial waters when he deals with the preexistence of the Son. He affirms that what is preexistent to Jesus is God who became incarnate in Christ. A strict preexistence would run contrary to his consubstantiality with us. Haight insists that there is no reason why God's personal self-communication, presence, and activity in Christ should not be understood as an ontological Incarnation, so long as Jesus' humanity is not diminished. He further notes that this ontological Incarnation is not to be viewed in an adoptionist sense because the presence of God as Spirit was evident in Christ from the first moment of his existence.

Whether or not there is a qualitative or a quantitative difference between Jesus and other humans is, according to Haight, a rather ambiguous issue today, since certain differences in degree may well constitute a qualitative difference. For example, he makes reference to the fact that the Spirit of God present in Jesus in a most unique and intense manner could very possibly convey what is intended by a qualitative difference. The question of the worship of Jesus and prayer to Jesus because he is divine is not really dealt with in sufficient detail; Haight simply says that worship moves through Jesus to its object who is God. Some of the conclusions Haight has drawn are as follows:

> Spirit Christology is faithful to the dominant New Testament language and to the definitions of Nicaea and Chalcedon. That is, no less than God is present and active in Jesus, who is undeniably consubstantial with our human condition.

> Spirit Christology is a viable option for today, and is in a number of ways more adequate for us at this time than Logos Christology.

> Spirit Christology would more easily allow us to make room for the possibility that God might also be at work through other mediations of salvation, that is, through other savior figures.

In the fourth issue of the 1992 *Theological Studies*, John H. Wright, professor emeritus at the Jesuit School of Theology at Berkeley, describes Haight's approaches to Spirit Christology as flawed and unacceptable because he seems to say that the indwelling of the Holy Spirit in Christ is what constitutes the divinity of Jesus.[36] Haight sees Jesus as a human person, pure and simple, who is filled with the Spirit from the first moment of his human existence, but there is in Christ no preexistent divine subject who acts in and through the human nature he has assumed. Therefore, Wright argues, Haight's position is consistent neither with the New Testament data that proclaim Jesus as Lord and reveal a Christology of divine sonship nor with the Councils of Nicaea and Chalcedon that define Christ as true God and true man, united in one divine person.

In an impressive volume published in 1999, *Jesus—Symbol of God*, Haight synthesizes his years of work in the field of Christology.[37] He employs as his controlling model or paradigm the notion of symbol. Whereas a sign merely points to something else, a symbol actually makes that something else present. He identifies Jesus as the concrete symbol of God, and by that he means that Jesus mediates through his human existence the vital and active presence of God into the world.

After he outlines four portrayals (i.e., prophet, teacher, charismatic healer, liberator) that have been employed over the years to clarify Christ's meaning and mission, Haight proceeds to review five principal New Testament Christologies that have been influential in developing and enriching our understanding of Jesus over the centuries. Paul's representation of Christ as the New Adam (Rom. 5:12–21; 1 Cor. 15:21–23), the Son of God image in Mark (1:1, 1:11, 9:7, 14:61), Luke's Spirit Christology (1:35, 3:22, 4:18–19; Acts 2:17ff.), and Jesus as the Wisdom of God (Phil. 2:6–11; Col. 1:15–20), do not necessarily call forth a three-stage Christology involving the notion of preexistence. Our author believes that these four theological positions leave the ontological status of Jesus open. But with the Logos theology of John, we witness a rather different perspective. The Logos is assigned its own distinctive existence, and this preexistent subject is the same subject who is Jesus of Nazareth. John's introductory narrative (1:1–18) tells a story that expresses the religious significance of Christ. Although it is poetic and imaginative in the most profound sense, it did prevail as the most influential paradigm among the Fathers of the church, and served as the ground for the position that was given dogmatic formulation at Nicaea and Chalcedon.

Haight states that the definition against Arius at Nicaea, although remaining normative, is no longer intelligible to our age in its present form. It was Arius who taught that the Logos was a creature and hence subordinate to God. The interpretation of the Nicene Creed proposed by Haight implies that the essence of the conciliar definition is captured and adequately reflected by affirming that not less than God was present and operative in Jesus. A reading of the creed, however, creates the implication that Christ is regarded as another, that is, a second divine figure—God of God, light of light, true God of true God through whom all things were made.[38] God's presence in the human person, Christ, does not seem to convey the full intent of Nicaea's declaration.

Regarding the definition of Chalcedon, Haight is convinced that its meaning can be communicated by stating the following: "Jesus was one human person with an integral human nature in whom not less than God, and thus a divine nature, is at work."[39] One wonders whether the words of Chalcedon depicting Christ as having two natures—without confusion or change, without division or separation—which come together, not in two persons, but in one person, that is, the person of the Word, are adequately reflected in Haight's interpretation.[40]

He carefully charts two christological models that he feels are viable in the postmodern age in which we live. (The postmodern era—which emerged in the last one-third of the twentieth century—is characterized by liberation theologies, process theologies, feminist theologies, inculturation theologies, and the increasing relevance of the study of other world religions.) In this context, our author proposes a Logos Christology, adapting somewhat the model of Karl Rahner. It begins from below with a transcendental anthropology that describes humankind as capable of reaching out beyond the heavens to the very reality of God. Jesus—within this context—is the human being who attained the summit, with God present and active in him. And he has thus opened the way for all, having been constituted as the medium of God's definitive salvation for humanity.

The second postmodern model proposed by Haight is his own adaptation of Spirit Christology that we have addressed earlier. It also begins from below with a historical consideration of Jesus, whose self-understanding and authority seemed to rise out of an abiding experience of God as Spirit, present and active in his life. Then, after the resurrection, this union between God as Spirit and Christ seems to tend toward identification. Spirit Christology perhaps reflects more clearly than Logos Christology that it is God at work in Jesus. According to Haight, "Jesus is divine dialectically, because the presence of God as Spirit pervades his being and action."[41] He further maintains that the presence of God in Jesus is indeed an ontological presence because where God is active, God is. The saving role of Jesus, according to this model, consists in the privileged disclosure of God, the presence and gift of God, that is expressed in the human history of Christ. Haight calls it a "pioneer soteriology" inasmuch as Jesus goes out ahead of us to show the way. The problems involved in the reconciliation of this model—and, to some extent, Haight's version of Rahner's Logos Christology—with the definitions of Nicaea and Chalcedon, have been dealt with above. Recently the Vatican has initiated an investigation of *Jesus—Symbol of God* regarding its Christology, its portrayal of the Trinity, and its apparent threat to the uniqueness of Jesus as universal savior.

A Summary

One of the earlier efforts to design an ascending Christology on the part of Catholic theologians was the work by three Dutch scholars, Ansfried Hulsbosch, Piet Schoonenberg, and Edward Schillebeeckx, in the 1960s. These three produced articles that appeared in the Dutch periodical *Tijdschrift voor Theologie* in 1966. Their studies were summarized by Robert North in a booklet entitled *In Search of the Human Jesus*, which was published in 1970 in the United States. In Hulsbosch's judgment the divinity of Jesus consists solely in the singular and unique perfection of his humanity, and no separate divine principle need be asserted to explain his divine character and prerogatives. The single reality of Christ has a created and a divine dimension. Although this divine dimension is eternal, Hulsbosch is unwilling to concede that the personal subjectivity of Jesus was a preexistent divine reality, distinct from anything human. Schoonenberg agrees partially with Hulsbosch in that there is not a person of the Son independent of the Incarnation. The intimations of preexistence in the New Testament are to be understood as references to the divine Wisdom operating with God from the beginning. Schillebeeckx has greater reservations regarding Hulsbosch's scheme because he feels that this approach fails to grasp the essence of the dogma of the hypostatic union, since Hulsbosch repudiates the two natures pattern.

The three scholars, however, affirm that the Council of Chalcedon adopted the word *person* without including the notion of a separate and distinct self-awareness, a position that is not compatible with modern psychology. Also, they note that the concept of preexistence alluded to in certain pericopes of the New Testament very probably traces its origin to the nonhypostatic Wisdom of Proverbs 8:22–31.

Three years after the appearance of the 1966 issue of the *Tijdschrift*, Piet Schoonenberg published his study on Christology and raised again the question of the two natures in Christ. There seems to be no evidence of dialogue within Jesus, between his divine and his human nature. If Apollinaris of Laodicea was condemned because he insisted that Jesus did not possess a human soul since the

Logos replaced it, how can we deny Jesus a created act of being? Would he indeed be truly human without such a created act of being? Schoonenberg is convinced that anhypostasia deprives Jesus of an essential dimension of manhood, and therefore he must be a human person, with individual and distinct human consciousness and freedom. How, then, can he be considered a divine person? If the Son of God does not possess an individual and distinct consciousness as a divine person in the Trinity, since all three persons share in a relative way the consciousness and freedom proper to God, then, Schoonenberg reasons, there are not two subjects in Christ that are "person" in the same manner. The dilemma of two natures in one person is addressed by positing a unique and absolutely unparalleled presence of God in this human person. This amounts to a Christology without duality, that is, a Christology of God's complete presence in the whole man Jesus.

For this theologian, the Word is enhypostatic in the man who is Christ. It is Bernard Lonergan's judgment, however, that Schoonenberg does not do justice to the christological dogmas. If the Dutch scholar means that Jesus was only a man and not the preexistent divine person, he would have fallen into the heresy of the Ebionites. In a study published about a decade later, Schoonenberg affirms that the two natures in Jesus, the divine and the human, mutually permeate each other. Christ is to be conceived of as a "God-man" person. The Logos perfects his humanity and is itself determined in a new way. The Word's mediational role between God and creation is brought to fulfillment in his being one person with Jesus' humanity. Christ now is truly Son, the only begotten of the Father.

Hans Küng's Christology was developed in his *On Being a Christian*. He, too, affirms that we must begin by asserting the full humanity of Jesus before we attempt to describe the relationship of Jesus to God. The heart of his proclamation, his values, and his fate can be charted reliably from the gospels. His public ministry was overshadowed by an abiding anticipation of the end-time and by the imminent coming of the kingdom. Jesus avoided the title "Messiah" because of its political overtones. He was not a social revolutionary, but rather lived as an itinerant preacher.

His Sermon on the Mount set out an ethic very different from that of the Pharisees and the scribes. Although Jesus did seem to restrict his saving work to the Jews, his mandate to love even one's enemies, as well as the parable of the good Samaritan (Luke 10:29–37), opened the door to a more universalist mission. In all likelihood he did not apply "Messiah" to himself, but his words and actions revealed a clear claim to messiahship. His approach to God was one of exceptional closeness and familiarity, and his use of "Abba" as applied to God was extraordinary. Küng describes the resurrection as an unambiguously supernatural event, unlike his portrayal of the virgin birth and the ascension. The appearances of the risen Lord generated the faith of his disciples, whose faith serves as the ground of our belief.

The title "Son of God" was initially understood in a functional sense and then developed into an ontological understanding under the influence of Greek thought. Regarding the notion of redemption, the explanation of Anselm (i.e., vicarious satisfaction) is not especially helpful today and should perhaps be replaced by concepts such as liberation and reconciliation that could be more meaningful to contemporary believers. Küng further notes that the move from a functional explanation of Christ's divinity to an ontological explanation that was given final form at Nicaea, Ephesus, and Chalcedon occurred because there was no other conceptual system available. The affirmations concerning divine sonship and preexistence are intended to assert that God is uniquely present and at work in Jesus, and to confirm the once-and-for-all character of his intimate relationship with the Father. Christ's humanity is set forth as the ultimate and definitive standard of human existence. His capacity for suffering, loneliness, insecurity, temptation, doubts, and possibility of error demonstrates the authentic humanity that he shares with us.

The first volume of the highly praised Christology of Edward Schillebeeckx was *Jesus: An Experiment in Christology*. The author traces Jesus' steps from the outset of his public life to the resurrection, and the profession on the part of the disciples that he is the Son of God. The principal purpose of the study is to discover and explain what belief in Jesus can mean to us today. The gospels reveal a number of divergent Christologies that are initially reflected in their selection and arrangement of materials. Schillebeeckx places a special emphasis on the Q source that was employed by Matthew and Luke in the writing of their gospels. They also made use of the Gospel of Mark that had been composed some ten or fifteen years before Matthew and Luke.

Schillebeeckx devotes a good deal of time to unfolding the meaning of the parables of Jesus, since they reveal most clearly his thoughts and hopes concerning the coming kingdom of God. The miracles of Jesus identify him as the last of the prophets who brings God's definitive offer of salvation to humankind. The healings and the expulsion of devils seem to require faith on the part of those who were healed, while the nature miracles, which are considered to be legendary, affirm the need for absolute trust in Jesus.

This theologian insists that there was some sort of gracious self-manifestation of the Lord after his death that led the disciples to believe that he was still alive. It was these appearances rather than the empty tomb that effectively demonstrated his bodily resurrection. Paul enumerates the various occasions when Jesus "made himself seen" (1 Cor. 15:5–8). These appearances were not merely projections of the mind and imagination of the disciples. They were objective events occasioned by the initiative of the risen Christ himself.

Schillebeeckx insists that Jesus must be referred to as a human person, since apart from a personally human mode of being, no one can be considered truly human. It cannot be maintained that Christ is anhypostatic (that he is without a human person). Rather, he is enhypostatic (the human person of Jesus is incorporated into the person of the Word). The term *hypostatic identification* is preferred to the words *hypostatic union*. The second person coming into human self-consciousness in Jesus brings about an identity of a finite, personally human mode of being and an infinite, divine mode of being, which for our author involves no contradiction. Nonetheless, how the man Jesus can be for us the form and aspect of a divine person, that is, the Son, remains an inscrutable mystery.

Schillebeeckx's second christological volume, *Christ: The Experience of Jesus as Lord*, could be more accurately described as an extended treatment of soteriology. However, he discusses in some detail the passages regarding the divinity of Jesus in, for example, Paul, Hebrews, and John. It is Schillebeeckx's judgment that although one or two writers of the Pauline school (e.g., those who composed Colossians and the Letter of Titus) seemed to affirm Christ's divinity, Paul himself does not speak of Jesus as God in unambiguous terms. The author of Hebrews, on the other hand, lays out very clearly the manner in which Jesus is the expression (or character) of God himself. The Gospel of John identifies Christ as the Word of God, preexistent with God, through whom all things were made. Because Jesus was so totally aware of God as Father, it is understandable that he considered himself to be the Son. Schillebeeckx is inclined to view the relationship between Jesus and God primarily in functional terms. What Jesus says and does reveals the mystery of his unity of life with the Father. Christ reveals God the Father by revealing himself.

In Walter Kasper's important contribution to contemporary Christology, *Jesus Christ*, he notes that it is time for a new approach to christological studies, and he begins his work with a review of Jesus' activity during his lifetime. Christ's relation to the Father was clearly unparalleled and actually amounted to a stunning revelation of the nearness of God. Unlike the rabbis of his day, he placed his word above the word of Moses and spoke on his own authority. On the basis of his word and his presence, we are to make our choice about God.

Kasper contends that it is possible to speak of a Christology from below in the New Testament because Jesus never referred to himself as the Messiah or the natural Son of God. Even in the Gospel of John, the unity between Father and Son is understood more as a unity of willing and knowing than as a metaphysical union. However, Kasper considers certain assertions in John as declarations of the divinity of Jesus (e.g., 20:28, 8:58, 10:30).

After reviewing the development of christological thought in the early councils, Kasper focuses on his own rendering of Spirit Christology. His emphasis on a more Spirit-centered approach to christological studies is an example of the attempt on the part of a number of theologians today to supplant, or at least to supplement the traditional Logos model, which they no longer deem to be completely adequate as the controlling pattern for Christology. It must be noted that, unlike some proponents of Spirit Christology, Walter Kasper's vision remains open to the preexistence of the Son, and to metaphysical statements regarding the consubstantiality of the Father and the Son.

Another more radical approach to Spirit Christology that departs somewhat from the classical christological and trinitarian framework is the effort of Roger Haight. He is convinced that we must adopt a broader view of the meaning of the Incarnation and be more attentive to some of the directions that have been taken recently, for example, political and liberation theology. The fun-

damental questions remain the same. Who was Jesus? How do we
describe his relation to the Father? What are the character and
scope of his mission? It is essential that we find a new meaning
for God's kingdom in our world, and the parables will be most
helpful in this search.

Haight proposes that the biblical symbol of God as Spirit, rather
than the Logos symbol, may well be a more effective paradigm
for disclosing the reality of Jesus for our age. The problem with
Logos Christology is that it makes the affirmation of the full and
integral humanity of Jesus more troublesome. We must be faithful
to both the biblical language and the declarations of Nicaea and
Chalcedon. At the same time, we must situate our Christology in
correlation with our contemporary world and its thought patterns.

The principal symbol of Spirit Christology is God as Spirit, the
creative power of God active in the world. According to Haight,
the Spirit is God's very own self, operating in and through Jesus.
He suggests that the subordinationism that frustrated christological development from the second through the fourth centuries was,
to some degree, the outgrowth of the Logos symbol itself when it
became objectified in the discourse of that period.

Haight affirms that the notion of *Spirit* more clearly reflects the
consubstantiality of the Son with the Father than does the term
Logos. He asserts that the definition of Nicaea can be translated
as follows: not less than God was present and active in Jesus.
Even the Chalcedonian definition (i.e., one person and two natures
in Christ) is just as effectively understood by means of the Spirit
symbol, because in our day we spontaneously accept Jesus as a
fully human person whose divinity can be identified as God present
and at work in him.

Haight's explanation of the preexistence of the Son has been
questioned because he affirms that what is preexistent to Jesus is
God who became incarnate in Christ. He declares that there is
no reason why God's personal self-communication and activity in
Jesus should not be understood as an ontological Incarnation, as
long as his humanity is not diminished. Haight is convinced that
Spirit Christology is faithful to the New Testament language and
to the definitions of Nicaea and Chalcedon, in that God is truly
present and active in Jesus who is consubstantial with us. Moreover, Spirit Christology allows us to make room for the possibility
that God might be at work in the universe through other medi-

ations of salvation, that is, other savior figures. He notes that in this postmodern era new christological models must be formulated, and he points to Karl Rahner's Logos Christology and his own Spirit Christology as alternatives.

Notes

1. Robert North, *In Search of the Human Jesus* (New York: Corpus Books, 1970).
2. Denzinger and Schönmetzer, *Enchiridion Symbolorum*, 126, 150.
3. Piet Schoonenberg, *The Christ*, trans. Della Couling (New York: Herder and Herder, 1971).
4. Ibid., 58.
5. Denzinger and Schönmetzer, *Enchiridion Symbolorum*, 3812.
6. Ibid., 556.
7. Willi Marxsen, *The Resurrection of Jesus of Nazareth* (Philadelphia: Fortress Press, 1970). The German edition was published in 1968.
8. Denzinger and Schönmetzer, *Enchiridion Symbolorum*, 801.
9. *Scripture and Christology*. A Statement of the Biblical Commission with a Commentary (New York: Paulist Press, 1986).
10. Ibid., 1.1.2.3 (5).
11. Bernard Lonergan, in *A Third Collection*, ed. Frederick Crowe (New York: Paulist Press, 1985), 74–99.
12. Ibid., 90.
13. Ibid., 95.
14. Piet Schoonenberg, "Denken über Chalcedon," *Theologische Quartalschrift* 160, no. 4 (Oct.–Dec. 1980): 295–305. See the summary in *Theology Digest* (Summer 1981): 103–7.
15. Hans Küng, *On Being a Christian*, trans. Edward Quinn (New York: Doubleday, 1976).
16. See Martin Hengel, *Studies in Early Christology* (Edinburgh: T & T Clark, 1995), 105–8.
17. Hans Küng, *Does God Exist?* trans. Edward Quinn (New York: Doubleday, 1978), 677–96.
18. Peter Hebblethwaite, *The New Inquisition? The Case of Edward Schillebeeckx and Hans Küng* (San Francisco: Harper and Row, 1980), 154–57.
19. Hans Küng, *Christianity: Essence, History, and Future*, trans. John Bowden (New York: Continuum, 1995), 162–96.
20. Schillebeeckx, *Jesus: An Experiment in Christology*, trans. Hubert Hoskins (New York: Seabury Press, 1979).
21. Raymond E. Brown, *An Introduction to the New Testament* (New York: Doubleday, 1997), 116–22.
22. Schillebeeckx, *Jesus*, 745–46.
23. Ted Schoof, ed., *The Schillebeeckx Case: Letters and Documents*, trans. Matthew J. O'Connell (New York: Paulist Press, 1984).
24. The issue that Schillebeeckx seems not to address is the challenge raised

in canon 5 of Constantinople II (553) which insists that there cannot be two subsistences or persons in Christ, and that the Word is the subsistence of the human nature of Jesus. Perhaps the author feels that his term *hypostatic identification* eliminates this problem. (See Denzinger and Schönmetzer, *Enchiridion Symbolorum*, 426.)

25. Edward Schillebeeckx, *Christ: The Experience of Jesus as Lord*, trans. John Bowden (New York: Crossroad, 1986).

26. Schillebeeckx enumerates the seven I am sayings as follows: John 6; John 7:1–8:59; John 9:1–10:21; John 10:1–6 and 10:22–29; John 11:25; John 14:6; John 15:1–10.

27. Edward Schillebeeckx, *The Interim Report on the Books, Jesus and Christ*, trans. John Bowden (New York: Crossroad, 1981).

28. Walter Kasper, *Jesus the Christ*, trans. V. Green (1976; reprint, Mahwah, N.J.: Paulist Press, 1985).

29. Denzinger and Schönmetzer, *Enchiridion Symbolorum*, 535.

30. Ibid., 150.

31. Philip Rosato, "Spirit Christology: Ambiguity and Promise," *Theological Studies* 38, no. 3 (Sept. 1977): 423–49.

32. Ibid., 429.

33. Ibid., 446–47.

34. Roger Haight, "Appropriating Jesus Today," *Irish Theological Quarterly* 59, no. 4 (1993): 241–63.

35. Haight, "Case for Spirit Christology," 257–87. For another approach to the subject that notably departs from the classical christological and trinitarian framework, see Geoffrey Lampe, *God as Spirit*, 2d ed. (London: SCM Press, 1983).

36. John H. Wright, "Roger Haight's Spirit Christology," *Theological Studies* 53, no. 4 (December 1992): 729–35.

37. Roger Haight, *Jesus—Symbol of God* (Maryknoll, N.Y.: Orbis Books, 1999).

38. Denzinger and Schönmetzer, *Enchiridion Symbolorum*, 125.

39. Haight, *Jesus—Symbol of God*, 461.

40. Denzinger and Schönmetzer, *Enchiridion Symbolorum*, 302.

41. Haight, *Jesus—Symbol of God*, 455 n. 59.

✷ *Chapter 4* ✷

Process Christology—
Another Direction

W. Norman Pittenger

It was the commendation of Bishop John A. T. Robinson that opened the door to process thought and attracted me in the late 1960s to the work of the Anglican theologian W. Norman Pittenger (1905–97), whose little volume, *Process-Thought and Christian Faith*, is a splendid introduction to Christianity as seen through the eyes of process categories.[1] Process thought is grounded in the root conviction that becoming rather than being or substance is *the* underlying metaphysical category. Reality itself is constituted by processes or events that are associated with other processes or events in a series of relationships forming the very construct of the universe. Although a number of process thinkers are rather obscure in the estimate of those schooled in Thomistic and Aristotelian categories, Norman Pittenger has a way about him that makes access into this evolutionary mode of thinking more feasible, and even inviting. Professor David Tracy some years ago praised the process tradition as being perhaps a somewhat more adequate vehicle for interpreting the fundamental Christian insight that God is love, and for facilitating the introduction of a sense of change and evolution into theological dialogue.[2] As a matter of fact, he noted that the use of process categories for the reformulation of the declarations of Chalcedon seems rather promising.[3]

Pittenger, who taught at the General Theological Seminary in New York and at King's College, Cambridge, set out a reasonably full treatment of his Christology in a work called *The Word Incarnate* in 1959.[4] He begins with four central affirmations:

Jesus is truly human, having lived a genuinely human life. Whatever he did was done under authentically historical conditions.

Christ is truly divine. God was present and acting in the total reality of Jesus, and his disciples were convinced that God was there.

Jesus is one person. From the gospels it is clear that there was no duality in his life.

Jesus is related to the general action and revelation of God in the world. His coming was not just the consequence of humankind's fall.

The author makes it clear that the Chalcedonian formula calls for a restatement since it no longer speaks convincingly to us today, and he warns that we must not become proponents of a simply verbal orthodoxy.

While it is true that a good deal can be learned about God and his purpose from our day-to-day experience in the world, there are times when God makes a unique and intensive disclosure of himself, which leads to a whole new range of comprehension concerning the divine nature and purpose. The advent of Jesus was not only such a special event, but it was the definitive revelation of God to humankind. By definitive, Pittenger means that through the Christ event God has given us a clue to all that he has done and will do for humanity. It is the New Testament as handed down by the church that affords us knowledge of the life and doings of Jesus and allows us to enter into the experience of the disciples. Was the divinity objectively present in Christ's manhood or was this a subjective interpretation on the part of the disciples? Pittenger affirms that in the wholeness of Christ's humanity the very being of God was known to be present and at work.

Jesus is portrayed as one who conceived of his mission as the proclamation of the imminent advent of the kingdom of God, which would replace the kingdoms of the world, and that this would perhaps be realized in the immediate future. He urged his hearers to live in watchful anticipation while working in the present for the alleviation of the pain and misery of their neighbors. The question of Jesus' identity is not entirely clear from the gospel accounts, but he is without doubt the principal agent in the coming of the kingdom. As a matter of fact, he is the kingdom incarnate. From the outset, he carries the authority of a divinely sent messenger, although it is not entirely clear how he envisioned his own vocation. Pittenger affirms that Christ's identity as the second person of the Trinity is not found explicitly in the earliest New Testament documents, but it is germinally present there. Certain narratives, such as the birth stories and the story of the empty tomb, are more legendary than factual, but they do serve to heighten the significance of Jesus and his mission. Although the resurrection appearances are confined to those who believe in Christ, they do proclaim that he who died on Calvary is now alive forever.

The development of the doctrine concerning Jesus is recapitulated in the central affirmation of our faith that he is truly human and truly divine. The definitions of the four great ecumenical councils (Nicaea, Constantinople I, Ephesus, and Chalcedon) proclaimed that what we encounter in Christ is the divinity itself, and that his humanity is of the same stuff as our own. When we declare, however, that Jesus is truly God, truly man, and truly the personal union of these two natures, these statements allow for various interpretations. The Alexandrians stressed the unity of the natures in Christ so much that their eminent doctor, Cyril, was fond of speaking of the one nature of the Word incarnate. According to the Antiochian school, our Lord was a man in whom the Word of God dwelt. Theodore of Mopsuestia of the Antiochian persuasion apparently taught that the indwelling of God in Christ was superior in degree and duration, but not in essential character, to the indwelling of God realized in the saints.

After describing the work of Leontius of Byzantium (ca. 480–543) as he understood it, Pittenger is not persuaded that there is any real difference between Leontius's enhypostasia and anhypostasia (frequently attributed to Cyril), since neither explanation provides for any natural personalizing of Jesus' humanity. The failure to posit a true, conscious, human center in Christ's humanity is bound to lead to the serious distortion and reduction of that humanity. According to Pittenger, if the Word in any fashion takes the place of that creaturely center instead of working in and through it, we are moving in the direction of Monophysitism. For then, the humanity would be lost in the divinity that possesses it. If the humanity of Jesus receives its personal, human center in and through the Word, the inevitable consequence of this position is anhypostasia, or the impersonal humanity of Christ. The Antiochian school protested against an anhypostatic manhood, for the experiencing center of Jesus' human life would not be properly human.

The concept of person is described as having undergone important changes since the fourth and fifth centuries. Today personhood is defined as the psychological center of subjective experience and the center of self-consciousness and self-direction. The term *person,* or *hypostasis,* in those days referred to a distinguishable mode of being and operation, and it did not carry with it the psychological connotations that it does today.

When we define *person* to mean the psychological center of human experience, this is seen to be indispensable in the human being who is Jesus. The argument used against Apollinaris of Laodicea that what Christ did not assume, he did not redeem, seems most applicable in our case. If Jesus did not possess a distinctly human psychological center of earthly experience, how could he have redeemed this critical dimension of human life for us? Pittenger also attests that no viable view of the Incarnation can be structured on the notion that some special avenues of human knowledge and perception, some hidden omniscience not common to humankind, were present in Jesus, for this would exempt him from a good number of the critical limitations defining the human condition.

Pittenger does not address in detail the miraculous deeds that the gospels attribute to Jesus, except to say that they—especially the nature miracles—bear traces of heightening on the part of the primitive Christian community. He deals at some length with the christological position of Charles Hartshorne (1897–2000), one of the founding fathers of the process movement. In chapter eight of his *Reality as Social Process,* written in 1953, Hartshorne speaks of Jesus as a unique symbol of the Christian view of divine love. Though he affirms that the Incarnation enshrines significant religious truth, such statements as "Jesus was God" or the "divinity of Jesus" are too ambiguous to serve as essential declarations of Christian belief. No one, Hartshorne insists, can be man and in every sense God. This would be no mystery, but simple contradiction.[5] Pittenger, on the other hand, teaches that Christ's divinity is to be found in his humanity, not plainly visible, but as operative in and through it. There is in Jesus a continuous divine operation and action in his humanity.

At this point Pittenger attempts a restatement of Christology in process terms. He describes process thought as a philosophy of movement wherein the fact of "becoming" is the central ingredient, and he notes that God must somehow be related to this constant becoming. He describes Hartshorne's concept of God in the following manner: God is always himself and is constantly related to the world. Actually the world is in him and he moves the world by his love. God is affected by the world in which he works and is related to all things most intimately. Perfection for Hartshorne consists in being oneself, through experiencing the fullest and richest sort of relationship with everything else. This defines perfection for God as well as for humankind.

Process thinkers describe the movement that they see in the world as emergent evolution. This notion postulates the recurring appearance of the genuinely new within the course of evolution. Each higher level in this developmental process emerges with a genuine element of novelty about it. Thus it is called "emergent" evolution. The drive animating the entire process for Pittenger is the Logos, the self-expressive dimension of the Deity. God is seen as the circumambient reality in this panentheistic view of the world. This metaphysics, according to the process thinkers, provides the optimal basis for the Christian view of the world. The whole of reality is in God, and yet God is not identified with it. His being is more than and in no way exhausted by the universe.

Existentialism is the other philosophical trend that attracts Pittenger. Man cannot let himself fall into any preordained scheme or regimen. He cannot explain his existence for he was "thrown" into the world, and his overriding concern must be to be true to himself. To be an authentic person he must decide—he must give his own life direction and be truly engaged. If he lets others or the torrents raging around him determine his direction, he sinks to the level of animality. Among the existentialists there are atheists (Sartre) and believers (Marcel). What distinguishes the believers is their abiding openness to Ultimate Reality. For the Christian existentialist, Christ is the clue to the meaning of life. He is the one for whom we must decide, and the one who ultimately engages us. It is Pittenger's judgment that these two philosophical trends are not mutually exclusive but, rather, they complement each other. He expresses the wish that a new christological statement be forged out on the basis of these two contemporary philosophical approaches, process thought and existentialism. The countless diffused activities of God in and for the human family are concentrated in Christ who is the decisive expression of Eternal Reality. He is divine in that he actualizes in human nature that transcendental divine principle that is working at the root of man's being, but which is only partially expressed in other members of the human race. The unity of the divine and the human in Christ reveals in an exemplary fashion the essential meaning of the whole process, as it quickens the realization of final convergence between God and humankind.

As the early Church Fathers abandoned the language of the Bible that portrayed God as close at hand and at work in the world, they adopted—in Pittenger's judgment—a more philosophical and antiseptic mode of expression, a language that reflected only a very modest knowledge of human psychology. We need for our age a christological statement that emphasizes the closeness of God to humanity, and humanity's striving to reach fulfillment in God. Jesus must be portrayed as the creature who represents the full actualization of the image of God in humankind, the true man in whom the Word has a perfect means of human self-expression. Christ is the one who in the full integrity of his manhood is so open to the Word of God that the Word possesses in that manhood the perfect instrument through whom he can be active in the world. Moreover, the humanity of Christ is the way in which we have access, as nowhere else, to the inmost nature of the divine. Pittenger feels that the term *Son* is only appropriate to the incarnate Lord, for in the discussion of the Godhead in itself and its distinctions the title is somewhat confusing. In the mystery of God there are distinctions or relationships. The Word is the action of God in self-expression, revelation, and redemption, while the Holy Spirit is the response to this self-expression, revelation, and redemption. In the Godhead, then, are three distinctive and essential modes of being and activity that are eternal—the Unoriginate Source, the Word, and the Holy Spirit.

Pittenger feels free to adopt the language of Paul Tillich when he says that the manhood of Jesus is utterly transparent to the Ground of Being (i.e., God), so that in him a "New Being" has entered into human history. For Tillich essential manhood has become existential in Jesus, who is a genuine emergent for he is the one who brings forth a new being. The movement of God to man and of man to God reached its culmination and fulfillment in Christ. Pittenger defines the term *omooúsios* as follows: what we know of God in Jesus is substantially the same as whatever there is of the divine operation anywhere else in creation, and the same as the Divine Reality itself. In other words, whatever is divine in Jesus is not a derivative or lesser divinity, but the same divinity as that of the Unoriginate Source. This process thinker conceives of the universe as being the result of a continuous process in which God reveals himself in creation, while Jesus is identified as the decisive revelation of the character and will of God.

Pittenger teaches that the eternal Word did exist with the Unoriginate Source before the birth of Jesus, but the Word did not supplant the human consciousness of Jesus. Nor is the Word his soul, his mind, or his ego. Pittenger asks how the presence of God in us and in Christ is different, and he responds that the difference is one of degree and not of kind. If Christ were different in kind, he would not really be able to identify with the common human condition. Pittenger then asks whether or not the work realized in the Incarnation has a wider application beyond our world and our human family on this planet. His response is that life on other planets, although possible, is still just a matter of speculation. If there is rational life elsewhere in the cosmos, it is not clear how Jesus would be related to such life, since Christ is not the whole of God's action in creation. Jesus, in a sense, defines but does not confine God in his relationship to the universe.

The question of the purpose of the Incarnation is not, according to Pittenger, to be restricted to redemption from sin. He holds that the primary purpose of the Word becoming flesh is the completion and the crowning of creation. The restoration and rehabilitation of human nature and its reconciliation with God, although important, is not the Incarnation's primary goal.

On the last page of his 1970 study, *Christology Reconsidered*, Pittenger states that this would be his final effort in the area of Christology.[6] In this work he reaffirms that Jesus was a genuine, historically conditioned, totally human being, and that the relationship between God and this man involved the most complete interpenetration, after the analogy of a personal union. That is, in the total being and action of Christ, both God and man are simultaneously and continually present and at work. Although we cannot take the miracle stories in the gospels at face value, Pittenger confesses that there was something behind them, but they were no doubt enhanced in the telling by the primitive Christian community. Jesus surely believed that certain kinds of illnesses (i.e., emotional disorders) were caused by demonic possession. In a number of cases, after he conveyed to those so afflicted the assurance of God's loving acceptance, these individuals in a good number of instances were apparently cured. However, it must be noted that the worldview of Jesus' day has broken down, along with much of the terminology and the thought patterns. It is our role to communicate the gospel message in a language that is comprehensible to the people of our time. We must take the conceptual patterns stated in static terms of substance and convert them into terminology that reflects activity and movement.

The gospels reveal a rather striking and highly probable portrait of a true man who preached, taught, healed, lived humbly, announced the kingdom, was ultimately crucified, and was believed by his followers to have risen from the dead. In the judgment of Pittenger, there are three things that we can say with assurance: (1) We are dealing with a genuine historical figure (2) about whom we know a great deal, and (3) what we know about him is in continuity with the primitive community's evaluation of him. Was Jesus without qualification God? Pittenger's answer is certainly not. He finds it impossible to accept either an anhypostatic Christology (no human person in Jesus), or an enhypostatic Christology (the presence in Christ of only a divine person who "personalizes" his humanity). In either case, the Lord's humanity would be compromised, for there would be no human psychological center, and thus he would not be fully human at all. The union between God and man in Jesus is one of total interpenetration. That is, both God and man are continuously present and operative in the one whom we call Jesus.

Pittenger describes the initial aim of Jesus—what he was originally destined to become—as the virtual embodiment of Love-in-action. This aim was embraced by Christ as his own subjective aim, and throughout his life he totally identified himself with it. He was deeply conscious of his background and was fully aware of his relationship with others. His teaching involved a reediting of the religious and moral tradition of the Jews, correcting its differences and bringing out its deepest meaning. His disciples received him as a teacher and a prophet, and after his death they identified him as the Messiah. God was present and acted with unique intensity toward humankind in the event of Jesus Christ, who is the outstanding example of the ceaseless love of God in all of creation. It is true that we cannot limit God's revelation to Jesus alone, for it is possible for humankind to achieve an authentic life without access to Christ. Indeed, it is unthinkable that God would not provide an opportunity for each and every human person—even those not encountering Jesus—to achieve authentic existence or salvation.

How is it, then, that Christ is decisive? From the Letter to the Ephesians it is obvious that the church is the continuation of the Incarnation and God's method of extending the activity of Jesus through time. The goal is to bring more and more of the human family into oneness with God, in terms of that specific spirit that is revealed out of the life of Jesus. The "at-one-ing" of God with humankind through the work of Christ is continued and extended through the church. This is not to deny that there are offerings of life and at-one-ment available to those outside the church. However, Jesus and his continuing activity in the church remain the exemplar of the at-one-ment process operative in the world. This is Pittenger's explanation of the decisive role of Christ. The divine action in the world of creative advance is given expression in a distinctive and unique fashion in the Christ event and in its continuation in the church. The qualitative distinctiveness of the Jesus event is the revelation through him of pure unbounded love that is very different in terms of intensity compared with other manifestations of love.

In and through the life of Jesus, God's chief way of acting centers on persuasion or lure, rather than coercion, thus providing the clue to the divine nature. Employing process terminology, Pittenger notes that it is God who provides the initial aim for human beings (i.e., the optimal self-realization of each individual), as well as the lure (i.e., the attraction to that aim). Each person can then decide to embrace his or her initial aim and respond to its lure, thus making this initial aim his or her subjective aim. The degree to which individuals wholeheartedly pursue and assimilate their subjective aim throughout their lives determines the extent to which they attain human fulfillment. As a process thinker, Pittenger continues to define himself as a panentheist, that is, one who holds that the universe is included in God's being although the universe does not exhaust God's being or creativity. He reaffirms his belief in Christ by asserting that Jesus was a human and historical event, and the point at which God acts in a manner unparalleled elsewhere. This, according to our author, is what the early Church Fathers meant when they declared that Christ was truly God and truly man.

John B. Cobb Jr.

After thirty-two years as a professor of process theology at the School of Theology at Claremont, California, John Cobb (b. 1925) retired in 1990. In 1975 he published his *Christ in a Pluralistic Age*, which is his most ample treatment of Christology.[7] In the introduction he identifies himself as a disciple of Alfred North Whitehead and admits that he is not attempting to formulate a complete Christology. Cobb maintains that life can best be organized around the process that he terms *creative transformation*, which is embodied in Christ in a preeminent way. A divine reality was present in Jesus, and for that reason he is called "Christ." His abiding concern for others was perhaps the most significant manifestation of his transcendence. After Dietrich Bonhoeffer (1906–45) the deity has been rather consistently reflected in the suffering Christ who became one with the outcasts and the oppressed of society. In the irrepressible surge among the downtrodden toward liberation, Christ can be observed.

Cobb stresses throughout the importance of making peace with religious pluralism, which need not necessarily lead to religious relativism. The affirmation of pluralism reflects an openness to other traditions, which has been a rare mindset in the history of religions. Christ should not be identified, according to Cobb, with any one system of belief that came into being under historically conditioned circumstances, but rather with the creative transformation of the whole theological enterprise that is moving us beyond every established denominational form.

Cobb then deals with Jesus as the incarnation of the Logos, that is, the incarnation of the divine. The Logos is defined as a dimension of God himself, the cosmic principle of order, the source of purpose and growth. In its transcendence it is boundless and eternal, but as immanent in creation it provides just the proper creative impulse optimal for every changing situation. Every human action or event incorporates elements from previous experiences, and it is the Logos that provides the new element, the lure that brings forth something novel. The Logos is the source of novelty, as one experience gives way to the next. To the extent that the new impulse is successful, we witness what Cobb calls a creative transformation. The Logos is the force within all things attracting them toward further actualization. Although the immanent Logos is active in all of creation, Cobb describes Christ as the most intensive expression of the Logos. He affirms that as one event or action follows another, there can only be either further actualization or erosion, depending on whether or not the lure of the Logos is responded to or ignored.

One can attribute to the Logos the transcendent characteristics of the deity, but the Logos is also active in the world as the principle of creative transformation. Cobb describes the Logos as an eternal dimension or facet of the deity, immersed in the world as the principle of continuing actualization in creation. He claims that substantialist modes of thought have impeded our comprehension of divine immanence. As expressed in created reality, God is the Logos who functions in the world as the immanence of the transcendent. The role of the Logos is to insert tension between what has been and what can be, thus challenging the fixed order to make way for the new. At each moment it is tending toward the optimal actualization for every given situation. If the creative impulses of the Logos are rejected, the possibilities of growth are thwarted. It is the Logos that makes us strive on and rejects our desire for stability.

Cobb reaffirms that Jesus is the privileged presence and expression of the Logos in the world. This is what he means when he calls Jesus "the Christ." Faith is the primal response to the acceptance of Jesus as the Christ, the new and ever-inviting divine reality. The meaning of love for Christians is exemplified by Jesus, whose life radiated a perennial concern for others, particularly the downtrodden and the oppressed. Our encounters with the words and actions of Jesus today through the New Testament provide us with the possibility of creative transformation. Wherever and whenever the words of Jesus are heard and taken seriously, an undying restlessness is introduced into human history. Faith for Jesus consisted in his personal response to the demands of his own proclamation, in terms of absolute trust and obedience. His preaching focused for the most part on the coming of the kingdom of God, which calls forth a decision now for repentance and a change of heart.

In spite of the fact that he spoke of the future, his expectations were not very clearly delineated. However, Jesus is portrayed as creatively transforming the Judaism of his day.

Cobb then undertakes to expand and deepen our understanding of the relation of Jesus to Christ, who is the perfect incarnation of the Logos. Without ceasing to be fully human, Jesus' ego was co-formed by the presence of the Logos, with the properties of each nature being preserved and being conjoined in one person. If the substance categories are put aside, it can be said that in Jesus, "who is a single person, the presence of the Logos and of his own past coalesce in each new act of self constitution."[8] In Cobb's view, the relation of believers to Jesus the Christ is expressed by St. Paul in a number of ways, but none so forcefully as in his poignant phrase, "in Christ." Through his passion, death, and resurrection, Jesus has created what Cobb calls "a field of force" into which believers can enter. To put on Christ is to initiate the process of identifying with him. To be in Christ is to realize Christ as the growing center of one's existence, to share in some degree in the distinctive relationship between Christ and God. Through Jesus we share in grace, peace, and joy with God, and we are taken up into the very sonship of Christ. According to Cobb we no longer have to justify ourselves because we are justified in Jesus. Paul was convinced that in the very center of our justified existence we discover the presence of Christ. No other New Testament writer has attempted to describe the profound identification between Christ and the justified believer as has Paul. In Cobb's estimate there are two traditions concerning Jesus coming out of the early church. The first is that of Jesus as teacher who reveals God and his will for us, for example, Justin, Cyril of Jerusalem, and John Chrysostom. According to the second tradition, Jesus is the one in whom the Logos entered history in an intensive manner to overcome the powers of evil by virtue of the field of force that he created, for example, Irenaeus, Athanasius, and Cyril of Alexandria. Through Jesus' words and field of force, the Logos is revealed in and through Jesus as the power of creative transformation.

Although Rudolf Bultmann taught that Jesus possessed a predominantly prophetic consciousness, it must be said that Jesus, unlike the prophets, proclaimed his message on his own authority. Cobb portrays Jesus as an individual who dared to act in the place of God. Although the Logos is incarnate in all things, the mode and function of that incarnation vary enormously. In a singular and intensive way, the divine Logos—a real dimension of the deity—was present and active in Jesus. In the key events of his life there was no tension in Jesus between his ego and the ever-new promptings of the Logos within him. The conscious center of his existence was at one with the divine aim, and thus God was immediately operative in the action. This unique structure of Jesus' existence was evident especially in the critical events of his life. Although there was on occasion some tension between his ego and the direction indicated by the Logos inasmuch as he was fully human, the "novum" in Jesus consisted in the full and singular presence of the Logos, and in the full and total union between the Logos and Jesus.

In Cobb's judgment Jesus operated from a very unique perspective. His ego was co-constituted (i.e., given shape and form) by the incarnate Logos. God's purpose for him was also his purpose, and not a threat to his personal goals as is often the case with us. Through our faith in him we are drawn into Jesus' field of force, confident that we will be justified, that is, rightly related to God. And we can only imagine what our lives would be if our egos would be so identified with the impulses of the Logos within us that at each moment we would be growing beyond our past and into a future that would completely actualize our human potential.

The church's understanding of Christ is reflected in the creeds of the early centuries. Cobb adopts Reginald Fuller's presentation in explaining the three stages of the initial Christian understanding of Christ.[9] The earliest Palestinian Christians stressed Jesus' earthly ministry, his death, resurrection, and ascension, and were awaiting his return. In the Hellenistic Jewish testimony the sending of Jesus was added as a preface to the narrative of his public life and death, his reign as Kurios, and the expectation of the parousia. Finally, the gentile formulation began with the preexistence of the Logos, the Incarnation, resurrection, ascension, his reign as Lord, and his ultimate return. Cobb notes that whereas the Nicene Creed described how Jesus is related to God, the creed of Chalcedon dealt with the relationship between Jesus and his human nature.

One of the earliest doctrinal deviations was modalism (third century), which treated the Father, Son, and Holy Spirit merely as the three forms in which the Godhead appears. Sabellius (third century) even arranged the modes in chronological order, that is, the Father created the world, the Son saved the world, and the Holy Spirit inspires believers. The Alexandrian scholar Origen taught that the Father generated the Logos, and from the Logos came the Spirit. The Logos was a divine being, but subordinate to the Father. The presbyter Arius from Alexandria precipitated the Council of Nicaea (325) by teaching that the Logos was the first of all creatures, but a creature nonetheless. Nicaea declared that the Logos was of the same substance as the Father, and was begotten eternally. John Cobb affirms that the Logos is indeed fully God.

The two basic approaches to Christology came out of Antioch and Alexandria. Whereas Antioch began with the man Jesus, Alexandria started with the divine Logos. The Antiochians held to a moral union between Jesus and God and spoke of the Logos as fully indwelling in Jesus. For them the divine and the human substances were extremely closely linked, but they still retained their distinct integrity. On the other hand, the Alexandrians began with the divine Logos and inquired into the manner in which the Logos assumed a human nature. They proclaimed the immanence of God in Jesus, but their substantialist formulations left them open to the suggestion that some human element in Jesus had been replaced by the Logos. Although Cyril of Alexandria wrote occasionally of the "one nature of the incarnate Word," after his death his followers taught that Jesus was composed *from* two natures and in the union became only one divine nature. The Council of Chalcedon (451) articulated the two natures/one person formula for Jesus, but the compromise remained ambiguous—capable, according to Cobb, of being read in one way by the Alexandrians and in another by the Antiochians.

Large segments of the Alexandrian contingent held fast to their monophysite faith (i.e., that in Christ there was only one nature— a divine nature), and they eventually became the Coptic church of Egypt. Significant numbers of the Antiochian party who were unable to accept the wording of Chalcedon—because for them the two natures in Christ constituted only a moral unity—broke off to form the Nestorian church, which still exists today, for example, in Iraq. It can be said that there were times prior to the Islamic and Mongol invasions when the monophysite and Nestorian churches were roughly comparable in size to the Chalcedonian church. Cobb notes that the fundamentally Alexandrian interpretation, confirmed at the Second Council of Constantinople (553), prevailed and the doctrine of what he terms "the impersonal humanity" of Jesus became traditional.

For John Cobb, the profession of the Chalcedonian faith that Jesus was one person, fully human and fully divine, without confusion, change, division, or separation, could only be believed by the sacrifice of the intellect. Although the Reformation of the sixteenth century did not modify or reject the creed, the Enlightenment did, by affirming a purely human Jesus. For the liberal Protestants of the nineteenth century, Jesus was a man like other men, except that he enjoyed a unique presence of God in him. With the rise of neo-orthodoxy in the twentieth century, the problem of accepting the classical Chalcedonian formulation reappeared, and it again became problematic to affirm what Cobb refers to as "a properly human selfhood" in Jesus. Cobb expresses admiration for the Catholic theologian Piet Schoonenberg because he teaches that it is not the human that became hypostatic in the divine person, but rather it was the divine that became hypostatic in the human person of Jesus. In Cobb's view, the optimal realization of the union between the immanent Logos and humanity was achieved in Jesus, because his humanity was in perfect harmony with the lure of the Logos. This union was such that the Logos and Jesus' humanity are joined in the one person who is Jesus. This full coalescence between Jesus' humanity and the Logos gives to this person an enhanced freedom which, it seems, knows no parallel in human history.

In addressing the question of Christ as the image of hope, John Cobb asserts that Friedrich Schleiermacher (1768–1834) was one of the first theologians to portray Christian faith as the full realization of our potentialities in this present life, rather than anticipating an existence beyond death. During the nineteenth century the scientific community seemed to find little room for the supernatural, and this in turn prompted even Christian academics to devote little time to the consideration of the afterlife. The emphasis was upon the quasi-limitless perfectibility of humankind in this life. However, after World War I, these vaunted claims of human progress seemed rather empty and even almost bizarre. With the advent of the neo-orthodoxy of Karl Barth and Emil Brunner, and especially with the resurgence of a theology of hope (e.g., Jürgen Moltmann) after World War II, the idea of an unlimited future began to expand once again and the prospects of creative transformation opened up new horizons. However, Cobb admonishes that fidelity to Christ calls Christians now to a deepening involvement in the transformation of the secular world, for it is here that the creative transformation of Christ currently operates. He analyzes the different approaches of Willi Marxsen and Wolfhart Pannenberg to the resurrection of Jesus and sides with the latter in affirming an actual resurrection from the dead for Jesus—without which there would be no Christian faith. For Pannenberg there will be in the new creation a community of persons who will enjoy the company of Christ in God. In this regard, Cobb parts company with his mentor, Whitehead, who seems to place the eschatological future within the confines of our own present world and time.

In 1990 John Cobb published a short rendering of his Christology "in story form," which enables a wider range of readers to appreciate the direction of his thought.[10] He stresses again the approach of the Antiochians versus the Alexandrians. While the first group taught that the Logos came to dwell in a human being, the latter insisted that the Logos assumed, that is, took to itself, an "impersonal humanity" that it personalized. The definition of Chalcedon, which according to Cobb is more Alexandrian than Antiochian, leaves us with a paradox or a mystery that has baffled believers ever since. There is for Cobb a significant difference between saying that God dwells in Jesus in a unique and unparalleled manner, and saying that Jesus is God.[11]

A Summary

Alfred North Whitehead and Charles Hartshorne in large part served as the inspiration for the development of W. Norman Pittenger's process theology. His extensive work, *The Word Incarnate*, represents a very accessible approach to his christological thought. Pittenger sets out the parameters of his study by affirming that although Jesus is truly human and truly divine, the Chalcedonian formulas are in need of a reworking because they no longer speak to us convincingly today. He warns us against becoming too attached to what he calls a merely verbal orthodoxy.

Dr. Pittenger's final effort in the field of Christology was published in 1970, *Christology Reconsidered*. He again emphasizes the need to express the gospel message and the meaning of Jesus in a language that is comprehensible to the people of our time. The conceptual patterns laid out in static terms of substance must be converted into terminology that is reflective of activity and movement. Pittenger poses the question as to whether Jesus was without qualification God, and he responds, "Certainly not!" He finds it impossible to accept either an anhypostatic Christology (i.e., no human person in Jesus), or an enhypostatic Christology (i.e., the presence in Christ of only a divine person who "personalizes" his humanity). In either case, the Lord's humanity would be compromised for there would be no human psychological center. The union between God and man in Jesus is one of total interpenetration. Both God and man are continuously present and active in him.

Another influential study, *Christ in a Pluralistic Age*, was published by John B. Cobb in 1975. He, too, considers himself a disciple of Alfred North Whitehead. It is Cobb's contention that life can most effectively take shape in and through the process he calls creative transformation, which is embodied in Christ in a preeminent manner. A divine reality was present and active in Jesus, and thus he was called "Christ." Jesus is described as the incarnation of the Logos, and the Logos is termed a dimension of God himself. As immanent in creation, the Logos provides the lure that brings forth the new elements in creation and in human activity.

The role of the Logos is to insert tension between what has been and what can be, challenging the fixed order to make way for the new. In every moment the Logos is tending toward the ideal actualization for every given occasion. Without ceasing to be human, Jesus' ego was co-formed by the presence of the Logos, with the properties of each nature preserved and conjoined in one person. Through his passion, death, and resurrection, Jesus has created what Cobb refers to as a "field of force" into which believers can enter and experience creative transformation. To put on Christ is to initiate the process of identifying with him, and to begin to share in the distinctive relationship between Christ and God. In Cobb's view we no longer need to justify ourselves because we are already justified in Jesus. Although his mentor, Whitehead, seems to exclude the possibility of an eschatological future beyond death, Cobb sides with Wolfhart Pannenberg in affirming an actual resurrection both for Jesus and for his faithful followers who will enjoy the company of Christ in God.

Notes

1. Norman Pittenger, *Process-Thought and Christian Faith* (New York: Macmillan, 1968).

2. Tracy, *Analogical Imagination*, 439–40.

3. Ibid., 336 n. 25.

4. W. Norman Pittenger, *The Word Incarnate* (New York: Harper and Brothers, 1959).

5. Charles Hartshorne, *Reality as Social Process* (Glencoe, Ill.: Free Press, 1953), 150–54.

6. Norman Pittenger, *Christology Reconsidered* (London: SCM Press, 1970), 153.

7. John B. Cobb Jr., *Christ in a Pluralistic Age* (Philadelphia: Westminster Press, 1975).

8. Ibid., 171.

9. Reginald Fuller, *Foundations of New Testament Christology* (New York: Scribner's, 1965), 243–57.

10. John B. Cobb Jr., *Doubting Thomas: Christology in Story Form* (New York: Crossroad, 1990).

11. For another recent approach to process Christology, see Marjorie H. Suchocki's *God. Christ. Church. A Practical Guide to Process Theology* (New York: Crossroad, 1989), 87–125.

✳ Chapter 5 ✳

Jesus as Liberator—
Liberation Christologies

Jon Sobrino

The first of the liberation theologians to be discussed is a Spanish Basque by birth, who studied in the United States and Germany. A longtime resident of El Salvador, Sobrino (b. 1925) has taught at the Central American University in San Salvador. His first significant work was *Christology at the Crossroads*, published in Spanish in 1976 and translated into English in 1978.[1] Sobrino begins by situating his study within the context of those authors who had a positive effect upon him. He has praise for the christological contribution of Karl Rahner but notes that he cannot be considered a political theologian. Rahner's emphasis is placed upon Christ's Incarnation and resurrection rather than on his passion and death. Jürgen Moltmann, whom Sobrino also admires, began his theologizing with the God of the future, and then turned his attention to the crucified God, that is, from hope in the future to the following of the historical Jesus.[2]

Sobrino affirms that Christology in Latin America has been strongly affected by the development of liberation theology, which has faced up to the Latin American reality of underdevelopment and widespread oppression. In that part of the world, Jesus has come to be identified as the "Liberator" who is to free his people from the political, social, and economic bondage in which they find themselves. Latin American theologians at this time are not especially interested in clarifying people's understanding of the traditional christological problems, such as the hypostatic union and the human and divine knowledge in Christ. Many see traditional theology as largely uninvolved with the real issues that touch the lives of the people. Rather, emphasis has been placed on those areas of Christology that can be focused on the paradigm of lib-

160

eration. Their concentration is centered therefore on the historical Jesus rather than on the glorified Christ.

In the estimate of Sobrino and others, we are now in the second phase of the Enlightenment. While the first phase effected the liberation of reason from dogmatic faith, the second looks toward the liberation of the whole person from a religious view that did not take a firm stand against pervasive social, economic, and political oppression. The mere verbal proclamation of God without accompanying action to realize the coming of his kingdom on earth is not sufficient. Orthopraxis must take priority over orthodoxy. Jesus announced that the kingdom of God is at hand and advocated a restructuring of the basic relationships among human beings. His cures, his miracles, and his forgiving sins are signs of the arrival of the kingdom (Matt. 11:5). The miracles are not so much exceptions to the known laws of nature. Rather, they are clear testimony to the active presence of God's saving action. The same liberating activity of the kingdom is revealed through the forgiving of sins, since those forgiven were living under oppression of one sort or another.

Jesus' attitude toward sin has two dimensions. He was not only committed to the healing of personal sin, but also to the eradication of social sin that fractures the bonds of brotherhood among humans and leads to oppression and servitude. It must be noted that Christ's anathemas were principally directed against the use of power, for example, by the Pharisees, the rich, and the priests. Sobrino asserts that our contact with Christ is not to be experienced primarily through cultic adoration, but through the following of Jesus in the day-by-day service of the kingdom. It is Sobrino's desire to avoid any Christology involving mere orthodoxy and an exclusively cultic relationship with God. We must live our faith through a concrete "praxis" that follows in the footsteps of Jesus, and we must be prepared to work for the transformation of the social and economic structures that enslave the poor and the helpless. We must work toward the day when God is acknowledged as Father of all, and when all humans deal with each other as brothers and sisters.

In Sobrino's judgment Jesus probably saw himself and his mission in the light of various Old Testament figures, especially the prophets, and later in his public life, as bearing a resemblance to the suffering servant of Yahweh. Possibly the only term he applied to himself was that of the "Son of man." The gospels do not provide us with enough data to determine clearly what Jesus thought about himself. However, we do know that his relationship with the Father constituted the central element of his identity. This "Abba" rapport reflects his absolute trust in the Father. He lived his life in and through that relationship, which was wholly different from that enjoyed by any other human. We can only plumb the depths of Jesus by observing his relationship with his Father, which was characterized by complete and unqualified trust and obedience.

As an introduction to his consideration of Jesus' faith, Sobrino notes that the gospels do not give us reason to predicate infused knowledge or the beatific vision of Christ, whose human knowledge was acquired through his life experiences. Although Thomas Aquinas held that Jesus did not possess faith because he enjoyed the beatific vision from the first moment of his conception (*Summa Theologiae*, III, q. 7. a. 3), our author attests that the observation in the Letter to the Hebrews (12:2) gives a strong indication that Jesus not only believed but has to be considered as the "originator, the pioneer, and the perfecter" of our faith. His faith constituted the very mode of his existence, and it underwent a process of development throughout his life. Sobrino teaches that there were two distinct phases in Christ's public life: the initial period wherein he preached and performed wonders that revealed the coming and the presence of the kingdom, and the second phase wherein the crowds abandoned him and the Jewish leaders refused to accept him. Sobrino refers to the crisis in Galilee, when Jesus departs for Caesarea Philippi and the Decapolis, as the turning point (Mark 8:27–33). After this Jesus concentrated on the disciples, while his conflicts with the priests and the Pharisees intensified. The coming of the kingdom seemed farther away and Jesus began to speak more and more of his own death at the hands of his enemies. Discipleship now became a summons to take up the cross with him.

Sobrino prefers to locate the temptations of Jesus later on in his public life rather than at the outset, for he feels that the urge to use power in the exercise of his mission was present through most of Christ's life. It was this overcoming of temptations throughout his earthly history that brought about in him a new and concrete sonship. Jesus affirmed that he did not know the day or the hour of the beginning of the endtime (Mark 13:32). His attitude was one of profound and exclusive confidence in the Father, and his response was nothing short of total obedience to the working out of his mission regarding the coming of the kingdom. Sobrino is inclined to describe Christ's divinity not so much in ontological terms, but rather in terms of his relationship with the Father, for that is what constitutes the very essence of his person. It is this unique and unrepeatable relationship with the Father that constitutes his participation in the divinity. Jesus becomes the Son of God in and through the unfolding of his human history.

In order to explain Christ's notion of God, we must look to his attitude in prayer, which assimilated a number of Old Testament traditions. Like the prophets, he was partial to the poor and to the downtrodden. From the apocalyptic tradition he drew the yearning for the renewal of all things by God at the end of time, and in the sapiential tradition he found the emphasis on the creative, loving God who allows the just and the unjust to grow up together. Jesus even experienced the absence of God in his prayer in the garden of Gethsemane and on the cross. In his parables he identifies God as a gracious and forgiving Father (Luke 15:11–24), but he makes very clear that God will not be manipulated through the use of hypocritical traditions that nullify his word (Mark 7:1–13). Those who had God neatly boxed into their traditions were excoriated by Jesus, who manifested from the outset a preference for the poor, the captives, the blind, and the oppressed (Luke 4:18–19). He denounced the Pharisees and the doctors of the law who made a habit of dominating others in no uncertain terms (Luke 11:37–53).

Cultic worship, in Sobrino's judgment, is inefficacious if it is not accompanied by the practice of love for other people (Hosea 6:6; Matt. 5:23–24). It is in the praxis of love for neighbor that we come to experience the transcendence of the Christian God. In the Gospel of Luke, the teaching on the greatest commandment (10:25–27) is followed immediately by the parable of the good Samaritan (10:29–37). Paul declares that the whole law is embodied in the injunction, "Love your neighbor as yourself" (Gal. 5:14). The first Letter of John insists that our response to God's love for us must be our love for one another (1 John 4:11). The locale of our praxis of love must not be some vague contemplative attitude, but the genuine and ongoing commitment to assist the poor and the oppressed in our world. For without the continuing praxis of love for our fellow men, we shall not be able to pray to the God of Jesus.

Sobrino emphasizes that the scandal of the cross was softened almost from the beginning, while the title "servant of Yahweh" was soon replaced with epithets reflecting Christ as risen from the dead. Throughout the history of theology, the stark message of the cross has been bypassed in favor of a Christian spirituality that highlighted the mystique of the cross and stressed the resurrection, which is not the last word in our salvation history because God is not yet all in all. Christian life must always be seen as a process of participating in the same painful course that characterized the earthly life of Jesus.

How then are we to understand Christ's resurrection? After reviewing briefly the positions of Bultmann, Marxsen, Pannenberg, and Boff, Sobrino seems to favor the approach of Jürgen Moltmann, who not only points to the resurrection of Jesus as the commencement of the universal resurrection but also sees it as the vindication of God's justice and the challenge to search for justice in the history of suffering. The New Testament accounts of the appearances of the risen Lord stress the conferral of a mission that includes a commitment to contribute to the transformation of the world that is to be achieved, to some extent, through our efforts. Because the world is as yet unredeemed, our praxis must seek to transform it. As we respond to this obligation, we must accept suffering and frustration in the face of contradiction. The grace offered by the risen Christ is not cheap grace, but costly grace that must take the cross seriously.

Sobrino expresses regret that Christology has for a very long time focused on the exaltation of Jesus here and now, and on a liturgy that views cultic worship as the preferred way to approach God, thus deemphasizing the abiding obligation of praxis directed at the elimination of injustice and oppression in the world. Further, we must see the sonship of Jesus more in terms of his concrete self-surrender through the various challenges and conflicts of his historical career, rather than in terms of some initial descent. He notes that in some Hellenistic communities, for example, Corinth, the risen Lord became so all-important that any interest in the historical Jesus seemed to vanish. Union with Christ was seen as being achieved no longer through concrete discipleship, but rather through participation in the sacraments. Paul corrected their views by affirming that following Jesus means conforming our lives to his. Christian freedom is a freedom to serve and to suffer, which necessitates immersing our lives in the task of transforming our world.

There is a clear distinction, in Sobrino's estimate, between religion and Christian faith. For him, religion involves a view of reality wherein everything is already given at the outset. God has certain definite and fixed characteristics, such as omnipotence and omniscience, and there is a privileged locale for direct access to the Deity, that is, Christian worship. A code of conduct is set out which, if followed, allows people to assure themselves of God's favor. Christian faith, on the other hand, is very different. The meaning of the essential elements is not given at the beginning. There is no direct access to God through the medium of cultic worship, for this can only come indirectly through service to human beings, particularly to the poor and the oppressed. Finally, there is no mechanism that will achieve a certain recompense or reward, because one must surrender all security and abandon oneself to God. Christian faith does not have a religious structure, and when it takes one on it ceases to be Christian. Sobrino attests that excessive concentration on the risen Christ has led Christian faith to take on a religious structure that has made it possible for Christians to forget about the historical Jesus of Nazareth.

In a number of later New Testament writings, for example, the Letter to the Ephesians and the Pastorals, the church occupies center stage while the figure of the historical Jesus recedes into the background. Sobrino notes that the Christian community began to see itself as a new religion, like Judaism and various species of paganism. Under the influence of the second-century apologists and thinkers like Clement of Alexandria (ca. 150–ca. 215), Christian faith was transformed into a vast theory of Christianity that attempted to explain the whole of reality. The emphasis placed on the Logos, the Word of God, overlooked the Jesus of history and neglected the wonder of the cross. Later on in the fourth century, Christianity became the official religion of the state. However, faith—to be authentic—must be a critical, praxis-oriented discipline deeply embedded in discipleship. The past has shown that Christian faith rather easily turns into religion if we neglect the concrete history of Jesus.

Liberation theology, in Sobrino's judgment, has not especially concerned itself with christological themes from a strictly dogmatic point of view. He notes that his book is not primarily structured around dogma. Although he expresses allegiance to the Chalcedonian formulations, he asks whether these markedly onto logical declarations threaten the position of Jesus in the real world of human beings. The language of 451 C.E. does not reflect the conflict-ridden life of Jesus and the process of human development that he experienced. His unique relationship with the Father is not really explained in any depth. Nor is Christ's unconditional trust in the Father given adequate attention. These conciliar statements miss much of the New Testament data that put flesh and blood on the historical figure of Jesus. For Sobrino, the divinity of Christ consists in the modality of his personal relationship with the Father which works itself out in history. In his obedient self-surrender to the Father to the very end of his earthly life, Jesus gradually took on his concrete personhood. He fashioned himself slowly and painstakingly as the Son of God. For Sobrino, he virtually became the Son of God in and through his concrete history. Jesus is thereby not only the Son of God, but the way to the Father, inasmuch as he reveals the very process of filiation, that is, the manner in which human beings can and do become children of God. The most pressing task of Christology is to reorientate believers so that their lives can reflect a continuing, advancing experience of discipleship.

Sobrino then attempts to fashion the outline of what he terms a "historical Christology." He notes that in Europe more recent political theologians, such as Johann-Baptist Metz, have been moving in this direction.[3] The same can be said of South American scholars such as Leonardo Boff. Are the gospels something for the intellect alone, or are they words to be realized in praxis as well? Is Christ first and foremost the sacrament of the Father, or is he primarily the way to the Father? Sobrino favors the latter approach. His Christology is less contemplative and more praxis oriented. This approach takes priority over any "intentional" sort of contact with Christ through prayer or worship. The theologies of liberation affirm that emphasizing the risen Lord and disregarding the historical Jesus turn Christianity into an abstract and largely theoretical discipline.

Jesus was situated in a world that bore cultural and social similarities to that of present-day Latin America, and it manifested a similar yearning for liberation, according to Sobrino. Christology must follow the events of Jesus' life in chronological order.

Before the Galilean crisis he freely engaged himself in proclaiming the good news, healing, comforting, inspiring, and also gathering together his disciples. After the crisis in Galilee (Mark 8:27–33; Matt. 16:13–20), which resulted in his departure from his homeland and his movement north across the Jordan toward Caesarea Philippi, changes began to take place in Christ's attitude, in the approach to his mission, and even in his conception of God and the kingdom.

In the first phase of his public life, he employed miracles as sources of power and signs of God's presence that were experienced as liberation from some type of oppression. After the crisis in Galilee, when he became keenly aware of the various pockets of opposition welling up against him, Jesus sensed that the sin-ridden situation was beginning to deprive him of his power. Sobrino affirms that Christ then began to feel a new sort of power coming over him, the power that springs from the sacrifice of one's life for others out of love. In the second phase of his ministry Jesus calls for the acceptance of his being, with his disappointments and failures, as he moves into an unknown future over which he has little control. Discipleship from this point on means following Jesus when it is not clear what part he will have in the ushering in of the kingdom.

This theologian does not deal with what he terms the absolute consciousness of Jesus (i.e., what he thought of himself). Rather, he focuses on Christ's relational consciousness, which would prompt us to deduce his thought patterns from his attitude toward the Father and toward the kingdom. Jesus had a unique personal consciousness regarding the kingdom and his role in its coming. He spoke on his own authority and expected people to follow him. His singular relationship with the Father differentiated him from all other humans, but it is not clear that he knew himself to be the eternal Son. Jesus' consciousness vis-à-vis the kingdom and vis-à-vis the Father evolved through his life experiences, and thus he became the prototypical human being and God's firstborn Son. The Letter to the Hebrews movingly describes Jesus' faith as a loyal surrender of himself to the Father throughout the varied experiences of his earthly existence.

Christ unmasked the domination of others in the name of religion on the part of the Jewish priests and the Pharisees. He emphasized that individuals could not feel secure simply through the performance of certain works, and he desacralized the locale where access to God could be achieved. For him such access was realized through the practice of liberating the poor and the oppressed from their bondage. Christ's conflict with the religious leaders of his day was deep indeed, and he was condemned to death as a political rebel because of it. In Sobrino's judgment the poverty that Christ witnessed during his life was the result of the fact that the rich did not share their wealth. Much of the oppression that his people suffered was due to the ponderous burdens placed upon them by the Pharisees. Sobrino notes that it was out of love that Jesus took his stand with the poor, as it was out of love that he took his stand against the rich.

Sobrino decries the fact that the scandal of the cross has been largely reduced to a cognitive mystery among Christians. Actually, the cross has produced a mystique of suffering rather than a mystique of following Jesus. The resurrection—which is principally attested to in the apparition narratives of the New Testament—defines God as a liberating power. Christ's risen presence reaffirmed the faith of the disciples and conferred on them a mission of active service in the transformation of the unredeemed world. Among Christ's titles of honor—Prophet, Servant of Yahweh, Lord, Logos, Son of God—none seems to be more fitting in our time than that of Liberator. It must be said that as the emphasis on the historical Jesus faded in favor of the risen and glorified Christ, the faith of many turned into a recitation of doctrine. Explicative theology replaced prayerful reflection on the work still to be done to transform the sinful world into the kingdom of God.

The Chalcedonian definition affirms that God and humankind are united in Jesus without division or confusion, and that the ultimate meaning of human existence is revealed in Christ. It is incumbent upon us at this time, says Sobrino, to reformulate the Christian message in more operational and functional terms. We should speak of the following of Jesus rather than the imitation of Jesus, and emphasize the difference between orthopraxis and orthodoxy. We must keep in mind that Christ had nothing but anathemas for abstract orthodoxy, which he regarded as meaningless without some praxis. For Sobrino the New Testament unambiguously affirms the supremacy of praxis over orthodoxy, as well as the critical need for praxis if orthodoxy is to become authentically Christian. The gospel account of the last judgment in Matthew 25:31–46 offers the clearest possible explanation of and rationale for the notion of Christian orthopraxis.

Jon Sobrino's theology as set forth in *Christology at the Crossroads* was questioned by Vatican officials because they felt that he denied the divinity of Christ and transformed him into a political revolutionary. However, the Jesuit's subsequent study, *Jesus in Latin America*, published in English in 1987, seems to reaffirm with conviction the full humanity and divinity of Christ.[4] In a more recent volume, *Jesus the Liberator*, published in Spanish in 1991 and translated into English in 1993, Sobrino returns to his familiar themes.[5] He underscores the vital importance of the preferential option for the poor highlighted at the Medellín Conference of Latin American bishops in 1968, and the priority that must be given to Jesus' special presence in the poor—a leading theme at the Puebla Conference of Latin American bishops in 1979. The kingdom of God in Latin America must focus first and foremost on the liberation of the poor and the oppressed. Sobrino stresses that Christ denounced the scribes, the Pharisees, the rich, and the priests who were representatives of what he calls the anti-kingdom. He insists that the origin of all dehumanization is structural or institutional injustice that can sometimes call for a violent response on the part of the downtrodden when no other remedy is available. After vividly portraying God's suffering in the agony and passion of the Third World, he turns his attention to the crucified people of the underdeveloped countries who are enslaved by the various powers that dominate those vast territories in connivance with the local authorities. The crucified people are like the suffering servant of Isaiah 53 in many ways. Their lands are being defaced and stripped of all their natural treasures and resources as the price of the other world's affluence. Yet the crucified people of Latin America and Africa are prepared to forgive their oppressors. They do not want to triumph over them but to share with them. The strong voice of Jon Sobrino continues to cry out for justice on behalf of the oppressed and forsaken who echo the cries for help of the suffering servant.

Leonardo Boff

Jesus Christ Liberator, published in 1972, was written in Brazil at a time when severe political repression was being aimed at large segments of the church.[6] Leonardo Boff (b. 1938) was considerably

limited in terms of what he could write at that time. An epilogue
was added to an English edition in 1978 when an atmosphere
of greater political tolerance in Brazil permitted him to set forth
more of his socioanalytical thought. A professor of theology in
Petropolis, Brazil, Boff received most of his theological education
at the University of Munich.

He sketches the return to the study of the historical Jesus on the
part of Bultmann and a number of his disciples and emphasizes
that from the New Testament writings the historical concreteness
and many of the details of Jesus' life and activity do shine through.
Jesus did possess a messianic consciousness, even if he did not
express it in explicit terms. In spite of the fact that the gospels are
attestations of faith rather than historical treatises, there is ample
information with which to construct a valid description of Jesus.
The Christology devised by the primitive community was nothing
more than a reflection upon what was revealed in the Jesus of
history.

According to *Jesus Christ Liberator*, Christ's message concerning the kingdom of God actually amounted to the promise of the
full realization of the whole of reality. (Later in the epilogue, Boff
identifies the promise of the kingdom as liberation from every kind
of stigma and oppression.) He complains that the revolutionary
message of Christ has been reduced in many cases to a decision
of faith made by individuals, with little relation to the pain and
anguish of the outside world. Christ's message possessed a political undercurrent—attacking all repressive situations of any sort.
The liberation proposed by Jesus relates to the public realm as
well as to the personal sphere. Over the years, the church has
fallen into the temptation of adopting the customs of pagan society, with authority patterns reflecting domination, and with the
use of lofty and honorific titles by those in positions of power
over others. Boff notes that the church is currently organized in
outmoded structures that imperil the very essence of the Christian
message.

Boff then addresses the development of Christian faith in Latin
America, a locale permeated by ecclesiological skepticism. All the
church models have been imported from Europe. So many of the
ecclesiastical traditions and institutions—which were functioning
at one time—have become ineffective and obsolete. They have become centers of a conservatism that has set up walls between faith

and the world, between the church and society. According to Boff large segments of the Latin American population have become marginalized, and hence it is imperative that the church take a more vital part in the upsurge of liberation that Latin American society is currently experiencing. Correct thinking, that is, orthodoxy, about Christ has taken priority over correct acting based on the example of Jesus, that is, orthopraxis. There has even been an ongoing exodus from the Catholic Church of a good number of the finest minds and the most energetic people because the ecclesiastical authorities have not supported the movements of liberation.

Jesus truly wanted to be God's full response to the needs of the human condition. His aim was to provide hope and consolation for those overcome by separation, pain, and death. The kingdom that he spoke of more than ninety times in the gospels was to be the fulfillment of hope at the end of time, when all alienation and evil would be overcome, and the old world would be transformed into the new (Luke 4:18–19, 21). Through his miracles and wondrous works, the kingdom of God was already beginning to appear (Luke 11:20). This kingdom was not a merely spiritual reality. If that were the case, Boff notes, he would not have created such enthusiasm among the ordinary folk. The theme of God's kingdom, which was a controlling idea among the Jews between 100 B.C.E. and 100 C.E., was given various interpretations. The Pharisees felt they could hasten the coming through the minute observance of the Mosaic law. The Essenes, on the other hand, were convinced that their total commitment to purification would accelerate the final event. Christ's preaching was very different. He never dwelt on nationalist notions, nor did he refer to the restoration of the kingdom of David (Acts 1:6–8). The temptation of a political messianism was not something to which he ever fell prey.

Jesus' two fundamental demands were the call to personal conversion and the restructuring of human relationships in society. In many ways he was saying "no" to the established order (Mark 2:27) and frequently opposed the intolerable burdens of pharisaical legalism (Matt. 23:3–5). On the contrary, Christ's repeated injunction is to love one another as God has loved us. In the Sermon on the Mount (Matthew 5–7) he does not in any way legitimate the status quo. It is, rather, a textbook of conduct for those who choose to follow him. Whereas the Pharisees, with their enormous influence throughout Israel, were neglectful of the weightier elements of the law such as mercy and fidelity (Matt. 23:23) and promoted social stratification against, for example, publicans, sinners, and even shepherds, Jesus moved spontaneously and consistently toward the marginalized who were much more responsive to him (Matt. 11:4–6). The Pharisees found Jesus' words threatening, and they largely turned away because accepting his message would have forced them to disestablish themselves.

For Christ, participation in Jewish worship was not a guarantee that one was right with God, nor did an exacting observance of the law provide the absolute security of God's favor. This could only come from a consistent disposition to love all, even one's enemies. Boff rather uniquely characterizes Jesus as a person endowed with eminent good sense, a creative imagination, and a singular talent for originality. His good sense was revealed in his uncanny ability to seek out the essentials in any situation. His directives were simple and clear, as was his mandate to love all, including one's oppressors. Jesus was deeply moved by the sorrow of the widow of Nain (Luke 7:11–17), felt the ingratitude of the Pharisees (Luke 7:36–50), and at times was roused to anger against them (Mark 8:11–13). Joy, indignation, friendship, generosity, toughness, spontaneity—all of these emotions were reflected in Christ's daily living.

There was a freedom and a certain spirit of nonconformity about Jesus when he pointed out what had been lost by the religious and moral complications created by his own people regarding their views, for example, on anger, divorce, and revenge (Matt. 5:21–42). His creative imagination broke through many of the structures that limited the vision of his contemporaries, even his disciples. When, for example, John the Apostle was upset by the efforts of someone attempting to drive out devils in Christ's name because he was not one of their company, Jesus replied that the individual should not be hindered, for he who is not against us is for us (Mark 9:38–40). A third quality lifted up by Boff is Christ's stunning originality in that he attempted to identify all as brothers and sisters of the same Father. Likewise, he desacralized piety and insisted that the way to salvation is through the service of one's neighbor, even one's enemies.

Boff deals at some length with the conflict between Jesus and the religious leaders of Israel that eventually led up to his apprehension and death. Because of his message and his miracles, he created a considerable following, which generated jealousy and ill will among the Jewish religious leaders. Some of them felt, as a matter of fact, that if they did not do something to curb his activities, everyone would come to believe in him, and the Romans would rob the Jews of their power and prerogatives (John 11:47–48). Christ's opposition to the teachings of the Pharisees prompted them to treat him with hostility, and they plotted to ensnare him in his speech so that they could report him to their authorities. His tendency to place himself above Moses, his practice of forgiving sin, and his miracles, aroused divisions among the people and united the Jewish leadership against him. Jesus clearly represented a danger to the established order, and thus there were attempts to arrest him (John 7:30) and to stone him (John 8:59). He was condemned by the Sanhedrin as a blasphemer for his liberal position regarding the Sabbath and his statements relating to the impending destruction of the temple. Christ's admission that he was the Son of the Blessed One prompted the priests to condemn him as guilty of blasphemy (Mark 14:61–64). Pilate, on the other hand, judged him to be a political enemy and, for this reason, condemned him to death.

Immediately after the crucifixion the apostles did not perceive any salvific significance in his death. They returned to Galilee and it was only after the resurrection that they began to understand that Christ died for our sins in accordance with the scriptures (1 Cor. 15:3). His resurrection constituted the revelation of total liberation for him and for all believers. For Boff the apparitions clarified for the disciples that the historical Jesus had risen and had shown himself to his followers with a real and bodily presence. Faith was the result of the impact of the apparitions on the disciples. The resurrection came to be seen as a pledge of future life for all true believers.

Boff then explores the question of the identity of Jesus who acted in the name and in the place of God. He taught with authority (Mark 1:22) and not as the scribes. The crowds were astonished at his teaching (Matt. 7:28), and his miracles prompted the same reaction (Matt. 9:33). They called him rabbi (Mark 9:5), and he reminded them of a prophet (Matt. 21:11). But how did he understand himself? In Boff's judgment Jesus came to realize toward the end of his life that he was a decisive factor in the breakthrough of the kingdom. Although the Lord never adopted the "Son of God" designation directly, his reference to the Father as Abba clearly implied an absolutely unique relationship. His use of the term "Son" (Mark 13:32; Matt. 11:27) reflected his profound experience of the Father and his own singular sonship. In the Synoptics, Jesus spoke of the "Son of man," which on a number of occasions had reference to another person identified with the final endtime. According to Boff, allusions to the Son of man who was to suffer and who has the power to forgive sins were probably inserted by the primitive community. The Palestinian Christian community had a predilection for the titles "Christ" and "Son of man," while the gentile Christians preferred "savior" and "Son of God." The latter title grounded the notion of Christ's preexistence (Phil. 2:5–11; Col. 1:15–17). The Gospel of John applied the concept "Logos" to Jesus to illustrate his relationship with the Father, as well as the fact that he is the unique revelation of the Father. It is Boff's view that Jesus was surely called God three times in the New Testament (Heb. 1:8; John 1:1; John 20:28) and possibly referred to as divine in five other pericopes (John 1:18; Titus 2:13; 1 John 5:20; Rom. 9:5; and 2 Pet. 1:1).

In his attempt to clarify the identity of "the human God and the divine human," Boff affirms that the ancient formulas are not enough. They must be expressed anew. The Council of Chalcedon (451), although it laid out the truth in succinct and lapidary sentences, did not make an effort to explain how the unity by way of person came about. In Boff's view the conscious center of the human "I" is grounded in the nature rather than in the person, a position resembling that of Paul Galtier alluded to in chapter 1. Boff does note, however, that the human person of Jesus is totally realized in the divine person of the Word. (It seems that he is using the term "human person" here in a rather imprecise sense, because he does not predicate two persons in Christ. The absence of a human person is pointed out as the highest perfection, creating space to be filled by the Word.) Boff attests that Chalcedon does not take into sufficient account the growth and evolution that Jesus experienced in his life in and through his dialogue with others, especially with the Father. Inasmuch as Christ is identified with the eternal Son of God, he was evidently without sin (John 8:46). Indeed, not only was he sinless, but he could not sin because he was the eternal Son.

Boff asks, where is the risen One today? His response is that he has penetrated the world in a much more profound manner (Matt. 28:20). According to Paul, he now lives in the form of Spirit (2 Cor. 3:17), and possesses a pneumatic body (1 Cor. 15:44). The resurrection has revealed the cosmic dimension of Christ, for in him all creation has come into existence (Col. 1:16–17), and he has revealed in himself the anticipated goal of all of creation. According to the Gospel of John, Jesus as Logos has unfolded the secret meaning of the entire universe. Moreover, the saving presence of the risen Lord is active wherever and whenever people seek after justice, for "whoever is not against us is for us" (Mark 9:40).

Boff then addresses the issue of the many titles of Jesus. There are some seventy in the New Testament, and still more have been added throughout the intervening centuries. Many of these, however, have lost their meaning, especially in certain parts of the world. For example, the title "Christ the King" has lost much of its significance for the oppressed classes who prefer to see him not as king but as advocate of the poor and the downtrodden. Because Jesus created a new humanity and preached a total liberation from all that alienates human beings, Boff suggests that a most appropriate title for the Lord today is that of "Liberator," whose task it is to raise up the poor and the marginalized of the world for whom he manifested such a preference during his earthly life. The parable of the anonymous Christians (Matt. 25:31–46) points the way for us and forcefully reveals the manner in which we can carry the liberating spirit of Jesus into our time and place.

Concerning the basic reason for the Incarnation, Boff sides with his Franciscan colleagues who consider it primarily as the crowning glory of creation, unlike the Thomists who first and foremost interpret it as a remedy for sin. The eternal person of the Son was always acting in the world from creation, but his presence was concentrated in Christ and was spread throughout the cosmos after the resurrection. Jesus is portrayed as the focal being in whom the total manifestation of God takes place within creation.

In 1978 Boff appended an epilogue to an English translation of his 1972 work. The "atmosphere of greater tolerance" in his homeland at that time allowed him to lay out in greater and more graphic detail the underpinnings of his thought. He holds that Christology today must entail a specific sociopolitical commitment to address and to break with the pervasive situation of oppression. Liberation Christology announces Christ as the Liberator and must be pledged to the economic, social, and political liberation of all those segments of society that are oppressed and dominated. This, notes Boff, includes the vast majority of people in Latin America who are suffering under inhuman living conditions, low income, unemployment, and lack of adequate health care, schools, and housing. He intimates that this widespread underdevelopment throughout Latin America is related to the progress achieved in the capitalist world, and to the high levels of consumption enjoyed by a relatively small number of elites.

There are, in Boff's judgment, two current approaches to Christology. The first he terms a "sacramental approach" that attempts a reinterpretation of basic christological dogmas and explores some of the liberative dimensions. It alludes to the larger problems and appeals for changes, but does not get down to the roots of the crisis. It can even engage in a criticism of the traditional images of Christ that tend to tolerate the whole phenomenon of colonization and domination, but there is no effort to explicitate a detailed analysis of underdevelopment, and therefore this theologizing carries little political force. The second approach is what he terms a "socioanalytical presentation of Christology" that is truly liberative inasmuch as it proposes to change the sociopolitical structures themselves. The social theory that he favors is the dialectical approach that bears the stamp of the Marxist tradition. This rationale stresses the notion of struggle and conflict, viewing the structure of society from the bottom up. It implies a break with the status quo and seeks to operate on structures, allowing for wider participation on the part of greater numbers of the people.

This approach to liberation Christology views the social, economic, and political emancipation of the dominated as indispensable for the coming of the kingdom. Boff views capitalism as a system wherein some nations by necessity are dependent on others. For the system to work, he holds that the peripheral nations must be kept in a state of dependence, and this amounts to domination. Boff asserts that they must break these ties and free themselves for a self-maintained national position. He claims that the forces of repression in Latin America have gained the upper hand and have blocked any organizational liberation movement, while the downtrodden majority has resorted to a culture of silence. This situation must be changed so that the oppressed can be liberated. Boff adds that liberation Christology of this sort has rarely found its way into print but has been passed around from hand to hand in mimeographed texts.

Boff places emphasis on the historical Jesus over the Christ of faith largely because of the structural similarities between Jesus' time and our own. Christ is portrayed as issuing an urgent call for the transformation of the social fabric. The way to the Father is clearly through orthopraxis. In the last days, God will install his reign in a final and definitive manner, liberating all who are dominated in one way or another, but it is up to us to inaugurate this transformation now as best we can. The program for liberation sketched by Jesus (Luke 4:16–22) makes it evident that God has a preference for the poor and the downtrodden. Christ's miracles were clearly signs of the ushering in of the kingdom, and his praxis had a social character that was aimed directly against the political, economic, and religious institutions of his day.

Like other liberation theologians, Boff affirms that access to God is not attained primarily through cultic worship or religious observance, but through service to the poor and the oppressed, for God lies hidden in those segments of society. The poor are declared blessed because poverty is the end product of unjust and enslaving relationships among human beings. Wealth is rejected because it is considered the result of the exploitation of the poor (Luke 16:9). All power that exercises domination over others is rejected out of hand (Luke 22:25–27). Although Jesus did not intend to occupy any position of political power, Boff warns that a takeover of political power should not necessarily be viewed as an improper way to seek justice and the redress of wrongs for the oppressed and the abject of our society. Because we in our day do not anticipate an impending parousia, we must therefore strive for justice and compassion in our world, and this task—especially in Latin America—will involve conflict and struggle, in order to release the poor from their underdeveloped economic and social condition.

In connection with his book *The Church: Charism and Power*, published in Portuguese in 1981 and translated into English in 1985, Leonardo Boff was ordered to come to Rome to discuss a number of the ecclesiological issues raised by the study. In spite of the intercession of the Brazilian Cardinals Lorscheider and Arns on his behalf, he was informed that he was to be silenced for a period of one year because of the dangers to sound doctrine in connection with his notions of the Catholic Church. Boff submitted to this restriction but left the ministry in 1992.

A Summary

A somewhat unique approach to the study of Jesus and his mission is that provided by the liberation theologians of Latin America. *Christology at the Crossroads* was the work of Jon Sobrino, a long-time resident of El Salvador. In Latin America, Jesus has become identified as the "Liberator," who is to free his people from the economic underdevelopment and widespread oppression in which they find themselves. Latin American theologians are not focusing on the traditional christological problems but are stressing instead those areas of Christology directly relating to the theme of liberation. They are, therefore, concentrating on the historical Jesus rather than the glorified Christ.

For Sobrino there is a considerable difference between religion and Christian faith. The past has shown that Christian faith can easily turn into religion if we neglect the concrete history of Jesus. Although he expresses his faith in the Chalcedonian definition, he feels that its markedly ontological language does not reflect adequately the New Testament data that puts flesh and blood on the historical figure of Jesus. The divinity of Christ consists in the modality of his personal relationship with the Father that works itself out in history.

Sobrino insists that Christ had a unique and unmatched personal consciousness regarding his relationship with the Father, but it is not clear that he knew himself to be the eternal Son. He spoke on his own authority and expected people to follow him. Jesus attacked the domination of others in the name of religion perpetrated by the Jewish leaders, especially the Pharisees, and for this he was ultimately condemned to death. In Sobrino's judgment it is tragic that the scandal of the cross has been largely reduced to a cognitive mystery among Christians. The message of Christ must be reformulated in more operational and functional terms. Jesus regarded abstract orthodoxy as meaningless without a sound commitment to praxis. The last judgment scene in Matthew 25:31–46 offers the most poignant explanation of the nature of Christian praxis. Sobrino's subsequent study, *Jesus in Latin America,* seemed to clear up a good many of the doubts about his position concerning the full humanity and full divinity of Christ.

The second liberation theologian examined is the Brazilian Leonardo Boff, who published his very popular *Jesus Christ Liberator* in 1972. Some years later, when the political oppression against the church in Brazil had been lifted, he added an epilogue in which he set forth his socioeconomic analysis more openly. Boff complains that the revolutionary message of Christ has frequently been reduced to a decision of faith made by individuals, with little relation to the anguish of the outside world. The liberation proclaimed by Jesus relates to the public realm as well as to the personal sphere. Unfortunately, all the church models, especially in Latin America, have been imported from Europe and have become ineffective and obsolete, as promoters of conservatism. Boff notes that while the Pharisees neglected certain important elements of the law such as mercy and fidelity (Matt. 23:23) and promoted social stratification, Jesus was drawn toward the marginalized, who were much more open to him (Matt. 11:4–6).

Christ is portrayed as a person gifted with eminent good sense, a creative imagination, and an outstanding talent for originality. Jesus' originality was especially demonstrated in his extension of the fatherhood of God to all men and women who could then view themselves as brothers and sisters in Christ. He also desacralized piety and taught that the way to salvation is through service to one's neighbor.

Although the crowds called him "rabbi" and he reminded them of a prophet, it is not easy to determine how Jesus understood himself. He was increasingly aware of his profound experience of the Father and of his own unique sonship. The early conciliar formulas that attempt to delineate the identity of Christ are, for Boff, no longer sufficient and need to be expressed anew. Chalcedon did not take into full account the growth and evolution experienced by Jesus during his earthly life, nor did it make an effort to explain how the unity by way of person came about. In Boff's judgment the absence of a human person in Christ is viewed as the highest perfection, creating space to be filled by the Word.

The resurrection has revealed the cosmic dimension of Christ, for he now penetrates the world in a much more profound manner. Because many of the titles applied to Jesus have lost their original significance in the intervening centuries, Boff suggests that the most appropriate name for the Lord today is that of Liberator, whose mission it is to raise up the poor and the marginalized of the world for whom he showed such a preference during his earthly sojourn.

Jesus is portrayed as issuing an urgent summons for the transformation of the social fabric. Orthopraxis is clearly the way to the Father. Christ's preference for the poor is dramatically charted out in his program for liberation (Luke 4:16–21). The poor are blessed because poverty is the result of unjust and enslaving relationships among human beings. Wealth is rejected as the consequence of the exploitation of the poor (Luke 16:9).

Notes

1. Paul E. Sigmund, *Liberation Theology at the Crossroads* (New York: Oxford University Press, 1990), 89–92.

2. Jon Sobrino, *Christology at the Crossroads*, trans. John Drury (Maryknoll, N.Y.: Orbis Books, 1978).

3. Moltmann, *The Crucified God*. The work was originally published in German in 1972.

4. See for example, Johann-Baptist Metz, *Theology of the World*, trans. W. G. Doepel (New York: Seabury Press, 1969), and *Faith in History and Society*, trans. David Smith (New York: Seabury Press, 1980).

5. Sigmund, *Liberation Theology at the Crossroads*, 91.

6. Jon Sobrino, *Jesus the Liberator*, trans. Paul Burns and Francis McDonagh (Maryknoll, N.Y.: Orbis Books, 1993).

7. Leonardo Boff, *Jesus Christ Liberator*, trans. Patrick Hughes (Maryknoll, N.Y.: Orbis Books, 1978), 264–95

✳ Chapter 6 ✳

Jesus versus Patriarchy— Feminist Christologies

Anne E. Carr

The feminist theological movement, which took its rise in the 1960s, has developed into a full-fledged and widely respected branch of the theology of liberation. Elizabeth Johnson described feminist Christology as a faith reflection "explicitly from the perspective and experience of women—based on the conviction that women share equally with men in the dignity of being human."[1] The question of the identity of Jesus is enriched "with yet another dimension when answered from the experience of believing women."[2]

In 1988 Anne Carr, a professor of theology at the University of Chicago Divinity School, published *Transforming Grace: Christian Tradition and Women's Experience*, in which she summarizes the contributions of Christian feminists since the 1960s.[3] She notes that the two groups of feminists, that is, those serving in the various ministries on campuses, hospitals, parishes, and so on, and the scholars in academia, have been working effectively together to level the playing field for women in the churches. It is nothing short of a struggle for justice to bring about a transformation of ecclesial structures, law, and attitudes, so that women can at last enjoy their rightful status as coequals with men.

No single effort has been as extensive worldwide as the international women's movement and the theology that has grown out of it. Feminist theology, which correlates the study of sacred scripture and tradition along with contemporary experience, emphasizes mutual cooperation and interdependence against the patriarchal, hierarchical patterns so prevalent in the churches today. Carr attests that in the judgment of some feminists the theology and the organizational fabric of the churches are so alienating to women that many of them have left their Christian communions. Ecclesial organization and law must reflect the radical equality of the sexes that is proclaimed by the gospel message. Given that the educational level among women has improved dramatically in the past generation or two, the need to address the question of the equal status of women is all the more urgent. A very serious tension exists in most of the churches between the patriarchal and hierarchical model and the egalitarian, inclusive model of organization.

In the 1960s the movement in the Christian churches encouraging the ordination of women and expanding the responsibilities in ministry attained a fair degree of success among the Presbyterians, the Methodists, the Episcopalians, the United Church of Christ, and others. In these denominations, the ministerial contributions of women in recent years have been considerable. Carr notes that similar efforts in the Catholic Church have not met with success. (As a matter of fact, Pope John Paul II's apostolic letter of May 22, 1994, *Ordinatio sacerdotalis*, and his pronouncement of May 18, 1998, *Ad tuendam fidem*, seem to close the door on any further public discussion of the issue of the priestly ordination of women.) Carr—whose study was published prior to these two papal letters—notes that traditions have been changed before. Church stands on usury, the persecution of heretics, slavery, vernacular liturgy, democracy, modern science, and modern developments in biblical exegesis—to name a few—have all been reversed in spite of very strong positions taken by central church authority to the contrary. To what extent, she asks, have sociological factors in the second and third centuries contributed to the rise of a special caste of male ecclesial ministers? A case can be made for the observation that the subordinate roles of women in the churches have simply been a reflection of the subjected position of women in society at large.

Many of the arguments that have been used in the past to demonstrate that women are not suitable candidates for the ordained priesthood do not seem, according to Carr, to be totally probative today. After all the scientific studies in biology, psychology, sociology, and anthropology have destroyed the assumption of female inferiority, the presumption of subordination persists institutionally. It is indeed curious that although the Christian churches generally have been slow to reflect in their structures and their law the full emancipation of women, the secular liberation of women has taken place more rapidly in Christian civil societies. In this context Carr asks whether the gospel message, which was submerged in oppressive cultural forms in the churches, was nonetheless able to act as a leavening agent in the corresponding secular societies.

Jesus' conduct as reflected in the New Testament was consistently inclusive of women as well as of other oppressed groups. His stance, as a matter of fact, was radically countercultural. He conversed with women in spite of the conventional restrictions against such practice (e.g., John 4:4–42; Mark 7:24–30). Jesus had women friends (Luke 10:38–42) and women disciples (Luke 8:1–3). Although Paul (or an interpolator shortly after Paul's death) urged women to be silent in church (1 Cor. 14:34), the Apostle of the Gentiles forcefully articulated the radical equality among all baptized Christians who are no longer Jew or Greek, slave or free, male or female, for all are one now in Christ Jesus (Gal. 3:28). Carr notes that in the early Christian congregations women played an active role in a wide variety of ministries, for example, as disciples, prophets, teachers, missionaries, patrons, and leaders of congregations. However, in the second century, with the emergence of the monarchical episcopate, there was a growing tendency in the churches to follow the patriarchal cultural patterns of Jewish and Hellenistic society that relegated women to a subordinate status, thus erasing the more egalitarian picture of the ministries as reflected in the gospels.

After the issue of admitting women into ecclesiastical ministries, the question of the language employed in the churches remains a great source of frustration for feminists. Inclusive language, when adopted, has been helpful, but the wording and the symbols of a largely patriarchal society still constitute a major grievance for women, for such symbols reveal how the churches fail to be responsive to the prerogatives and the dignity of more than one-half of their membership. A third issue that is problematic for the feminists is the maleness of Jesus. Many stress that Christ has always been seen primarily as human, and not initially as male. Some, however, continue to wonder whether or not Jesus can be a role model for contemporary women. They ask, "In what sense is Jesus the savior of women?" The majority of feminists respond that Christ can be shown to be in every instance supportive of the full humanity of women.

Although the christological positions of St. Thomas Aquinas are not prejudicial to females since they principally emphasize the fact that Christ was fully human and fully divine, in part 3 of the *Summa Theologiae* he declares that "the male sex is more noble than the female sex. But lest the female sex be disparaged [*contemneretur*], it was fitting that Christ should assume his flesh from a woman."[4] According to Carr, Aquinas affirms that the male is the normative sex and that woman is a somewhat defective human being. In this regard the Angelic Doctor adheres to the patterns of medieval, feudal society that assimilated the prevailing patriarchal system.

The assumption of the inferiority of women was maintained without question by Tertullian, Clement of Alexandria, Augustine, and other Church Fathers. Medieval theology generally held fast to the view of the inequality of the sexes that was as regressive as the doctrine of Aristotelian biology. In spite of this overriding theological bias, there were some exceptions to the dominance of males, in that well into the twelfth century ordained deaconesses and abbesses occasionally exercised power in the church that was normally reserved to male clerics. Except for a few passages in Vatican II's *Pastoral Constitution on the Church in the Modern World* (e.g., no. 29), this most recent ecumenical council did not really deal with the question of the ecclesial status of women.

Anne Carr affirms that her focus is on a Christology "from below" that concentrates on the unfolding life of the historical Jesus as it is related in the gospels. At the same time, she seems to endorse a Christology "from above," because she speaks of the birth of a God among us in the humble form of an infant. Jesus thus establishes for us a twofold solidarity with God and with the people, especially the downtrodden and the marginalized. His primary message is one of liberation for all people. Carr notes that this message is sometimes forgotten in our persistent focus on the metaphysics of Christ's inner being. Throughout his life on earth, Jesus transcends all the gender stereotypes to which women are opposed, and through the resurrection Christ transcends all the limits of human existence.

Carr deals with four of the principal symbols that are traditionally expressive of Jesus. The first, which is Christ as the Word of God, is often thought of as an exclusively male symbol. However, because of the significance for women of verbal communication and dialogue, the Word can be a suitable symbol of mutuality and reciprocity, which would appropriately reflect female attributes. Carr reminds her readers that in the Old Testament's Wisdom of Solomon (ca. 50 B.C.E.) and in Philo of Alexandria (ca. 25 B.C.E.–50 C.E.), the terms *Logos* (Word) and *Sophia* (Wisdom) are virtually interchangeable.

The image of Jesus as sacrificial victim is a difficult one for feminists to identify with, unless his sacrificial death is seen as one entered into freely and as a result of the manner in which he consciously lived. The third symbol that must be reinterpreted somewhat by feminists is that of Jesus as servant. Although there is nothing intrinsically demeaning about service to others, it must be portrayed as an option freely and lovingly chosen, in a social frame of reference that clearly reveals it as not having been imposed by persons or circumstances from without.

The final image that Carr sets forth is that of Jesus as Son. For the feminists, this is more problematic because it is suggestive of the patriarchal culture that has sanctioned the rule of male over female, and the primacy of sons over daughters. As a result of this patriarchal milieu, women have been ordered to be subject to their husbands and fathers, and told to be submissive, in spite of the fact that they have also been promised that they have been made partakers of a wondrous equality in Christ through baptism. This pervasive suggestion of male superiority over women is totally overshadowed when it is situated in the rich relational context of the life, death, and resurrection of Jesus. The feminist understanding of love and reciprocity provides an ideal response to the damaging effects of a noninclusive Christology. Carr reminds her readers that women find that the Jesus as reflected in the New Testament is not always the same by any means as the Christ who is mediated through the structures, practices, and language of the churches.

Carr then addresses the important question of the meaning of salvation in the Christian context. She describes the classical view held, for example, by Irenaeus (ca. 140–ca. 200), as the recapitulation of the whole of human life by Christ. His total transformation of every phase of human existence shattered the hold of the demonic powers over humankind once and for all. In the light of this view of salvation, women can see themselves as engaged in a great struggle with forces and prejudices that seem to transcend them,

were it not for the inclusive and egalitarian pattern of human re-
latedness revealed by Jesus, which will eventually overcome every
tendency to subordinate and enslave.

The second approach is the satisfaction theory of St. Anselm
that insists that the sin of humankind requires an infinite satisfaction since the one offended is God. Therefore no one less than a
God-man was necessary in order to make amends. In this context
Carr adds that the whole of Jesus' life must be viewed as redemptive, not just his passion and death, but the total service of Jesus on
earth and his daring reversals of the patriarchal patterns, as well
as the ministrations of the risen Lord whose activity continues to
the end of time.

In contrast to the rather legalistic thesis of Anselm, which has
had a controlling influence for a thousand years, Carr proposes the
theory of moral exemplarity advanced by Peter Abelard. Christians
are invited to fashion their lives after the model of Jesus, and, to
the extent that we are successful in this effort, our actions will in
fact transform our being and exercise a profound effect upon the
whole relational context in which we live. Feminists see this view
of Abelard as an ideal explanation of the salvation brought into
the world by Christ.

In a short article entitled "Feminist Views of Christology"
published in 1996, Carr returns to the same themes that she
emphasized in *Transforming Grace*.[5] Among the feminists, the revolutionary group continues to insist that Christianity is essentially
patriarchal and, therefore, cannot change. The reformists, on the
other hand, hope to find a way to think of Jesus in nonandrocentric
terms and have focused on the female figure of Wisdom (Sophia),
that rather mysterious individual of the latter Old Testament. Jesus
as "Sophia's prophet" offers them a new and different christological image, while other feminists have shown a preference for
the risen Christ who transcends sexual differences. Paul refers to
Jesus as the Wisdom of God (1 Cor. 1:24), while John fashions
Jesus' long discourses on the Sophia pattern of the Old Testament
wisdom books. For feminists this opens up the possibility of po-
sitioning Christ in a nonandrocentric framework. Although the
feminist vision of genuine mutuality and reciprocity among men
and women is widely affirmed, it must be said that there is hardly
any consensus concerning the best avenues toward the realization
of that goal.

Among those numerous themes proposed by women, Carr has recently emphasized that the humanity rather than the maleness of Jesus remains prominent.[6] Also, the popularity of Sophia Christology—which interprets Christ in such a way that his sex is as humanly contingent as his race or historical environment—has contributed much to the ongoing dialogue. Along with Joan Chittister, Carr advocates a feminist spirituality for both men and women, emphasizing respect for others, equality, mutuality, and the elimination of patriarchy and domination from the fabric of Christian teaching and institutions.

Elisabeth Schüssler Fiorenza

One of the more influential of the American feminist theologians is Elisabeth Schüssler Fiorenza (b. 1938), a professor of scripture and interpretation at the Harvard University Divinity School. In 1983 she published *In Memory of Her: A Feminist Theological Reconstruction of Christian Origins*, which attempts to revise our understanding of the role of women in the New Testament narratives.[7] Schüssler Fiorenza's principal goal is to rediscover primitive Christian history as a history of women as well as men. She believes that this effort to reinsert women into the earliest days of the Christian movement will lead to a fuller and more reliable knowledge of Christian beginnings. She asks whether women as well as men were key contributors to the development of the Jesus movement, and she replies that women are revealed in the New Testament writings as not only followers of Christ, but as leading members of the primitive churches.

Inasmuch as all of the earliest Christian documents were written from a patriarchal point of view, a critical shift is necessary in order that the biblicists and historians can appreciate the old data from a new perspective. Schüssler Fiorenza sees the feminist theological enterprise as an indispensable part of the theology of liberation. *In Memory of Her: A Feminist Theological Reconstruction of Christian Origins,* looks initially into the role of women in the first Palestinian Christian communities and then charts that development in the Greco-Roman churches. The assigning of principally familial responsibilities to women in the Roman world was due to the fact that they were considered as an inferior group in antiquity, for the most part incapable of occupying public leadership positions in society. Schüssler Fiorenza aims to show that the important functions that they performed in the first Christian communities stood in stark contrast to the patriarchal traditions of the Greco-Roman world.

The Jesus movement, as reported in the gospel accounts, gathered itself together after the resurrection of Christ to continue his work of renewal within Israel and then expanded into the neighboring territories to include non-Jews. Schüssler Fiorenza attempts to reconstruct the experience of those Jewish women who contributed to the development of the Christian phenomenon at the very beginning. She warns, however, that the New Testament sources must be viewed as androcentric, patriarchal texts that are largely reflective of the experience and viewpoint of the male writers. Jewish women labored under the limitations placed upon their sex in the dominant cultures of the time.

There were a good number of Jewish renewal movements active in the first century C.E.—the Pharisees, the Sadducees, the Essenes, the Qumran community, and the apocalyptic prophets—that were committed to the fulfillment of Israel's hopes for national independence. Unfortunately there is little information on the part that women played in those various movements. However, the Old Testament Book of Judith—a fictional account written in the first century B.C.E.—reveals a woman of considerable power and prestige who inherited her husband's estate and managed it through a woman subordinate (8:10). Judith's victory over Holofernes was viewed as a victory for all the people. The portrait of this shrewd and courageous woman must have encouraged the Jews during their subjugation by the Romans.

The kingdom proclaimed by Jesus was intended for all, especially the oppressed and the powerless. It was inclusive of all, that is, women, the have-nots, and the castoffs of society. The kingdom was present and active whenever Jesus cast out devils, healed the sick, and forgave sins (Matt. 11:4–6), but the full inbreak of the kingdom would only be realized in the future. Jesus opened out the kingdom to the poor (Mark 12:41–44), the sick (Luke 13:10–17), tax collectors, sinners, and prostitutes (Matt. 21:31). He broke bread not only with women but also with notorious sinners. Indeed, it can be said that the outcasts of Jewish society were heavily represented among his followers, and many of these were women.

In the parable of the workers in the vineyard (Matt. 20:1–16) the goodness of God to one and all is graphically portrayed, as well as the equal status of all in God's eyes. It is Matthew who identifies Jesus with the Sophia of the late Old Testament wisdom literature. The divine Sophia (or Wisdom) offers salvation to all who receive her. She sends apostles and prophets, makes all things new, and receives all who accept her as friends of God (Wis. 7:27). Sophia is an intimate associate in the wondrous works of God (Wis. 8:4). According to Schüssler Fiorenza it is likely that Jesus understood himself as the prophet of Sophia whose yoke is easy and whose burden is light (Matt. 11:28–30). The Palestinian movement recognized Jesus as the prophet of Sophia who wills the wholeness of everyone and envisions a discipleship of equals. Jesus' death is seen by the movement as the result of his all-inclusive and persistent struggles as Sophia's prophet.

The Galilean disciples apparently received gentile followers very early on. The Syro-Phoenician woman in Mark (7:24–30) proposed that Jews and Gentiles break bread together, and it seems that Jesus found her arguments plausible, for she went home to find her demon-possessed daughter healed. This apparently gentile woman became the "foremother" of all gentile Christians. The Galilean women who followed Jesus did not flee like the men after he was apprehended and crucified (Mark 16:1–6). Moreover, the Lord first showed himself to Mary of Magdala after his resurrection (Mark 16:9–10). In the first century, although patriarchy was firmly established in the societal fabric of Jewish life, the all-inclusive context of the Palestinian Jesus movement did liberate women, giving them more freedom and a greater sense of equality. In God's eyes men and women are no longer to relate to each other in terms of patriarchal domination but as individuals who live in the gracious presence of God (Mark 12:18–27).

Christian discipleship abolished the patriarchal prerogatives and established a new familial community (Mark 3:31–35). In a discipleship of equals all the structures of domination are to be eliminated (Matt. 23:8–12). "Call no one father, for you have but one Father in heaven" (Matt. 23:9). Schüssler Fiorenza notes that the address "father" employed so widely in the church has caused scandal to feminists because the mandate of Jesus "to call no one father" has been ignored and disobeyed. It is hoped that the reevaluation of the first-century world in Palestine and the rediscovery of the role of women in the development of the early

Christian movement will assist the feminists in their task of build-
ing an unassailable foundation for a community of equals in the
church.

The sources for the assessment of the role of women in the
Greco-Roman churches are the Pauline letters and the Acts of the
Apostles. Although Luke portrays women in Acts as mere support-
ers of Paul's mission, the Pauline literature reveals women as not
only patronesses of various Christian communities, but actual missionaries who preached the gospel and were very much involved in
the expansion of the faith throughout the Roman world. The community at Antioch—whose early leader was Barnabas—seemed to
be the focal point for the evangelization of the Gentiles. As a matter of fact, the Antiochian church could well have been responsible
for carrying the gospel to Rome. Mary, a cousin of Barnabas, was
apparently a leader in one of the house churches in Jerusalem (Acts
12:12–17). These house churches were frequently placed under the
direction of wealthy women converts who were eager to support
them, and the first congregations gathered in their houses. Prisca
and her husband, Aquila, were probably responsible for founding
a few house churches (1 Cor. 16:19), while Apphia was one of
the leaders of a house church in Colossae (Philem. v. 2). By join-
ing the Christian movement, affluent women were able to acquire
prominence and influence that they did not enjoy in the patriarchal Roman society. These women who founded and maintained
the house churches were considered members of a community of
equals. Among the twenty-five persons greeted by Paul in Romans
16, eight were women.

The second significant role played by women in the Greco-
Roman churches was their participation in missionary activity.
Paul attests that women labored side by side with him in the work
of evangelization (Phil. 4:2–3), while missionary titles were applied by Paul to women such as Prisca (co-worker) and Phoebe
(deaconess). As a matter of fact, Phoebe, the deaconess of the
church at Cenchreae (the port city of Corinth), was highly praised
as a colleague by Paul and was recommended to the church
in Rome (Rom. 16:1–2). Schüssler Fiorenza attests that Phoebe
seemed to be the official entrusted with the preaching duties and
the management of the congregation at Cenchreae. Prisca and
Aquila, Junia and Andronicus, two missionary couples, are refer-
enced by Paul as co-missionaries, while Andronicus and Junia are

called "apostles," and indeed described as "outstanding among the apostles" (Rom. 16:3–7). There is clear evidence, therefore, in the Pauline letters that women were active as missionaries and leaders, teachers and founders of house churches in the first century C.E.

The early Christian missionary movement identified the risen Lord with the Spirit of God and the Sophia of God (1 Cor. 1:24). According to Schüssler Fiorenza, the wisdom Christology of the Christian missionary endeavor identified Jesus as the divine Sophia herself. She claims that it is Sophia Christology that is expressed in the pre-Pauline hymns, for example, Philippians 2:6–11. Early Christians proclaimed Christ-Sophia as the controller of the principalities and powers and the center of the new creation (Col. 1:15–20). It is the Christian community that has become the true temple of God (2 Cor. 6:16–17). All Christian believers are referred to as the holy ones, and all are sons and daughters in a community of equals (2 Cor. 6:18). Through baptism Christians are led into the "force field" of the Holy Spirit, and because they share the same baptism they are all equals (Gal. 3:28). In Schüssler Fiorenza's judgment the feminists have begun to reconstruct the history of women in primitive Christianity. Through baptism women enter into a discipleship of equals who are called to care for the oppressed and the downtrodden of the earth. However, as long as women are excluded from the ministry, she affirms that the discipleship of equals will not be fully achieved. For women, the "Eden image," that is, the homemaker image, must now give way to the "Exodus image" that calls women to leave the servitude of the patriarchal family and march in solidarity with the poor women of the world. It is only when believing women are joined by all those who affirm the vision of the people of God as a discipleship of equals that the gospel will be credibly proclaimed in the entire world.

In 1994 Schüssler Fiorenza revisited the christological arena with the publication of *Jesus: Miriam's Child, Sophia's Prophet: Critical Issues in Feminist Christology.*[8] Neither she nor Anne Carr seems to show much interest in the traditional concerns of Christology, for example, the explanation of Jesus' divinity and his humanity, the relationship between his human and divine knowledge, the question of preexistence. Their concentration focuses rather on the manner in which Jesus dealt with the men and women of his day. What divine attitudes and attributes did he reveal in his dealings with his contemporaries and with the societal structures of first-century Palestine? Was he crucified because he so consistently fought against the prevailing patriarchal culture of his day? These seem to be the questions that challenge the feminists, and it can be said that their concern for such issues extends and enriches the portrait of Jesus offered by the more traditional studies.

Schüssler Fiorenza approaches her treatment of Jesus from the point of view of the need to establish the radical equality of the sexes. She joins the great body of feminist theologians the world over in affirming that it is not enough merely to analyze the structures of domination in the societal fabric, but it is necessary to transform those systems of domination in order to create a community of equals by eliminating the many oppressive strictures. In her penchant for neologisms she introduces the term *kyriarchy* to signify the rule of masters, lords, fathers, and husbands over their subordinates. It is the concerns of women, perennially found at the bottom of the kyriarchal pyramid, that animate the feminist movement throughout the world.

The challenge of the feminists is to question and possibly re-place the patriarchal forms of Christianity that have controlled Christian thought for nearly two thousand years. They fully realize the immensity of their task, which amounts to the overturning of the thought patterns of an ancient society. Further, they intend to make clear that the hierarchical and patriarchal Christian religion has been largely exclusive of women.

The primary difficulty confronting feminist theologians is the dilemma of the maleness of Jesus that challenges them on many levels. The conventional attributes of men (i.e., self-assertion and independence) have long been contrasted against the traditional characteristics of women (e.g., humble service and dependence), and this relegation of women to "selfless femininity" has been reinforced over the centuries by Christian preaching. Although changes have been occurring recently in the secular world, women have been customarily directed toward the private domain, while men were schooled for life in the public sphere. Male and female were, in effect, "biologized" in the churches and in theological discussion. Schüssler Fiorenza laments that women have been excluded from ordination within the Catholic communion on the grounds of anatomical sex. The Pauline injunction that there should no longer be slave or free, male or female, but that all should be one in Christ Jesus has to be given far greater currency in the church. Rosemary Radford Ruether's haunting question, "Can a male savior bring salvation to women?" still gives many feminists pause today. Some feminists hold that they can be religious, but not Christian, because Christianity is radically sexist. Schüssler Fiorenza affirms that we cannot ground a viable feminist Christian theology on Jesus' preferential option for the poor but, rather, it is crucial that it be based on the energetic struggle of like-minded men and women for the transformation of the kyriarchal patterns within the church.

Schüssler Fiorenza then addresses the second issue of the feminists, which is the claim that traditional Jesus scholarship produces the seeds of anti-Semitism. Charting the striking ideological differences between the teachings of Christ and the positions espoused by the Pharisees and Sadducees leads one to the conclusion that the preaching of Jesus—as it is portrayed in the New Testament—is anti-Semitic. This is also the case with regard to the feminists' depiction of Jesus as the liberator of women vis-à-vis the patriarchal social fabric of Judaism. However, Christ's struggle to emancipate Jewish women from their subordinated status need not be seen as an attack against Jewish culture as such, but rather as a confrontation with the kyriarchal structures of domination embedded in the entire imperial colonial system of the first century C.E. Jesus should be seen as standing in the vanguard of the struggle for justice and freedom from the patriarchal oppression of women and the have-nots so prevalent in antiquity.

A third actively debated issue among feminists has to do with the theology of the cross. Whenever Christianity engages in the glorification of suffering, this can validate those relationships of domination that over the years have reinforced the feminine vocation to submission and self-sacrifice. The injunction of 1 Peter 2:18–23 that calls for slaves to endure even the unjust sufferings inflicted on them by their masters has often been repeated through the centuries as counsel to underlings and women. Schüssler Fiorenza asks whether the symbol of the suffering Son has facilitated innumerable acts of violence against women and children in the name of religion. It is crucial, she adds, to reformulate feminist approaches to the sufferings of Christ within a different and more creative context that will not revive those destructive undercurrents of submission and subjugation.

It is difficult for us to comprehend how Jesus understood his own death. All four gospels indicate that he was accused of the political crime of sedition, and as a result the authorities felt free to affix the judgment, "King of the Jews," to his cross. Also, some attested that he intended to destroy the Jerusalem temple. However, apparently the underlying cause for his apprehension and crucifixion was the threat that his teachings had lifted up against the Jewish and, ultimately, the Roman imperial system of domination. The first- and second-generation Christians shifted the culpability for his death from the Romans to the Jewish leaders and the Jewish people.

Christ's resurrection is viewed by feminists as the ultimate justification for him and for all the oppressed and subjugated who are striving for something better. Schüssler Fiorenza emphasizes that Mary of Magdala and the other women made the first announcement of the resurrection after their moving experience at the empty tomb, thus highlighting the faithful witness of women. They were directed to search out the risen presence of Christ who is "going before you into Galilee, and there you will see him" (Matt. 28:7).

She then directs her attention to the Sophia tradition and what it can offer to clarify and enrich our understanding of Jesus and notes that the feminist theologians have made great strides in unearthing the primitive strains of Sophia-Wisdom. Whereas the female figure of Wisdom can be observed often in later Old Testament and first-century Jewish writings, Sophia is only barely visible in early Christian literature. According to Schüssler Fiorenza, Wisdom was identified as a female figure not only by the gender of the Greek and Hebrew nouns, but also through the cultural change experienced in Israel in the postexilic period. The transition from a rather authoritarian monarchy to a much more loosely knit society based to a great extent on familial ties is revealed in such passages as the portrait of the ideal Jewish homemaker (Prov. 31:10–31) and in the hymn to Lady Wisdom who offers the food and drink that enrich the lives of her guests (Proverbs 9). Sophia is presented in the wisdom literature as a divine-like figure who in no way threatens the rigid monotheism of Israel.

Schüssler Fiorenza insists that in the New Testament Jesus saw himself as Sophia's offspring or prophet (Luke 7:35; Matt. 11:28–30). As a matter of fact, Jesus himself declares that someone greater than the wise Solomon is in your midst (Luke 11:31).

Schüssler Fiorenza asks if Jesus and Sophia in the Gospel of Matthew are identical, since the conflation of the two appears to be rather complete (Matt. 23:34–36). The Gospel of John seems to portray the Logos as the son of Sophia, or perhaps as her replacement. Yet by employing the Father-Son language so consistently, the Fourth Gospel seems to reduce the importance and influence of Lady Wisdom.

Feminist theologians have been at work to revive and reinstate the New Testament Sophia tradition that has almost entirely disappeared in the Christian theology of the West. This ancient and venerable biblical strain is extremely important for the development of feminist Christology. For it is through the Sophia tradition that the feminine dimensions of the divine can be most emphatically expressed. However, the work of the feminists in this regard is just beginning. The revival of the image of the divine Sophia should do wonders to animate what Schüssler Fiorenza refers to as the "ossified masculine language about God and Christ." It is crucial that feminist theologians take pains to situate their studies within the context of the liberation movement that affirms the equal status of men and women the world over.

A Summary

The feminist movement, which arose in the late 1960s, has become an important subset of the theology of liberation. In her *Transforming Grace: Christian Tradition and Women's Experience*, Anne Carr summarizes the contributions of the feminists since Vatican II. She characterizes the movement as a worldwide struggle to change church law, church structures, and ecclesiastical attitudes so that women can finally enjoy their rightful status as coequals with men.

Those Protestant churches that have encouraged the ordination of women have been quite happy with the ministerial contributions of women in recent years. Although the Catholic Church has adopted what seems to be a definitive posture against the priestly and diaconal ordination of women, Carr notes that a fair number of longstanding positions over the years have been reversed, for example, usury, the persecution of heretics, slavery, religious freedom, to name a few. A case can also be made for the assertion that the subordinate roles of women in the churches have resulted simply as a reflection of the subjugated position of women in society at large.

The conduct of Jesus as reported in the New Testament was consistently inclusive of women as well as of other oppressed groups. Although the established rhetoric and the symbols of a largely patriarchal society still constitute a major grievance for women, it is the maleness of Jesus that looms as a continual problem. Carr notes that St. Thomas Aquinas taught that the male is the normative sex and that woman is a somewhat defective human being. Such a stance had already been affirmed in the early centuries by a number of the Church Fathers. Except for a few passages in the *Pastoral Constitution on the Church in the Modern World* of Vatican II, even this most recent council did not really deal with the issue of the ecclesial status of women.

In her treatment of the major symbols expressive of Jesus, Carr insists that they have to be reinterpreted in such a way that they are more meaningful to women. For example, the image of Jesus as Son is quite suggestive of the patriarchal culture that has sanctioned the role of male over female and the primacy of sons over daughters. The feminists' understanding of love and reciprocity provides an ideal response to the damaging effects of such a noninclusive Christology.

Among the feminists is a revolutionary group that insists that Christianity is essentially patriarchal and therefore cannot change. The reformists, on the other hand, are hopeful of finding a way to think of Jesus in nonandrocentric terms and have concentrated on the female figure of Wisdom (Sophia). Jesus as Sophia's prophet offers them a new and striking christological image, while other feminists have shown a preference for the image of the risen Christ who transcends sexual differences. Feminists agree that a true mutuality and reciprocity among men and women in the churches is the objective, but there is little consensus as to how that goal can be achieved.

In her 1983 *In Memory of Her: A Feminist Theological Reconstruction of Christian Origins*, Elisabeth Schüssler Fiorenza researches the role of women in the New Testament narratives. She emphasizes that women are portrayed not only as followers of Christ but as leading members of the primitive churches. The role of women is studied in the first Palestinian communities, and then in the Greco-Roman churches. Although several Jewish renewal movements were operating in the first century C.E., little information is available on the roles that women played in these developments. However, the Book of Judith paints a picture of a woman of considerable power and prestige, which must have encouraged the Jews during the period of their subjugation by the Romans.

Schüssler Fiorenza emphasizes that Jesus understood himself as the prophet of Sophia, whose yoke is easy and whose burden is light (Matt. 11:28–30). The Syro-Phoenician woman in Mark (7:24–30) is seen as the "foremother" of all gentile Christians. Moreover, the Galilean women who followed Jesus did not flee after he was scourged and crucified, as did the male disciples (Mark 16:1–6). The all-inclusiveness of the Palestinian Jesus movement liberated women, giving them a greater sense of equality not experienced elsewhere in Jewish society.

In the Greco-Roman communities women were involved as missionaries, teachers, deaconesses, and leaders of house churches. Paul attests that women labored side by side with him in the work of evangelization (Phil. 4:2–3). Indeed, missionary titles were applied by Paul to such women as Prisca, Phoebe, and Junia. Schüssler Fiorenza concludes that there is ample evidence in the Pauline letters that women were actively involved in the establishment and administration of many of the Christian communities in the first century C.E.

Schüssler Fiorenza does not show much interest in the traditional issues of Christology. She and most feminists focus principally on the manner in which Jesus dealt with and related to the men and women of his day. Their abiding concern is the transformation of the systems of domination within the church, which are especially harmful and prejudicial to women. Along with many feminist theologians, Schüssler Fiorenza notes that a major difficulty is the dilemma of the maleness of Jesus that challenges them on many levels. Moreover, the relegation of women to "selfless femininity" has been reinforced over the centuries by Christian preaching. This theologian insists that a viable feminist Christian theology cannot be based on Christ's preferential option for the poor, but rather must be grounded in the continuous struggle of like-minded men and women for the transformation of the patterns of domination within the church.

According to Schüssler Fiorenza the Sophia tradition offers

much to enrich our understanding of Jesus. While Lady Wisdom is presented in later Old Testament literature as a divine-like figure, Jesus saw himself as Sophia's offspring or prophet (Luke 7:35; Matt. 11:28–30). However, in the Gospel of John, the consistent use of the Father-Son image seems to diminish the importance and influence of Sophia. Nonetheless, this venerable and ancient biblical strain is central for the development of feminist Christology, because the Sophia figure will be able to re-enkindle the "ossified masculine language of God and Christ."

Notes

1. Elizabeth A. Johnson, *Consider Jesus: Waves of Renewal in Christology* (New York: Crossroad, 1990), 97.

2. Ibid.

3. Anne E. Carr, *Transforming Grace: Christian Tradition and Women's Experience* (San Francisco: Harper and Row, 1988).

4. Thomas Aquinas, *Summa Theologiae*, pars IIIa., 3d ed. (Madrid: Biblioteca de Autores Cristianos, 1964), q. 31, a. 4, ad primum.

5. Anne E. Carr, "Feminist Views of Christology," *Chicago Studies* 35, no. 2 (August 1996): 128–40.

6. Anne Carr, " 'Who Do You Say That I Am?' Contributions to Christology from Contemporary Women," *Chicago Studies* 38, no. 2 (Summer/Fall 1999): 165–76.

7. Elisabeth Schüssler Fiorenza, *In Memory of Her: A Feminist Theological Reconstruction of Christian Origins* (New York: Crossroad, 1983). For a review of the first phase of feminist theology, see Susan A. Ross and Mary Catherine Hilkert, "Feminist Theology: A Review of Literature," *Theological Studies* 56, no. 2 (June 1995): 327–52.

8. Elisabeth Schüssler Fiorenza, *Jesus: Miriam's Child, Sophia's Prophet: Critical Issues in Feminist Christology* (New York: Continuum, 1994).

An Afterword

In this study I have attempted to select and review a representative group of theologians whose work is very highly regarded by their peers. They approach the discipline of Christology differently because they are honestly striving, from the vantage point of their respective faith traditions, to make more understandable and appealing the central doctrine of Christianity, that Christ the Lord is true God and true man. Every era from postapostolic times has struggled to unravel this mystery and render it as intelligible as possible for the believers of each age. As was the case in the first four or five Christian centuries, the last several generations have witnessed a considerable resurgence in christological studies. We understand that the Incarnation is an unfathomable reality, but this does not prevent men and women of good will from attempting to make their faith ever more comprehensible. The more we grasp the dimensions of the Incarnation, the more fully we can enter into it, and thus deepen and enrich our faith. Orthopraxis must always be grounded in orthodoxy. The richer our faith is, the more vibrant our motivation to follow in the footsteps of the Galilean.

The early chapters of this study focus on the mystery of Jesus' ontological constitution. How is his humanity different from or superior to ours? Was his human existence activated by the divine Word, or does he possess a human act of existence as we do? Did he as a human being possess a superhuman knowledge, or was his knowledge—especially of the future—limited? How are we to define his divinity? Was he adopted as the divine Son at some point by the Father, or is he the eternal Son? In what sense are he and the Father one?

The latter chapters of the book do not so much concentrate on the metaphysical constitution of Jesus. Theirs is more of a practical or functional approach. Where do we find Jesus today in our world? What is he asking us to accomplish in order to follow his example? What kind of mission is he inviting us to undertake? Is he beckoning us into our world to reshape its political structures and the way we deal with one another in society? All of these questions have been asked by these various theologians, and they await our answer.

It is my hope that this study will tempt readers to pursue those theologians who impress them most, so that their appreciation of the life and mission of Jesus will grow and radiate new light and graciousness into their lives.

Bibliography

Note: The New Testament quotations in the text are my translations from the *Novum Testamentum, Graece et Latine*, edited by Augustinus Merk, S.J.

Alberigo, Giuseppi, et al. *Decrees of the Ecumenical Councils.* Vol. 1. Washington, D.C.: Georgetown University Press, 1990.

Aquinas, Thomas. *Summa Theologiae.* 3d ed. Pars IIIa. Madrid: Biblioteca de Autores Cristianos, 1964.

Barth, Karl. *Church Dogmatics. A Selection.* Compiled by Helmut Gollwitzer. 1st Amer. ed. translated and edited by G. W. Bromiley. Louisville, Ky.: Westminster/John Knox, 1994.

———. *Credo.* Foreword by Robert McAfee Brown. New York: Scribner's, 1962.

———. *The Doctrine of Creation. Church Dogmatics.* Vol. 3, part 2. Edited by G. W. Bromiley and T. F. Torrance. Translated by Knight, Bromiley, Reid, and Fuller. Edinburgh: T & T Clark, 1960.

———. *The Doctrine of Reconciliation. Church Dogmatics.* Vol. 4, part 1. Edited by G. W. Bromiley and T. F. Torrance. Translated by G. W. Bromiley. Edinburgh: T & T Clark, 1956.

———. *The Doctrine of the Word of God. Church Dogmatics.* Vol. 1, part 1. Translated by G. T. Thomson. New York: Scribner's, 1936.

———. *The Epistle to the Romans.* Translated by E. C. Hoskyns. 6th ed. New York: Oxford University Press, 1968.

———. *The Humanity of God.* Translated by J. N. Thomas and T. Wieser. Louisville, Ky.: John Knox Press, 1960.

Bauckham, Richard. *The Theology of Jürgen Moltmann.* Edinburgh: T & T Clark, 1995.

Berger, Peter L. *The Heretical Imperative.* New York: Doubleday, 1979.

Boff, Leonardo. *Jesus Christ Liberator.* Translated by Patrick Hughes. Maryknoll, N.Y.: Orbis Books, 1978.

Bonhoeffer, Dietrich. *Letters and Papers from Prison.* Edited by E. Bethge. New York: Collier Books, 1972.

Bornkamm, Günther. *Jesus of Nazareth.* Translation of 3d ed. by Irene and Fraser McLuskey with James M. Robinson. New York: Harper and Row, 1960.

Boyer, Charles. *De Verbo Incarnato.* 2d ed. Rome: Gregorian University, 1952.

Braaten, Carl E., and Philip Clayton, eds. *The Theology of Wolfhart Pannenberg.* Minneapolis: Augsburg Publishing, 1988.

Bromiley, Geoffrey W. *Introduction to the Theology of Karl Barth.* Grand Rapids, Mich.: Eerdmans, 1979.

Brown, Raymond E. *An Introduction to New Testament Christology.* Mahwah, N.J.: Paulist Press, 1994.

————. *An Introduction to the New Testament.* New York: Doubleday, 1997.

————. *Jesus—God and Man.* New York: Macmillan, 1967.

Bultmann, Rudolf. *Essays Philosophical and Theological.* Translated by James C. G. Grieg. London: SCM Press, 1955.

————. *Jesus and the Word.* Translated by Louise P. Smith and Erminie H. Lantero. New York: Scribner's, 1958.

————. *New Testament and Mythology and Other Basic Writings.* Edited and translated by Schubert Ogden. Philadelphia: Fortress Press, 1984.

————. *Theology of the New Testament.* Vol. 1. Translated by Kendrick Grobel. London: SCM Press, 1952.

————. *Theology of the New Testament.* Vol. 2. Translated by Kendrick Grobel. London: SCM Press, 1955.

Carr, Anne E. "Feminist Views of Christology." *Chicago Studies* 35, no. 2 (August 1996): 128–40.

————. *Transforming Grace: Christian Tradition and Women's Experience.* San Francisco: Harper and Row, 1988.

————. " 'Who Do You Say That I Am?' Contributions to Christology from Contemporary Women." *Chicago Studies* 38, no. 2 (Summer/Fall 1999): 165–76.

Charlesworth, James. *Jesus Within Judaism.* New York: Doubleday, 1988.

Clements, Keith W. *Friedrich Schleiermacher: Pioneer of Modern Theology.* London: Collins Liturgical Publications, 1987.

Cobb, John B., Jr. *Christ in a Pluralistic Age.* Philadelphia: Westminster Press, 1975.

————. *Doubting Thomas: Christology in Story Form.* New York: Crossroad, 1990.

Denzinger, H., and A. Schönmetzer. *Enchiridion Symbolorum.* 32nd ed. Freiburg: Herder, 1963.

Dunn, James D. G. *Christology in the Making.* 2d ed. Grand Rapids, Mich.: Eerdmans, 1989.

Green, Clifford, ed. *Karl Barth: Theologian of Freedom.* London: Collins Liturgical Publications, 1989.

Grenz, Stanley J. *Reason for Hope: The Systematic Theology of Wolfhart Pannenberg.* New York: Oxford University Press, 1990.

Griffin, David R. *A Process Christology.* Lanham, Md.: University Press of America, 1990.

Grillmeier, Aloys, and Theresia Hainthaler. *Christ in Christian Tradition.* Translated by Pauline Allen and John Cawte. Vol. 2, part 2. Louisville, Ky.: Westminster/John Knox, 1995.

Haight, Roger. "Appropriating Jesus Today." *Irish Theological Quarterly* 59, no. 4 (1993): 241–63.

————. "The Case for Spirit Christology." *Theological Studies* 53, no. 2 (June 1992): 257–87.

————. "The Impact of Jesus Research on Christology." *Louvain Studies* 21 (1996): 216–28.

————. "Jesus and Salvation: An Essay in Interpretation." *Theological Studies* 55, no. 2 (June 1994): 225–73.

————. *Jesus—Symbol of God.* Maryknoll, N.Y.: Orbis Books, 1999.

———. "The Situation of Christology Today." *Ephemerides Theologicae Lovanienses* 69, no. 4 (December 1993): 315–34.

———. "Two Types of Christology." *Chicago Studies* 38, no. 2 (Summer/Fall 1999): 117–27.

Harnack, Adolf. *Adolf von Harnack: Liberal Theology at Its Height*. Edited by Martin Rumscheidt. London: Collins Liturgical Publications, 1989.

———. *What Is Christianity?* Translated by Thomas Bailey Saunders. Philadelphia: Fortress Press, 1986.

Hartshorne, Charles. *Reality as Social Process*. Glencoe, Ill.: Free Press, 1953.

Hebblethwaite, Peter. *The New Inquisition? The Case of Edward Schillebeeckx and Hans Küng*. San Francisco: Harper and Row, 1980.

Hengel, Martin. *Studies in Early Christology*. Edinburgh: T & T Clark, 1995.

Ihm, Claudia Carlen, ed. *Papal Encyclicals*. Vol. 4, *1939–58*. Ann Arbor, Mich.: Pierian Press, 1990.

Johnson, Elizabeth A. *Consider Jesus: Waves of Renewal in Christology*. New York: Crossroad, 1990.

Johnson, Roger A. *Rudolf Bultmann: Interpreting Faith for the Modern Era*. London: Collins Liturgical Publications, 1987.

Käsemann, Ernst. *Essays on New Testament Themes*. Translated by W. J. Montague. London: SCM Press, 1964.

Kasper, Walter. *Jesus the Christ*. Translated by V. Green. 1976. Reprint, Mahwah, N.J.: Paulist Press, 1985.

Knox, John. *The Humanity and Divinity of Christ*. 1967. Reprint, Cambridge: University of Cambridge, 1992.

Krasevac, Edward. "Christology from Above and Christology from Below." *The Thomist* 51, no. 2 (April 1987): 299–306.

Küng, Hans. *Christianity: Essence, History, and Future*. Translated by John Bowden. New York: Continuum, 1995.

———. *Credo*. Translated by John Bowden. New York: Doubleday, 1993.

———. *Does God Exist?* Translated by Edward Quinn. New York: Doubleday, 1978.

———. *On Being a Christian*. Translated by Edward Quinn. New York: Doubleday, 1976.

Lampe, Geoffrey. *God as Spirit*. 2d ed. 1977. Reprint, London: SCM Press, 1983.

Lonergan, Bernard. "Christ as Subject: A Reply." In *Collected Papers by Bernard Lonergan*, ed. Frederick Crowe, 164–97. New York: Herder and Herder, 1967.

———. "Christology Today: Methodological Reflections." In *A Third Collection*, ed. Frederick Crowe, 74–99. New York: Paulist Press, 1985.

———. *De Constitutione Christi Ontologica et Psychologica*. Rome: Gregorian University, 1964.

———. "The Dehellenization of Dogma." In *A Second Collection*, ed. W. Ryan and B. Tyrrell, 11–32. Philadelphia: Westminster Press, 1974.

———. *De Verbo Incarnato*. Rome: Gregorian University, 1961.

———. *Doctrinal Pluralism*. Milwaukee, Wis.: Marquette University Press, 1971.

———. "Origins of Christian Realism." In *A Second Collection*, ed. W. Ryan and B. Tyrrell, 239–61. Philadelphia: Westminster Press, 1974,

Macquarrie, John. *Christology Revisited.* Harrisburg, Pa.: Trinity Press International, 1998.

———. *Jesus Christ in Modern Thought.* London: SCM Press, 1990.

———. *Principles of Christian Theology.* 2d ed. New York: Scribner's, 1977.

Marxsen, Willi. *The Resurrection of Jesus of Nazareth.* Philadelphia: Fortress Press, 1970.

Merk, Augustinus, S.J., ed. *Novum Testamentum, Graece et Latine.* 5th ed. Rome: Pontifical Biblical Institute, 1944.

Metz, Johann-Baptist, and Jürgen Moltmann. *Faith and the Future.* Maryknoll, N.Y.: Orbis Books, 1995.

Moltmann, Jürgen. *The Crucified God.* Translated by R. A. Wilson and John Bowden. San Francisco: HarperCollins, 1991.

———. "The 'Crucified God': God and Trinity Today." In *New Questions on God,* ed. Johannes B. Metz, 26–37. New York: Herder and Herder, 1972.

———. *Jesus Christ for Today's World.* Translated by Margaret Kohl. Minneapolis: Fortress Press, 1994.

———. *Theology of Hope.* Translated by James W. Lëitch. San Francisco: Harper and Row, 1975.

———. *The Way of Jesus Christ.* Translated by Margaret Kohl. London: SCM Press, 1990.

North, Robert. *In Search of the Human Jesus.* New York: Corpus Books, 1970.

O'Collins, Gerald. *Christology.* New York: Oxford University Press, 1995.

O'Collins, Gerald, and Edward G. Farrugia. *A Concise Dictionary of Theology.* New York: Paulist Press, 1991.

Pannenberg, Wolfhart. *The Apostles' Creed: In the Light of Today's Questions.* Translated by Margaret Kohl. Philadelphia: Westminster Press, 1972.

———. *An Introduction to Systematic Theology.* Grand Rapids, Mich.: Eerdmans, 1991.

———. *Jesus—God and Man.* 2d ed. Translated by L. Wilkins and D. Priebe. Philadelphia: Westminster Press, 1977.

———. *Systematic Theology.* Vol. 2. Translated by Geoffrey W. Bromiley. Grand Rapids, Mich.: Eerdmans, 1994.

Pittenger, W. Norman. *Christology Reconsidered.* London: SCM Press, 1970.

———. *Process-Thought and Christian Faith.* New York: Macmillan, 1968.

———. *The Word Incarnate.* New York: Harper and Brothers, 1959.

Rahner, Karl. *Foundations of Christian Faith.* Translated by William V. Dych. New York: Crossroad, 1986.

———. *Theological Investigations.* Vol. 1. Translated by Cornelius Ernst. London: Darton, Longman and Todd, 1961.

———. *Theological Investigations.* Vol. 5. Translated by Karl-H. Kruger. London: Darton, Longman and Todd, 1966.

———. "The Two Basic Types of Christology." In *Theological Investigations,* vol. 13, translated by David Bourke, 213–23. New York: Seabury Press, 1975.

Robinson, James M. *A New Quest of the Historical Jesus.* London: SCM Press, 1959.

Robinson, John A. T. *Honest to God.* Philadelphia: Westminster Press, 1963.

———. *The Human Face of God.* Philadelphia: Westminster Press, 1973.

Rosato, Philip. "Spirit Christology: Ambiguity and Promise." *Theological Studies* 38, no. 3 (Sept. 1977): 423–49.

Ross, Susan A., and Mary Catherine Hilkert. "Feminist Theology: A Review of Literature." *Theological Studies* 56, no. 2 (June 1995): 327–52.

Schillebeeckx, Edward. *Christ: The Experience of Jesus as Lord.* Translated by John Bowden. New York: Crossroad, 1986.

———. *Church: The Human Story of God.* Translated by John Bowden. New York: Crossroad, 1990.

———. *The Interim Report on the Books, Jesus and Christ.* Translated by John Bowden. New York: Crossroad, 1981.

———. *Jesus: An Experiment in Christology.* Translated by Hubert Hoskins. New York: Seabury Press, 1979.

Schleiermacher, Friedrich. *The Christian Faith.* Translated from the 2d German ed. Edited by H. R. MacKintosh and J. S. Stewart. Edinburgh: T & T Clark, 1986.

Schoof, Ted, ed. *The Schillebeeckx Case: Letters and Documents.* Translated by Matthew J. O'Connell. New York: Paulist Press, 1984.

Schoonenberg, Piet. *The Christ.* Translated by Della Couling. New York: Herder and Herder, 1971.

———. "Denken über Chalcedon." *Theologische Quartalschrift* 160, no. 4 (Oct.–Dec. 1980): 295–305.

Schüssler Fiorenza, Elisabeth. *In Memory of Her: A Feminist Theological Reconstruction of Christian Origins.* New York: Crossroad, 1983.

———. *Jesus: Miriam's Child, Sophia's Prophet: Critical Issues in Feminist Christology.* New York: Continuum, 1994.

Schweitzer, Albert. *The Quest of the Historical Jesus.* Translated by W. Montgomery. New York: Macmillan, 1968.

Scripture and Christology. A Statement of the Biblical Commission with a Commentary. New York: Paulist Press, 1986.

Sigmund, Paul E. *Liberation Theology at the Crossroads.* New York: Oxford University Press, 1990.

Sobrino, Jon. *Christology at the Crossroads.* Translated by John Drury. Maryknoll, N.Y.: Orbis Books, 1978.

———. *Jesus the Liberator.* Translated by Paul Burns and Francis McDonagh. Maryknoll, N.Y.: Orbis Books, 1993.

Suchocki, Marjorie Hewitt. *God. Christ. Church. A Practical Guide to Process Theology.* New York: Crossroad, 1989.

Tillich, Paul. *The Shaking of the Foundations.* New York: Scribner's, 1948.

Tracy, David. *The Analogical Imagination.* New York: Crossroad, 1986.

Vorgrimler, Herbert. *Understanding Karl Rahner.* Translated by John Bowden. New York: Crossroad, 1986.

Welch, Claude. *Protestant Thought in the Nineteenth Century.* Vol. 1, 1799–1870. New Haven: Yale University Press, 1972.

———. *Protestant Thought in the Nineteenth Century.* Vol. 2, 1870–1914. New Haven: Yale University Press, 1985.

Wright, John H. "Roger Haight's Spirit Christology." *Theological Studies* 53, no. 4 (December 1992): 729–35.

Index of Scripture References

General Index